Contents

Contents

Contents

Part I

The Job

Thank you for agreeing to be a coach in the YMCA Winners program of YMCA Youth Super Sports. The job is challenging, but with effort and enthusiasm, you'll find it very rewarding. In part I we'll tell you more about YMCA Youth Super Sports—the best sports program in America, if you don't mind us saying so. As we share with you our philosophy about sports programs for young people in chapter 1, you'll see why we think YMCA Youth Super Sports is special. In chapter 2 we'll present you with your job description and request that you bring the YMCA philosophy to life as you teach basketball to your players.

Welcome to YMCA Youth Super Sports

Welcome to the YMCA Youth Super Sports program! As a YMCA Winners basketball coach you'll be charged with teaching players the skills and rules of the game in ways that make their participation fun and exciting. You see, we want them to play basketball not only this season, but for many years to come. And we want you to have fun coaching basketball because we'd like you to help us again next season.

Okay, let's get started. In this guide you'll find essential information about coaching basketball the YMCA way. In the next section we'll explain more about the best sports program in America—YMCA Youth Super Sports—and especially the YMCA Winners program, which you'll be a part of. Next is your "job description" for being a YMCA Winners basketball coach. Then we'll show you how to teach basketball using the games approach and provide you with a curriculum and three sets of practice plans, one each for 8- to 9-year-olds, 10- to 11-year-olds, and 12- to 13-year-olds. (While YMCA Winners is also for 14- to 16-year-olds, the instruction and information needed for this age group is at a higher level than for the other age groups. See appendix A for resources that you can use for 14- to 16-year-olds.) In the last part we'll explain how to teach the four main components of the basketball curriculum: tactics and skills, rules and traditions, fitness, and character development. And throughout the book, Lucky, the YMCA Youth Super Sports mascot, will help illustrate key points. We hope that by seeing Lucky on these pages, you'll be reminded to keep the fun in your practices and games.

Please read the entire guide carefully and consult it regularly during the season. And if your YMCA offers you the opportunity to participate in a YMCA Winners Basketball Coaches Course, be there. The 4-hour clinic will help you use our "games approach" to teaching basketball.

Let's begin by defining YMCA Youth Super Sports, outlining the YMCA's philosophy of youth sports, and taking a closer look at the three parts of YMCA Youth Super Sports: YMCA Rookies, YMCA Winners, and YMCA Champions.

YMCA Youth Super Sports

We've named the program YMCA Youth Super Sports because we're confident it's the best-designed sports program available anywhere for young people ages 4 to 16. We built the program by bringing together the knowledge of sport scientists who've spent their careers studying young people's sports, with the practical wisdom of YMCA youth sports directors who have guided literally millions of youngsters through sports programs. Our objective for YMCA Youth Super Sports is to help young people not only become better players, but also become better people. We recognize that not every player can be on the winning team, but every kid can be a winner in YMCA Youth Super Sports. That's why our motto for the program is

BUILDING WINNERS FOR LIFE

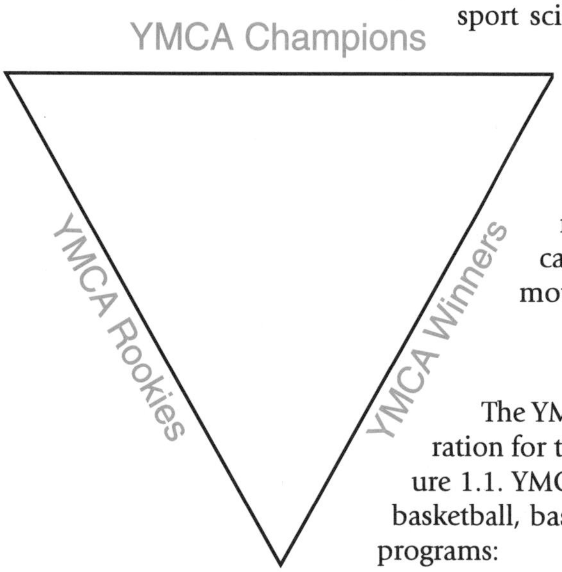

The YMCA triangle, representing spirit, mind, and body, is the inspiration for the YMCA Youth Super Sports program triangle shown in figure 1.1. YMCA Youth Super Sports is currently designed for five sports—basketball, baseball, softball, soccer, and volleyball—and consists of three programs:

Figure 1.1 YMCA Youth Super Sports triangle.

YMCA Rookies—A precompetitive, instructional program to teach 4- to 7-year-old boys and girls the basic skills and rules of the game.

YMCA Winners—The YMCA's unique, values-based competitive sports program for young people ages 8 to 16.

YMCA Champions—An innovative opportunity for 8- to 16-year-olds to demonstrate personal achievement in and through sport.

All three programs have been carefully crafted to maximize the potential for youngsters to have a positive and beneficial experience under your leadership. We now recognize that sport is not just a frivolous game in young athletes' lives; it influences them profoundly. Through YMCA Youth Super Sports we want to help young people *develop* character, not *become* "characters." We want to help them learn to **care** about others, to be **honest,** to show **respect,** and to be **responsible.**

Of course, sport doesn't teach these things to young people automatically. But it does provide opportunities to learn about and develop these values when skillful leadership is provided by volunteer adults like you.

4

The YMCA Philosophy of Youth Sports

So you see, YMCA Youth Super Sports is not just another sports program. We have a mission, and that mission is stated in our Seven Pillars of YMCA Youth Super Sports.

◎ **Pillar One—Everyone Plays**. We do not use tryouts to select the best players, nor do we cut kids from YMCA Youth Super Sports. Everyone who registers is assigned to a team. During the season everyone receives equal practice time and plays at least half of every game.

◎ **Pillar Two—Safety First.** Although kids may get hurt playing sports, we do all we can to prevent injuries. We've modified each sport to make it safer and more enjoyable to play. We ask you to make sure the equipment and facilities are safe, and to teach the sport as we've prescribed it so that the skills taught are appropriate for your athletes' developmental levels. We ask you to gradually develop your players' fitness levels so they are conditioned for the sport. And we ask you to constantly supervise your players and stop any unsafe activities.

◎ **Pillar Three—Fair Play**. Fair play is about playing by the rules—and more. It's about you and your players showing respect for all involved in YMCA Youth Super Sports. It's about you being a role model of good sportsmanship and guiding your players to do the same. Remember, we're more interested in developing children's character through sports than developing a few highly skilled players.

◎ **Pillar Four—Positive Competition.** We believe competition is a positive process when the pursuit of victory is kept in the right perspective. When adults make decisions that put the best interests of the players before winning the contest—*that's* the right perspective. Learning to compete is important for youngsters, and learning to cooperate in a competitive world is an essential lesson of life. Through YMCA Youth Super Sports we want to help kids learn these lessons.

◎ **Pillar Five—Family Involvement.** YMCA Youth Super Sports encourages parents to be involved appropriately in their child's participation in our sports programs. In addition to parents being helpful as volunteer coaches, referees, and timekeepers, we encourage them to be at practices and games to support their child's participation. To help parents get involved appropriately, YMCA Youth Super Sports offers parent orientation programs.

◎ **Pillar Six—Sport for All.** YMCA Youth Super Sports is an "inclusive" sports program. That means that youngsters who differ in various characteristics are to be included rather than excluded from participation. We offer sports programs for kids who differ in physical abilities by matching them with kids of similar abilities and modifying the sport. We offer programs to all youngsters regardless of their race, gender, religious creed, or ability. We ask our adult leaders to encourage and appreciate the diversity of children in our society and to encourage the kids and their parents to do the same.

◎ **Pillar Seven—*Sport for Fun*.** Sports are naturally fun for most kids. They love the challenge of mastering the skills of the game, playing with their friends, and competing with their peers. Sometimes when adults become involved in

youth sports they overorganize and dominate the activity to the point that it destroys young people's enjoyment of the sport. If we take the fun out of sports for our children, we are in danger of the kids taking themselves out of sports. Remember, the sports are for the kids; let them have fun.

 # YMCA Rookies

YMCA Rookies is a skill-development program that prepares children ages 4 to 7 to participate in YMCA Winners, the competitive sports program, and YMCA Champions, the personal sports achievement program. The coaches for YMCA Rookies focus on teaching players the basics of the game in an environment where they can focus on learning the sport, not performing to win.

Too often today kids are thrust into *competitive* sports programs with little instruction on the basics of the sport (both the skills and the rules of the game). Perhaps they participate in a few practice sessions, but often they do not obtain sufficient instruction or time to develop basic skills in a precompetitive environment. Then, too, many programs do not sufficiently modify the sport to meet the physical and mental abilities of kids.

The consequence of such an introduction to sports is that kids who have had early opportunities for instruction and who are physically more gifted often succeed, while those without these advantages are more likely to fail. We designed YMCA Rookies to address these problems by providing a positive introduction to sports for all children.

 # YMCA Winners

YMCA Winners is the values-based competitive program in YMCA Youth Super Sports. It's for young people ages 8 to 16, with the competition grouped in these age ranges:

◎ 8 to 9

◎ 10 to 11

◎ 12 to 13

◎ 14 to 16

The objectives for YMCA Winners are the same as those for YMCA Rookies: learning the tactics and skills of the game, the rules and traditions of the sport, important fitness concepts, and character development. However, in YMCA Winners they are achieved along with competition with other players and teams. Here's an overview of each area of focus in YMCA Winners:

◎ **Individual Skills.** These skills include both basic and more advanced skills as players learn the sport and advance through the program.

◎ **Tactics and Team Skills.** Players will also learn appropriate skills that involve more than one participant and are necessary in using team tactics.

◎ **Rules and Traditions.** YMCA Winners teaches players the rules of the sport as they learn the basic skills. They also learn the sport's basic protocols and traditions, or the proper actions to take that show courtesy and avoid injury.

◎ **Fitness.** The YMCA Winners program includes Fitness Circles where coaches lead activities and discussions and provide tips related to fitness, training, flexibility, nutrition, and preventing injuries.

◎ **Character Development.** Players in YMCA Winners will participate in Team Circles during each practice as well. The ideas discussed in the Team Circles also work in conjunction with the YMCA's Character Development resources and incorporate the concepts of caring, honesty, respect, and responsibility.

Players practice the individual and team skills by using games that keep kids active, learning, and having fun. These three elements—being active, learning, and having fun—are heightened by using the games approach to coaching basketball. We'll describe this approach in detail in chapter 8.

To ensure having the highest quality coaches, referees, and sport administrators, YMCA Youth Super Sports offers training and educational resources for all adults involved in YMCA Winners. The purpose of this training is to emphasize the positive objectives of the program and to de-emphasize the winning-at-all-costs mentality that leads to so many negative practices in youth sports programs.

The training offered to adults involved in the program is just one aspect that makes YMCA Winners unique. Another is the modifications we've made to the sports so that players progress through the program in developmentally appropriate ways. Modifying the sports increases the likelihood that athletes will experience success and reduces the risk of injury.

 # YMCA Champions

YMCA Champions is an innovative program that encourages and recognizes personal achievement in YMCA sports among kids ages 8 to 16. As shown in table 1.1, for young people to earn an award they must demonstrate their mastery of the sport in four areas, or domains; and within each sport, they have the opportunity to earn three levels of awards.

TABLE 1.1

The YMCA Champions Program

Levels	CONTENT DOMAINS			
	Knowledge	Skill	Participation	Character
Bronze				
Silver				
Gold				

The four content domains are the following:

1. **Knowledge.** Participants must show that they understand the rules and protocol of the sport and related fitness and health concepts.

2. **Skill.** Athletes must demonstrate their mastery of the physical skills of the sport through "game-like" skill tests.

3. **Participation.** Players must participate for a given amount of time in practices and contests for each of the three levels.

4. **Character.** Participants must demonstrate character development through caring, honesty, respect, and responsibility.

In each sport, participants begin at the Bronze Level, the initial level of achievement. Once the Bronze Award is obtained in that sport, they can move on to the Silver and Gold levels. Participants can be working on a Bronze Award in one sport, a Silver Award in another sport, and a Gold Award in a third sport if they wish. They are encouraged to progress through the levels as rapidly as they can.

The players' progress is monitored by YMCA Champions coaches who act as mentors for the athletes. YMCA Champions coaches are assisted by Gold Leaders, players 14 years old or older who have earned the Gold Award in that sport. Gold Leaders are trained to assist younger players in their preparation for being tested in the four domains; they also assist the Champions coaches conducting the evaluations.

Once players have earned a Gold Award, they are eligible to join the YMCA Gold Club. The club is both an honorary and service club, and it provides opportunities for leadership. The Gold Leaders would come from the YMCA Gold Club.

As a YMCA Winners coach you will play an important role in encouraging young people to participate in YMCA Champions. That encouragement will come not just by urging them to participate, but by helping them learn the basics of the sport while having fun and building their self-worth.

Your Job Description

Now you have an overview of YMCA Youth Super Sports. You also know that in YMCA Winners, players learn basketball tactics, skills, and rules while being introduced to competition against other teams. You'll teach your players the tactics and skills involved in basketball, but your obligations won't stop there. You'll also

◎ prepare them to compete;

◎ make decisions about starting lineups and sub-stitutions;

◎ direct youngsters in competition;

◎ make tactical decisions during contests;

◎ relate to opposing coaches, players, referees, and parents; and

◎ help your players handle both success and failure—lessons essential for adult living.

Your Duties As a Coach

Your duties begin with ensuring that the Seven Pillars of YMCA Youth Super Sports are in place. These pillars, covered in more detail in chapter 1, are

◎ Everyone plays.

◎ Safety first.

◎ Fair play.

◎ Positive competition.

◎ Family involvement.

◎ Sport for all.

◎ Sport for fun.

Your duties also extend beyond those pillars. As a YMCA Winners basketball coach, you'll be called upon to:

1. **Provide a safe physical environment.** Playing basketball holds an inherent risk, but as a coach you're responsible to regularly inspect the practice and competition areas (see the checklist for facilities and support personnel in chapter 6).

2. **Communicate in a positive way.** You'll communicate not only with your players, but with parents, referees, and administrators as well. Communicate in a way that is positive and that demonstrates you have the best interests of the players at heart. Chapters 4 and 5 will help you communicate effectively and positively.

3. **Teach the tactics and skills of basketball.** We'll show you an innovative games approach to teaching and practicing the tactics and skills young athletes need to know—an approach that kids thoroughly enjoy. We ask you to help all players be the best they can be. In chapter 5 we show you how to teach basketball skills. In chapters 10, 11, and 12 we provide practice plans for 8- to 9-year-olds, 10- to 11-year-olds, and 12- to 13-year-olds, respectively. In chapter 13 we provide descriptions of all the skills you'll need to teach and to help you detect and correct errors that players typically make.

4. **Teach the rules and traditions of basketball.** We'll ask you to teach your players the rules and traditions of basketball. By traditions we mean the actions to take to show courtesy and avoid injury—in short, to be a good sport. You'll find the rules and traditions for YMCA Winners Basketball in chapter 14.

5. **Direct players in competition.** This includes determining starting line-ups and a substitution plan, relating appropriately to referees and to opposing coaches and players, and making tactical decisions during games (see chapter 6). Remember that the focus is not on winning at all costs, but in coaching your kids to compete well, do their best, and strive to win within the rules.

6. **Help your players become fit and value fitness for a lifetime.** We want you to help your players be fit so they can play basketball safely and successfully. We also want your players to learn to become fit on their own, understand the value of fitness, and enjoy training. Thus, we ask you not to make them do push-ups or run laps for punishment. Make it fun to get fit for basketball, and make it fun to play basketball so they'll stay fit for a lifetime. In chapter 15 we'll give you some tips on basic fitness for your players.

7. **Help young people develop character.** Character development includes learning respect, responsibility, and honesty, and learning to care about others. These intangible qualities are no less important to teach than learning to shoot the ball well. We ask you to teach these values to children (a) by conducting Team Circles that are built into every lesson plan, and (b) by demonstrating and encouraging behaviors that express these values at all times. Chapter 16 will give you more suggestions about teaching character.

Tools of Effective Basketball Coaches

Have you purchased the traditional coaching tools—things like whistles, coaching clothes, sport shoes, and a clipboard? They'll help you coach, but to be a successful coach you'll need five other tools that cannot be bought. These tools are available only through self-examination and hard work; they're easy to remember with the acronym COACH:

C   Comprehension

O   Outlook

A   Affection

C   Character

H   Humor

Comprehension

Comprehension of the rules, tactics, and skills of basketball is required. It is essential that you understand the basic elements of the sport. To assist you in learning about the game, we describe rules, tactics, and skills in part IV. We also provide a season plan and individual practice plans in chapters 9 through 12. In the chapters on practice plans, you'll find a variety of games and skill practices to use in developing basketball skills.

To improve your comprehension of basketball, take the following steps:

◎ Read the sport-specific section of this book in chapters 13 and 14.

◎ Consider reading other basketball coaching books, including those available from the YMCA Program Store.

◎ Contact any of the organizations listed on page 304.

◎ Attend basketball clinics.

◎ Talk with more experienced coaches.

◎ Observe local college, high school, and youth basketball games.

◎ Watch basketball games on television.

In addition to having basketball knowledge, you must implement proper training and safety methods so your players can participate with little risk of injury. Even then, injuries may occur. And more often than not, you'll be the first person responding to your players' injuries, so be sure you understand the basic emergency care procedures described in chapter 7. Also, read in that chapter how to handle more serious sports injury situations.

 # Outlook

This coaching tool refers to your perspective and goals—what you are seeking as a coach. The most common coaching objectives are (a) to have fun, (b) to help players develop their physical, mental, and social skills, and (c) to win. Thus your *outlook* involves the priorities you set, your planning, and your vision for the future.

While all coaches focus on competition, we want you to focus on *positive* competition, keeping the pursuit of victory in perspective by making decisions that first are in the best interest of the players, and second, will help to win the game.

So how do you know if your outlook and priorities are in order? Here's a little test for you:

Look over your answers. If you most often selected "a" responses, then having fun is most important to you. A majority of "b" answers suggests that skill development is what attracts you to coaching. And if "c" was your most frequent response, winning is tops on your list of coaching priorities. If your priorities are in order, your players' well-being will take precedence over your team's win-loss record every time.

The American Sport Education Program (ASEP) has a motto that fits well with the philosophy of YMCA Youth Super Sports, and it will help you keep your outlook in the best interest of the kids on your team. It summarizes in four words all you need to remember when establishing your coaching priorities:

ATHLETES FIRST, WINNING SECOND

This motto recognizes that striving to win is an important, even vital, part of sports. But it emphatically states that no efforts in striving to win should be made at the expense of the athletes' well-being, development, and enjoyment.

Take the following actions to better define your outlook:

1. Determine your priorities for the season.

2. Prepare for situations that challenge your priorities.

3. Set goals for yourself and your players that are consistent with those priorities.

4. Plan how you and your players can best attain those goals.

5. Review your goals frequently to be sure that your are staying on track.

Which situation would you be most proud of?

a. Knowing that each participant enjoyed playing basketball.

b. Seeing that all players improved their basketball skills.

c. Winning the league championship.

Which statement best reflects your thoughts about sports?

a. If it isn't fun, don't do it.

b. Everyone should learn something every day.

c. Sports aren't fun if you don't win.

How would you like your players to remember you?

a. As a coach who was fun to play for.

b. As a coach who provided a good base of fundamental skills.

c. As a coach who had a winning record.

Which would you most like to hear a parent of a player on your team say?

a. Mike really had a good time playing basketball this year.

b. Nicole learned some important lessons playing basketball this year.

c. Willie played on the first-place basketball team this year.

Which of the following would be the most rewarding moment of your season?

a. Having your team not want to stop playing, even after practice is over.

b. Seeing one of your players finally master the skill of dribbling without constantly looking at the ball.

c. Winning the league championship.

 ## Affection

This is another vital tool you will want to have in your coaching kit: a genuine concern for the young people you coach. It involves having a love for kids, a desire to share with them your love and knowledge of basketball, and the patience and understanding that allow each individual playing for you to grow from his or her involvement in sports. Again, two of the pillars of YMCA Youth Super Sports are that *everyone* plays and *everyone* has fun.

There are many ways to demonstrate your affection and patience, including these:

- ◎ Make an effort to get to know each player on your team.

- ◎ Treat each player as an individual.

- ◎ Empathize with players trying to learn new and difficult skills.

- ◎ Treat players as you would like to be treated under similar circumstances.

- ◎ Be in control of your emotions.

- ◎ Show your enthusiasm for being involved with your team.

- ◎ Keep an upbeat and positive tone in all of your communications.

 # Character

The fact that you have decided to coach young basketball players probably means that you think participation in sports is important. But whether or not that participation develops character in your players depends as much on you as it does the sport itself. How can you build character in your players?

Having good character means modeling appropriate behaviors for sports and life. That means more than just saying the right things. What you say and what you do must match. There is no place in coaching for the "Do as I say, not as I do" philosophy. Challenge, support, encourage, and reward every youngster, and your players will be more likely to accept—even celebrate—their differences. Be in control before, during, and after all practices and contests. And don't be afraid to admit that you were wrong. No one is perfect!

Consider the following steps to being a good role model:

- ◎ Take stock of your strengths and weaknesses.

- ◎ Build on your strengths.

- ◎ Set goals for yourself to improve on those areas you would not like to see mimicked.

- ◎ If you slip up, apologize to your team and to yourself. You'll do better next time.

We'll help you address issues of character development with your players in the Team Circles of your practice sessions. The practice plans in chapters 10 through 12 will help you lead discussions on a variety of topics surrounding character development and good sporting behavior.

You also have available a wide range of resources through the YMCA Character Development materials, which include books, posters, videos, and more. To learn more about what resources might help you develop your athletes in the four key areas (caring, honesty, respect, and responsibility), contact the YMCA Program Store.

 **Humor**

Humor is an often-overlooked coaching tool. For our use it means having the ability to laugh at yourself and with your players during practices and contests. Nothing helps balance the tone of a serious skill-learning session like a chuckle or two. And a sense of humor puts in perspective the many mistakes your players will make. So don't get upset over each miscue or respond negatively to erring players. Allow your athletes and yourself to enjoy the ups, and don't dwell on the downs.

Here are some tips for injecting humor into your practices:

◎ Make practices fun by including a variety of activities.

◎ Keep all players involved in games and skill practices.

◎ Consider laughter by your players a sign of enjoyment, not waning discipline.

◎ Smile!

Part II

Coaching Essentials

Now you know your coaching duties and you're ready to coach. Whoa! Not quite yet. We've got some essential information to cover about coaching that will help you be a better coach and make your coaching experience more enjoyable. In chapter 3, we'll provide you with information on the physical, social, emotional, and cognitive development of your players. In chapter 4, we'll give you some tips on communicating effectively with your players and the adults you'll be working with. Whether you're a veteran coach or a novice, you'll find it beneficial to review the teaching principles for sports skills presented in chapter 5. Because coaching involves more than just teaching skills, we present essential coaching principles for you in chapter 6. And chapter 7 will remind you of your duties to provide your players with a safe experience.

Coaching 8- to 16-Year-Olds

One of the challenges of coaching youngsters is that you need to relate to them as children, not miniature adults. To do this, you need to understand where they are in their development physically, socially, emotionally, and cognitively. Among any team you coach, you're going to find children who mature relatively early for their age as well as those who mature relatively late. A player may be quite intellectually mature and quick to understand basketball tactics and the skills required to carry them out, but she may be slow in physical development and thus have a hard time successfully executing the skills. Another player may be well developed physically but underdeveloped emotionally. Dealing with such a potpourri of physical, social, emotional, and cognitive ranges in your players is one of the main challenges of coaching.

The more familiar you are with the physical capabilities and mindset of youngsters, the better you'll be able to communicate with them and help them grow through their experience in basketball. The following lists detail children's physical, social, emotional, and cognitive development. Understand that each child will not conform to the characteristics at any given age—and, of course, this doesn't mean the child is abnormal. These lists provide a *general* understanding of children's developmental characteristics and should help you better relate to children and better coach them.

8- to 11-year-olds

Physical Characteristics

Many children from ages 8 to 11 are growing rapidly, and this growth is accompanied by changes in dexterity, coordination, and muscle strength. Girls particularly are showing signs of oncoming adolescence. The ages of 10 and 11 are awkward for many children, as muscle strength lags behind growth. Some of the physical characteristics of 8- to 11-year-old children include

- increased strength in arms, hands, and fingers;

- accelerated development of skills in the use of small muscles;

- improved execution of gross motor skills such as running, jumping, throwing, catching, kicking, and batting;

- improved reaction time; and

- improved endurance.

Social and Emotional Characteristics

Life gets more complicated for children during these years. Some handle changes well, while others have trouble adjusting to new expectations that come along with being in school and growing older. Discipline can be a problem at this age as children grapple with new responsibilities and demands. There is a strong tendency for children to compare themselves to others, which can lead to conformity. Children at these ages seldom strive to be different from their peers. Here are some common general traits that characterize children at ages 8 through 11:

- They don't like playing alone; they respond well to group activities.

- They feel loyal to their team.

- They like variety and get bored more easily than they used to.

- They make social comparisons and use these to help define their self-concept.

- They appreciate the link between moral rules and social conventions.

- They are more attentive to peer groups but still want approval of adults.

- They don't like to be criticized by adults.

- They don't want to be different from their friends.

Development characteristics are adapted from the following:

From Berk, Laura E., *Development Through the Lifespan.* Copyright © 1998 by Allyn & Bacon. Adapted by permission.

From Humphrey, James H., *Sports for Children: A Guide for Adults.* Copyright © 1993 by Charles C Thomas, Publisher, Ltd. Adapted by permission.

◎ They compete more with their siblings and are sensitive to perceived imbalances in parental attention.

◎ They become more responsible and dependable.

◎ They like challenge and adventure.

◎ They don't like to be treated as children.

◎ They tend to blame others first.

◎ They want to be recognized for their accomplishments.

◎ They are inclined toward "hero worship" and can be inspired by others.

◎ They compare their skills to those of others, and lesser-skilled players withdraw from their group.

Cognitive Characteristics

Children make great cognitive strides from ages 8 through 11. Adults are often amazed at how quickly children learn and how well they can remember. Cognitive character traits of children during this period typically include

◎ an increased attention span;

◎ stronger memory skills;

◎ improved self-evaluative skills;

◎ rapid increases in vocabulary;

◎ a finer, more discriminating sense of humor;

◎ an improved ability to understand sophisticated concepts such as double meaning of words, metaphors, and analogies;

◎ a tendency to think in concrete rather than abstract terms;

◎ a desire for simple, clear-cut reasons for decisions made by others;

◎ a readiness to learn from failure (if the consequences aren't too great); and

◎ a greater likelihood to quit because of perceived failure.

 ## 12- to 16-year-olds

Physical Characteristics

Physical awkwardness continues during the ages 12 through 16, especially for boys as they begin the main growth spurt of their lives during these years. Some girls will have begun their growth spurt before the age of 12, but many continue up to age 15. Other physical characteristics common among kids during this period include the following:

◎ They continue to gain skills that use small muscles.

◎ Girls reach peak of growth spurt by 14 and slow way down by 15 or 16.

◎ Girls' motor performance gradually increases, then levels off.

◎ Boys begin growth spurt by 12 to 14 and often continue until 16 or 17.

◎ In both genders, strength and endurance increase, though girls add more body fat than muscle.

Social and Emotional Characteristics

Some of the traits that surfaced in children during the years from 8 through 11 peak prominently during ages 12 through 16. They outgrow some of the other tendencies of their earlier youth as they begin to compare themselves (favorably) to adults. During this period they tend to

◎ identify better with adolescents of their gender,

◎ see more weaknesses and faults in adults,

◎ see themselves as adults rather than children,

◎ begin to develop a truer picture of morality,

◎ feel the pressure from their peers, and

◎ care more about their personal appearance and how they look compared to others.

Cognitive Characteristics

As they strive to become more adult, adolescents value and use their intellects and become much more critical in their thinking. They tend to

◎ reflect more about abstract issues and perceived injustice;

◎ acquire and sometimes cultivate a social conscience;

◎ grasp irony and (perhaps overuse) sarcasm;

◎ argue and reason more effectively;

◎ become more self-focused, idealistic, and critical; and

◎ use language better.

 ## Be Patient

No matter what age children you're coaching, few virtues are more valuable to a coach than patience. As they test and repeatedly push their limits, children from ages 8 to 16 can try a coach's patience much more than younger children. Whereas young children usually embrace adult instruction and guidance, older children and adolescents are often encouraged by their peers to resist it. This makes your job more challenging but also more rewarding when you succeed.

Communicating Effectively

In chapter 2 you learned about the tools needed to COACH: Comprehension, Outlook, Affection, Character, and Humor. These are the essentials for effective coaching; without them, you'd have a difficult time getting started. But none of those tools will work if you don't know how to use them with your athletes—and this requires skillful communication. This chapter examines what communication is and how you can become a more effective communicator-coach.

What's Involved in Communication?

Coaches often mistakenly believe that communication involves only instructing players to do something, but verbal commands are only a small part of the communication process. More than half of what is communicated is nonverbal. So remember, when you are coaching, *actions speak louder than words.*

Communication in its simplest form involves two people: a sender and a receiver. The sender transmits the message verbally, through facial expressions, and possibly through body language. Once the message is sent, the receiver must assimilate it successfully. A receiver who fails to attend or listen will miss parts, if not all, of the message.

How Can I Send More Effective Messages?

Young athletes often have little understanding of the rules and skills of basketball and probably even less confidence in playing it. So they need accurate, understandable, and supportive messages to help them along. That's why your verbal and nonverbal messages are so important.

Verbal Messages

"Sticks and stones may break my bones, but words will never hurt me"—this old saying simply isn't true. Spoken words can have a strong and long-lasting effect. And coaches' words are particularly influential because youngsters place great importance on what coaches say. Perhaps you, like many former youth sports participants, have a difficult time remembering much of anything you were told by your elementary school teachers, but you can still recall several specific things your coaches at that level said to you. Such is the lasting effect of a coach's comments to a player.

Whether you are correcting misbehavior, teaching a player how to pass the ball, or praising a player for good effort, there are a number of things you should consider when sending a message verbally. They include the following:

◎ Be positive and honest.

◎ State it clearly and simply.

◎ Say it loudly enough, and say it again.

◎ Be consistent.

Be Positive and Honest

Nothing turns people off like hearing someone nag all the time, and athletes react similarly to a coach who gripes constantly. Kids particularly need encouragement because they often doubt their ability to perform in sports. So look for and tell your players what they did well.

But don't cover up poor or incorrect play with rosy words of praise. Kids know all too well when they've erred, and no cheerfully expressed cliché can undo their mistakes. If you fail to acknowledge players' errors, your athletes will think you are a phony.

A good way to correct a performance error is first to point out what the athlete did correctly. Then explain in a positive way what he or she is doing wrong and show him or her how to correct it. Finish by encouraging the athlete and emphasizing the correct performance.

Be sure not to follow a positive statement with the word *but*. For example, don't say, "That was good location on your pass, Kelly. But if you follow through a little more, you'll get a little more zip on the ball." Saying it this way causes many kids to ignore the positive statement and focus on the negative one. Instead, say something like "That was good location on your pass, Kelly. And if you follow through a little more, you'll get a little more zip on the ball. That was right on target. That's the way to go."

State It Clearly and Simply

Positive and honest messages are good, but only if expressed directly in words your players understand. "Beating around the bush" is ineffective and inefficient. And if you do ramble, your players will miss the point of your message and probably lose interest. Here are some tips for saying things clearly.

◎ Organize your thoughts before speaking to your athletes.

◎ Explain things thoroughly, but don't bore them with long-winded monologues.

◎ Use language your players can understand. However, avoid trying to be hip by using their age group's slang vocabulary.

Say It Loudly Enough, and Say It Again

Talk to your team in a voice that all members can hear and interpret. A crisp, vigorous voice commands attention and respect; garbled and weak speech is tuned out. It's okay, in fact, appropriate, to soften your voice when speaking to a player individually about a personal problem. But most of the time your messages will be for all your players to hear, so make sure they can! An enthusiastic voice also motivates players and tells them you enjoy being their coach. A word of caution, however: Don't dominate the setting with a booming voice that distracts attention from players' performances.

Sometimes what you say, even if stated loudly and clearly, won't sink in the first time. This may be particularly true with young athletes hearing words they don't understand. To avoid boring repetition yet still get your message across, say the same thing in a slightly different way. For instance, you might first tell your players, "Play tighter defense!" If they don't appear to understand, you might say, "When your opponent is one pass away from the ball, you need to cut off the passing lane." The second form of the message may get through to players who missed it the first time around.

Be Consistent

People often say things in ways that imply a different message. For example, a touch of sarcasm added to the words "way to go" sends an entirely different message than the words themselves suggest. It is essential that you avoid sending such mixed messages. Keep the tone of your voice consistent with the words you use. And don't say something one day and contradict it the next; players will get their wires crossed.

Nonverbal Messages

Just as you should be consistent in the tone of voice and words you use, you should also keep your verbal and nonverbal messages consistent. An extreme example of failing to do this would be shaking your head, indicating disapproval, while at the same time telling a player, "Nice try." Which is the player to believe, your gesture or your words?

Messages can be sent nonverbally in a number of ways. Facial expressions and body language are just two of the more obvious forms of nonverbal signals that can help you when you coach.

Facial Expressions

The look on a person's face is the quickest clue to what he or she thinks or feels. Your players know this, so they will study your face, looking for any sign that will tell them more than the words you say. Don't try to fool them by putting on a happy or blank "mask." They'll see through it, and you'll lose credibility.

Serious, stone-faced expressions are no help to kids who need cues as to how they are performing. They will just assume you're unhappy or disinterested. Don't be afraid to smile. A smile from a coach can give a great boost to an unsure athlete. Plus, a smile lets your players know that you are happy coaching them. But don't overdo it, or your players won't be able to tell when you're genuinely pleased by something they've done or when you're just putting on a smiling face.

Body Language

What would your players think you were feeling if you came to practice slouched over, with head down and shoulders slumped? Tired? Bored? Unhappy? What would they think you were feeling if you watched them during a contest with your hands on your hips, your jaws clenched, and your face reddened? Upset with them? Disgusted with a referee? Mad at a fan? Probably some or all of these things would enter your players' minds. And none of these impressions is the kind you want your players to have of you. That's why you should carry yourself in a pleasant, confident, and vigorous manner. Such a posture not only projects happiness with your coaching role but also provides a good example for your young players who may model your behavior.

Physical contact can also be a very important use of body language. A handshake, a pat on the head, an arm around the shoulder, or even a big hug are effective ways of showing approval, concern, affection, and joy to your players. Youngsters are especially in need of this type of nonverbal message. Keep within the obvious moral and legal limits, but don't be reluctant to touch your players and send a message that can only truly be expressed in that way.

How Can I Improve My Receiving Skills?

Now, let's examine the other half of the communication process—receiving messages. Too often people are very good senders and very poor receivers of messages. As a coach of young athletes, it is essential that you be able to fulfill both roles effectively.

The requirements for receiving messages are quite simple, but the requirements for receiving skills are perhaps less satisfying and therefore underdeveloped compared to sending skills. People seem to naturally enjoy hearing themselves talk more than hearing others talk. But if you read about the keys to receiving messages and make a strong effort to use them with your players, you'll be surprised by what you've been missing.

Attention!

First, you must pay attention; you must want to hear what others have to communicate to you. That's not always easy when you're busy coaching and have many things competing for your attention. But in one-to-one or team meetings with players, you must really focus on what they are telling you, both verbally and nonverbally. You'll be amazed at the little signals you pick up. Not only will such focused attention help you catch every word your players say, but you'll also notice your players' moods and physical states, and you'll get an idea of your players' feelings toward you and other players on the team.

Listen CARE-FULLY

How we receive messages from others, perhaps more than anything else we do, demonstrates how much we care for the sender and what that person has to tell us. If you care little for your players or have little regard for what they have to say, it will show in how you attend and listen to them. Check yourself. Do you find your mind wandering to what you are going to do after practice while one of your players is talking to you? Do you frequently have to ask your players, "What did you say?" If so, you need to work on your receiving mechanics of attending and listening. But if you find that you're missing the messages your players send, perhaps the most critical question you should ask yourself is: Do I care?

 ## Providing Feedback

So far we've discussed separately the sending and receiving of messages. But we all know that senders and receivers switch roles several times during an interaction. One person initiates a communication by sending a message to another person, who then receives the message. The receiver then switches roles and becomes the sender by responding to the person who sent the initial message. These verbal and nonverbal responses are called feedback.

Your players will be looking to you for feedback all the time. They will want to know how you think they are performing, what you think of their ideas, and whether their efforts please you. Obviously, you can respond in many different ways. How you respond will strongly affect your players. They will respond most favorably to positive feedback.

Praising players when they have performed or behaved well is an effective way of getting them to repeat (or try to repeat) that behavior in the future. And positive feedback for effort is an especially effective way to motivate youngsters to work on difficult skills. So rather than shouting and providing negative feedback to a player who has made a mistake, try offering players positive feedback, letting them know what they did correctly and how they can improve.

Sometimes just the way you word feedback can make it more positive than negative. For example, instead of saying, "Don't shoot the ball that way," you might say, "Shoot the ball this way." Then your players will be focusing on what to do instead of what not to do.

You can give positive feedback verbally and nonverbally. Telling a player, especially in front of teammates, that he or she has performed well, is a great way to boost the confidence of a youngster. And a pat on the back or a handshake can be a very tangible way of communicating your recognition of a player's performance.

Who Else Do I Need to Communicate With?

Coaching involves not only sending and receiving messages and providing proper feedback to players, but also interacting with parents, fans, game referees, and opposing coaches. If you don't communicate effectively with these groups of people, your coaching career will be unpleasant and short-lived. So try the following suggestions for communicating with these groups.

Parents

A player's parents need to be assured that their son or daughter is under the direction of a coach who is both knowledgeable about the sport and concerned about the youngster's well-being. You can put their worries to rest by holding a preseason parent-orientation meeting in which you describe your background and your approach to coaching.

If parents contact you with a concern during the season, listen to them closely and try to offer positive responses. If you need to communicate with parents, catch them after a practice, give them a phone call, or send a note through the mail. Messages sent to parents through players are too often lost, misinterpreted, or forgotten.

Parents should take an active, supportive role in YMCA Youth Super Sports. The appendix to the *YMCA Youth Super Sports Parents Training Guide*, "YMCA Youth Super Sports Parent's Guidelines," contains essential information about the YMCA Youth Super Sports program, including YMCA Rookies, YMCA Winners, and YMCA Champions. It also includes the parent's code of conduct and a description of how parents can assist and support their children's participation in YMCA Youth Super Sports.

Fans

The stands probably won't be overflowing at your contests, but that only means that you'll more easily hear the few fans who criticize your coaching. When you hear something negative said about the job you're doing, don't respond. Keep calm, consider whether the message had any value, and if not, forget it. Acknowledging critical, unwarranted comments from a fan during a contest will only encourage others to voice their opinions. So put away your "rabbit ears" and communicate to fans—through your actions—that you are a confident, competent coach.

Prepare your players for fans' criticisms. Tell them it is you, not the spectators, they should listen to. If you notice that one of your players is rattled by a fan's comment, reassure the player that your evaluation is more objective and favorable—and the one that counts.

Contest Referees

How you communicate with referees will have a great influence on the way your players behave toward them. Therefore, you need to set an example. Greet referees with a handshake, an introduction, and perhaps some casual conversation about the upcoming contest. Indicate your respect for them before, during, and after the contest. Don't make nasty remarks, shout, or use disrespectful body gestures. Your players will see you do it, and they'll get the idea that such behavior is appropriate. Plus, if the referee hears or sees you, the communication between the two of you will break down.

Opposing Coaches

Make an effort to visit with the coach of the opposing team before the game. During the game, don't get into a personal feud with the opposing coach. Remember, it's the kids, not the coaches, who are competing. And by getting along well with the opposing coach, you'll show your players that competition involves cooperation.

Teaching Principles

Coaching basketball is about teaching tactics, skills, fitness, values, and other useful things. Coaching basketball is also about "coaching" players before, during, and after contests. Teaching and coaching are closely related, but there are important differences. In this chapter we'll focus on principles of teaching and, especially, on teaching the skills of basketball. Many of the principles we discuss apply to teaching tactics, fitness concepts, and values—all elements of our Winners curriculum. Most of the other important teaching principles deal with communication; we covered those in chapter 4. Then, in chapter 6, we will discuss the principles of coaching, which refer to your leadership activities during contests. Chapter 8 addresses how to teach tactics in a new way, using the games approach.

 ## Teaching Basketball Skills

Many people believe that the only qualification needed to teach a skill is to have performed it. It is helpful to have performed a particular skill, but there is much more than that to teaching successfully. And even if you haven't performed the skill before, you can still learn to teach successfully with the useful acronym IDEA:

I Introduce the skill.

D Demonstrate the skill.

E Explain the skill.

A Attend to players practicing the skill.

These are the basic steps of good teaching. Now we'll explain each step in greater detail.

Introduce the Skill

Players, especially young and inexperienced ones, need to know what skill they are learning and why they are learning it. You should therefore take these three steps every time you introduce a skill to your players:

1. Get your players' attention.
2. Name the skill.
3. Explain the importance of the skill.

Get Your Players' Attention

Because youngsters are easily distracted, use some method to get their attention. Some coaches use interesting news items or stories. Others use jokes. And others simply project a sense of enthusiasm that gets their players to listen. Whatever method you use, speak slightly above the normal volume and look your players in the eye when you speak.

Also, position players so they can see and hear you. Arrange the players in two or three evenly spaced rows, facing you and not some source of distraction. Then ask if all of them can see you before you begin.

Name the Skill

Although you might mention other common names for the skill, decide which one you'll use and stick with it. This will help avoid confusion and enhance communication among your players.

Explain the Importance of the Skill

Although the importance of a skill may be apparent to you, your players may be less able to see how the skill will help them become better basketball players. Offer them a reason for learning the skill and describe how the skill relates to more advanced skills.

> The most difficult aspect of coaching is this: Coaches must learn to let athletes learn. Sport skills should be taught so they have meaning to the child, not just meaning to the coach.
>
> *Rainer Martens, Founder of American Sport Education Program*

Demonstrate the Skill

The demonstration step is the most important part of teaching sport skills to players who may have never done anything closely resembling the skill. They need a picture, not just words. They need to see how the skill is performed.

If you are unable to perform the skill correctly, have an assistant coach, one of your players, or someone skilled in basketball perform the demonstration. These tips will help make your demonstrations more effective:

◎ Use correct form.

◎ Demonstrate the skill several times.

◎ Slow down the action, if possible, during one or two performances so players can see every movement involved in the skill.

◎ Perform the skill at different angles so your players can get a full perspective of it.

◎ Demonstrate the skill with both the right and left hands.

Explain the Skill

Players learn more effectively when they're given a brief explanation of the skill along with the demonstration. Use simple terms and, if possible, relate the skill to previously learned skills. Ask your players whether they understand your description. A good technique is to ask the team to repeat your explanation. Ask questions like: "What are you going to do first?" "Then what?" Watch for looks of confusion or uncertainty, and repeat your explanation and demonstration of those points. If possible, use different words so that your players get a chance to try to understand the skill from a different perspective.

Complex skills often are better understood when they are explained in more manageable parts. For instance, if you want to teach your players how to perform the crossover dribble, you might take the following steps:

1. Show them a correct performance of the entire skill, and explain its function in basketball.

2. Break down the skill and point out its component parts to your players (see chapter 13 to break down skills).

3. Have players perform each of the component skills you have already taught them, such as controlling the dribble at knee level, dribbling with the head up to see the rim, and protecting the ball with the body and the nondribbling hand.

4. After players have demonstrated their ability to perform the separate parts of the skill in sequence, reexplain the entire skill.

5. Have players practice the skill in game-like conditions.

One caution: Young players have short attention spans, and a long demonstration or explanation of the skill will bore them. So spend no more than a few minutes combined on the introduction, demonstration, and explanation phases. Then get the players active in a game that calls on them to perform the skill. The total IDEA should be completed in 10 minutes or less, followed by games in which players practice the skill.

Attend to Players Practicing the Skill

If the skill you selected was within your players' capabilities, and you have done an effective job of introducing, demonstrating, and explaining it, your players should be ready to attempt the skill. Some players may need to be physically guided through the movements during their first few attempts. Walking unsure athletes through the skill in this way will help them gain confidence to perform the skill on their own.

Your teaching duties don't end when all your athletes have demonstrated that they understand how to perform the skill. In fact, a significant part of your teaching will involve observing closely the hit-and-miss trial performances of your players. In the next section we'll guide you in shaping players' skills, and then we'll help you learn how to detect and correct errors, using positive feedback. Keep in mind that your feedback will have a great influence on your players' motivation to practice and improve their performance.

Remember, too, that players need individual instruction. So set aside a time before, during, or after practice to give individual help.

Helping Players Improve Skills

After you have successfully taught your players the fundamentals of a skill, your focus will be on helping them improve that skill. Players will learn skills and improve upon them at different rates, so don't get too frustrated. Instead, help them improve by shaping their skills and detecting and correcting errors.

Shaping Players' Skills

One of your principal teaching duties is to reward positive behavior—in terms of successful skill execution—when you see it. A player makes a good pass in practice, and you immediately say, "That's the way to extend! Good follow-through!" This, plus a smile and a "thumbs up" gesture, go a long way toward reinforcing that technique in that player.

However, sometimes you may have a long, dry spell before you have any correct technique to reinforce. It's difficult to reward players when they aren't executing skills correctly. How can you shape their skills if this is the case?

Shaping skills takes practice on your players' part and patience on your part. Expect your players to make errors. Telling your player who made the great pass that she did a good job doesn't ensure that she'll make that pass the next time. Seeing inconsistency in your players' techniques can be frustrating. It's even more challenging to stay positive when your athletes repeatedly perform a skill incorrectly or lack enthusiasm for learning. It can certainly be frustrating to see athletes who seemingly don't heed your advice and continue to make the same mistakes. And when an athlete doesn't seem to care, you may wonder why you should.

Please know that it is normal to get frustrated at times when teaching skills. Nevertheless, part of successful coaching is controlling this frustration. Instead of getting upset, use these six guidelines for shaping skills:

1. Think small initially. Reward the first signs of behavior that approximate what you want. Then reward closer and closer approximations of the desired behavior. In short, use your reward power to shape the behavior you seek.

2. Break skills into small steps. For instance, in learning to dribble, one of your players does well in keeping the ball close to his body, but he's bouncing the ball too high and not shielding it with his body and nondribbling hand. Reinforce the correct technique of keeping the ball close, and teach him how to dribble at knee level. When he masters that, focus on getting him to shield the ball from defenders.

3. Develop one component of a skill at a time. Don't try to shape two components of a skill at once. For example, in rebounding, players must first block their opponents out, then go for the ball. They should focus first on blocking out by putting their back against their opponent's chest, spreading a wide base, putting the hands up, and then going on for the ball. Athletes who have problems mastering a skill often do so because they're trying to improve two or more components at once. Help these athletes to isolate a single component.

4. As athletes become more proficient at a skill, reinforce them only occasionally, and reinforce only the best examples of the skill behavior. By focusing only on the best examples, this will help them continue to improve once they've mastered the basics.

5. When athletes are trying to master a new skill, temporarily relax your standards for how you reward them. As they focus on the new skill or attempt to integrate it with other skills, the old well-learned skills may temporarily degenerate.

6. If, however, a well-learned skill degenerates for long, you may need to restore it by going back to the basics.

Coaches often have more skilled players provide feedback for teammates as they practice skills. This can be effective, but proceed with caution: you must tell such players exactly what to look for when their teammates are performing the skills. You must also tell them the corrections for the common errors of that skill.

We've looked at how to guide your athletes as they learn skills. Now let's look at another critical teaching principle that you should employ as you're shaping skills: detecting and correcting errors.

Detecting and Correcting Errors

Good coaches recognize that athletes make two types of errors: learning errors and performance errors. *Learning errors* are ones that occur because athletes don't know how to perform a skill; that is, they have not yet developed the correct motor program in the brain to perform a particular skill. *Performance errors* are made not because athletes don't know how to do the skill, but because they made a mistake in executing what they do know. There is no easy way to know whether a player is making "learning" or "performance" errors. Part of the art of coaching is being able to sort out which type of error it is.

The process of helping your athletes correct errors begins with your observing and evaluating their performances to determine if the mistakes are learning or performance errors. For performance errors, you need to look for the reasons that your athletes are not performing as well as they know how. If the mistakes are learning errors, then you need to help them learn the skill, which is the focus of this section.

There is no substitute for knowing skills well in correcting learning errors. The better you understand a skill—not only how it is done correctly but what causes learning errors—the more helpful you will be in correcting mistakes.

One of the most common coaching mistakes is to provide inaccurate feedback and advice on how to correct errors. Don't rush into error correction; wrong feedback or poor advice will hurt the learning process more than no feedback or advice. If you are uncertain about the cause of the problem or how to correct it, continue to observe and analyze until you are more sure. As a rule, you should see the error repeated several times before attempting to correct it.

Correct One Error at a Time

Suppose Jill, one of your forwards, is having trouble with her shooting. She's doing some things well, but you notice that she's extending her arm on too flat a trajectory, resulting in too low an arc, and not squaring up to face the basket on all of her shots. What do you do?

First, decide which error to correct first, because athletes learn more effectively when they attempt to correct one error at a time. Determine whether one error is causing the other; if so, have the athlete correct that error first, because it may eliminate the other error. In Jill's case, however, neither error is causing the other. In such cases, athletes should correct the error that will bring the greatest improvement when remedied—for Jill, this probably means squaring up to the basket. Improvement here will likely motivate her to correct the other error.

Use Positive Feedback to Correct Errors

The positive approach to correcting errors includes emphasizing what to do instead of what not to do. Use compliments, praise, rewards, and encouragement to correct errors. Acknowledge correct performance as well as efforts to improve. By using the positive approach, you can help your athletes feel good about themselves and promote a strong desire to achieve.

When you're working with one athlete at a time, the positive approach to correcting errors includes four steps:

1. Praise effort and correct performance.

2. Give simple and precise feedback to correct errors.

3. Make sure that the athlete understands your feedback.

Let's take a brief look at each step.

Step 1: Praise Effort and Correct Performance.   Praise your athlete for trying to perform a skill correctly and for performing any parts of it correctly. Praise the athlete immediately after he or she performs the skill, if possible. Keep the praise simple: "Good try," "Way to hustle," or "Good form," "Good extension," "That's the way to follow through." You can also use nonverbal feedback, such as smiling, clapping your hands, or any facial or body expression that shows approval.

Make sure you're sincere with your praise. Don't indicate that an athlete's effort was good when it wasn't. Usually an athlete knows when he or she has made a sincere effort to perform the skill correctly, and perceives undeserved praise for what it is—untruthful feedback to make him or her feel good. Likewise, don't indicate that a player's performance was correct when it wasn't.

Step 2: Give Simple and Precise Feedback.   Don't burden a player with a long or detailed explanation of how to correct an error. Give just enough feedback so the player can correct one error at a time. Before giving feedback, realize that some athletes will readily accept it immediately after the error; others will respond better if you slightly delay the correction.

For errors that are complicated to explain and difficult to correct, try the following:

◎ Explain and demonstrate what the athlete should have done.

◎ Explain the cause or causes of the error, if this isn't obvious.

◎ Explain why you are recommending the correction you have selected, if it's not obvious.

Step 3: Make Sure the Athlete Understands Your Feedback. If the athlete doesn't understand your feedback, he or she won't be able to correct the error. Ask him or her to repeat the feedback and to explain and demonstrate how it will be used. If the athlete can't do this, be patient and present your feedback again, and have the athlete repeat the feedback after you're finished.

Step 4: Provide an Environment that Motivates the Athlete to Improve. Your players won't always be able to correct their errors immediately even if they do understand your feedback. Encourage them to "hang tough" and stick with it when corrections are difficult or they seem discouraged. For more difficult corrections, remind them that it will take time, and the improvement will happen only if they work at it. Look to encourage players with low self-confidence. Saying something like, "You were dribbling at a much better speed today; with practice, you'll be able to keep the ball closer to you and shield it from defenders," can motivate a player to continue to refine his or her dribbling skills.

Some athletes need to be more motivated to improve. Others may be very self-motivated and need little help from you here at all; with them you can practically ignore Step 4 when correcting an error. While motivation comes from within, look to provide an environment of positive instruction and encouragement to help your athletes improve.

A final note on correcting errors: Team sports such as basketball provide unique challenges in this endeavor. How do you provide individual feedback in a group setting using a positive approach? Instead of yelling across the court to correct an error (and embarrassing the player), substitute for the player who erred. Then make the correction on the sidelines. This type of feedback has three advantages:

◎ The player will be more receptive to the one-on-one feedback.

◎ The other players are still active, still practicing skills, and unable to hear your discussion.

◎ Because the rest of the team is still playing, you'll feel compelled to make your comments simple and concise—which, as we've said, is more helpful to the player.

This doesn't mean you can't use the team setting to give specific, positive feedback. You can do so to emphasize correct group and individual performances. Use this team feedback approach *only* for positive statements, though. Keep any negative feedback for individual discussions.

Speaking of negative feedback, there are times when you'll have to deal with players who are misbehaving in practice. In the next section we'll help you handle these situations.

Dealing With Misbehavior

Athletes will misbehave at times; it's only natural. Following are two ways you can respond to misbehavior: through extinction or discipline.

Extinction

Ignoring a misbehavior—neither rewarding nor disciplining it—is called extinction. This can be effective under certain circumstances. In some situations, disciplining young people's misbehavior only encourages them to act up further because of the recognition they get. Ignoring misbehavior teaches youngsters that it is not worth your attention.

Sometimes, though, you cannot wait for a behavior to fizzle out. When players cause danger to themselves or others or disrupt the activities of others, you need to take immediate action. Tell the offending player that the behavior must stop and that discipline will follow if it doesn't. If the athlete doesn't stop misbehaving after the warning, discipline.

Extinction also doesn't work well when a misbehavior is self-rewarding. For example, you may be able to keep from grimacing if a youngster kicks you in the shin, but he or she still knows you were hurt. Therein lies the reward. In these circumstances, it is also necessary to discipline the undesirable behavior.

Extinction works best in situations where players are seeking recognition through mischievous behaviors, clowning, or grandstanding. Usually, if you are patient, their failure to get your attention will cause the behavior to disappear.

On the other hand, be alert that you don't extinguish desirable behavior. When youngsters do something well, they expect to be positively reinforced. Not rewarding them will likely cause them to discontinue the behavior.

Discipline

Some educators say we should never discipline young people, but should only reinforce their positive behaviors. They argue that discipline does not work, that it creates hostility and sometimes develops avoidance behaviors that may be more unwholesome than the original problem behavior. It is true that discipline does not always work and that it can create problems when used ineffectively, but when used appropriately, discipline is effective in eliminating undesirable behaviors without creating other undesirable consequences. You must use discipline effectively, because it is impossible to guide athletes through positive reinforcement and extinction alone. Discipline is part of the positive approach when these guidelines are followed:

◎ Discipline in a corrective way to help athletes improve now and in the future. Don't discipline to retaliate and make yourself feel better.

◎ Impose discipline in an impersonal way when athletes break team rules or otherwise misbehave. Shouting or scolding athletes indicates that your attitude is one of revenge.

◎ Once a good rule has been agreed upon, ensure that athletes who violate it experience the unpleasant consequences of their misbehavior. Don't wave discipline threateningly over their heads. Just do it.

◎ Warn an athlete once before disciplining.

◎ Be consistent in administering discipline.

◎ Don't pick disciplines that may cause you guilt. If you can't think of an appropriate discipline right away, tell the player you will talk with him or her after you think about it.

◎ Once the discipline is completed, don't make athletes feel they are in the doghouse. Make them feel that they're valued members of the team again.

◎ Make sure that what you think is discipline isn't perceived by the athlete as a positive reinforcement.

◎ Never discipline athletes for making errors when they are playing.

◎ Never use physical activity—running laps or doing push-ups—as discipline. To do so only causes athletes to resent physical activity, something we want them to learn to enjoy throughout their lives.

◎ Discipline sparingly. Constant discipline and criticism cause athletes to turn their interests elsewhere and to resent you as well.

Coaching Principles

Contests provide the opportunity for your players to show what they've learned in practice. Just as your players' focus shifts on contest days from learning and practicing to *competing,* so your focus shifts from teaching skills to coaching players as they perform those skills in contests. Of course, the contest is a teaching opportunity as well, but the focus is on performing what has been previously learned.

In the last chapter you learned how to teach your players basketball tactics and skills; in this chapter we will help you coach your players as they execute those tactics and skills in contests. We'll provide important coaching principles that will guide you throughout the game day—before, during, and after the contest.

Before the Contest

Just as you need a practice plan for what you're going to do each practice, you need a game plan for what to do on the day of a game. Many inexperienced coaches focus only on how they will coach during the contest itself, but your preparations to coach should include details that begin well before the first play of the game. In fact, your preparations should begin during the practice before the contest.

Preparations at Practice

During the practice a day or two before the next contest, you should do two things (besides practicing tactics and skills) to prepare your players: decide on any specific team tactics that you want to employ, and discuss pre-game particulars such as what to eat before the game, what to wear, and when to be at the gym.

Deciding Team Tactics

Some coaches see themselves as great military strategists guiding their young warriors to victory on the battlefield. These coaches burn the midnight oil as they devise a complex plan of attack. There are several things that are wrong with this approach, but we'll point out two errors in terms of deciding team tactics:

1. The decision on team tactics should be made with input from the players.

2. Team tactics at the YMCA Winners level don't need to be complex.

Perhaps you guessed right on number 2 but were surprised by number 1. Why should you include your players in deciding tactics? Isn't that the coach's role?

It's the coach's role to help youngsters grow through the sport experience. Giving your athletes a chance to give their input on team tactics helps them to learn the game. It gets them involved at a planning level that often is reserved solely for the coach. It gives them a feeling of ownership; they're not just "carrying out orders" of the coach. They're executing the plan of attack that was jointly decided. Youngsters who have a say in how they approach a task often respond with more enthusiasm and motivation.

Don't dampen that enthusiasm and motivation by concocting tactics that are too complex. Keep tactics simple, especially at the younger levels. Focus on maintaining good court balance, penetrating the defense, setting screens to get players open, taking good shots on offense, and cutting off passing lanes on defense.

As you become more familiar with your team's tendencies and abilities, help them focus on specific tactics that will help them play better. For example, if your team has a tendency to stand around and watch the action, emphasize moving more and spreading out the attack. If they are active and moving throughout the game, but not in any cohesive fashion, focus them on setting screens, penetrating the defense, and looking to open up passing lanes.

If you're coaching 12- and 13-year-olds, you might institute certain plays that your team has practiced. These plays should take advantage of your players' strengths. Again, give the players some input as to what plays might be employed in a game.

Discussing Precontest Particulars

Players need to know what to do before a contest: what they should eat on game day and when; what clothing they should wear to the game; what equipment they should bring; what time they should arrive at the gym. Discuss these particulars with them at the practice before a contest. Here are guidelines for discussing these items:

◎ **Pregame Meal.** Carbohydrates are easily digested and absorbed, and are a ready source of fuel. Players should eat a high-carbohydrate meal, ideally about three to four hours before a game to allow the stomach to empty completely. This won't be possible for games held in early morning; in this case, athletes should still eat food high in carbohydrates, such as an English muffin, toast, or cereal, but not eat so much that their stomachs are full. An athlete's pregame meal shouldn't include foods that are spicy or high in fat content.

◎ **Clothing and Equipment.** Instruct players to wear their team shirts or uniforms, shorts, suitable shoes, and sweats.

Players may not wear equipment with projecting metal or other hard plates or with exposed sharp edges. They also may not wear pads containing hard or unyielding materials, even if covered with soft padding.

◎ **Time to Arrive.** Your players will need to adequately warm up before a game; instruct them to arrive 20 minutes before a game to go through a team warm-up (see "The Warm-Up" later in this chapter).

Facilities and Support Personnel

Although the site coordinator and referees have responsibilities regarding facilities and equipment, it's wise for you to know what to look for to make sure the contest is safe for the athletes. You should arrive at the gym 25 to 30 minutes before game time so you can check the court, check in with the site coordinator and referees, and greet your players as they arrive to warm up. The site coordinator and referees should be checking the facilities and preparing for the contest. If referees aren't arriving before the game when they're supposed to, inform the site coordinator. A facilities checklist includes the following:

Gymnasium Facilities

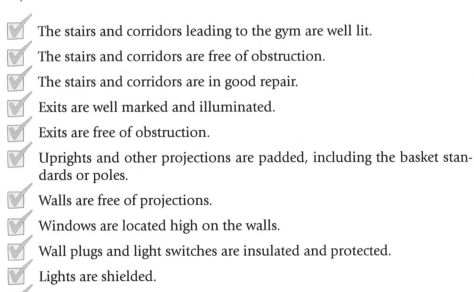

The stairs and corridors leading to the gym are well lit.

The stairs and corridors are free of obstruction.

The stairs and corridors are in good repair.

Exits are well marked and illuminated.

Exits are free of obstruction.

Uprights and other projections are padded, including the basket standards or poles.

Walls are free of projections.

Windows are located high on the walls.

Wall plugs and light switches are insulated and protected.

Lights are shielded.

Lighting is sufficient to illuminate the playing area well.

☑ The heating/cooling system for the gym is working properly and is monitored regularly.

☑ Ducts, radiators, pipes, etc. are shielded or designed to withstand high impact.

☑ Tamper-free thermostats are housed in impact-resistant covers.

☑ If there is an overhanging track it has secure railings with a minimum height of three feet, six inches.

☑ The track has direction signs posted.

☑ The track is free of obstructions.

☑ Rules for the track are posted.

☑ Projections on the track are padded or illuminated.

☑ Gym equipment is inspected prior to and during each use.

☑ The gym is adequately supervised.

☑ Galleries and viewing areas have been designed to protect small children by blocking their access to the playing area.

☑ The gym (floor, roof, walls, light fixtures, etc.) is inspected on an annual basis for safety and structural deficiencies.

☑ Fire alarms are in good working order.

☑ Fire extinguishers are up to date, with note of last inspection.

☑ Directions are posted for evacuating the gym in case of fire.

Communicating With Parents

The groundwork for your communication with parents will have been laid in the Parent Orientation Program, through which parents learn the best ways to support their kids'—and the whole team's—efforts on the court. As parents gather in the gym before a contest, let them know what the team has been focusing on during the past week and what your goals are for the game. For instance, perhaps you've worked on the "give-and-go" play in practice this week; encourage parents to watch for improvement and success in executing this play and to support the team as they attempt all tactics and skills. Help parents to judge success not just based on the contest outcome, but on how the kids are improving their performances.

If parents yell at the kids for mistakes made during the game, make disparaging remarks about the referees or opponents, or shout instructions on what tactics to employ, ask them to refrain from making such remarks and to instead be supportive of the team in their comments and actions.

After a contest, briefly and informally assess with parents, as the opportunity arises, how the team did based not on the outcome, but on meeting performance goals and playing to the best of their abilities. Help parents see the contest as a process, not solely as a test that's pass/fail or win/lose. Encourage parents to reinforce that concept at home.

Unplanned Events

Part of being prepared to coach is to expect the unexpected. What do you do if players are late? What if *you* have an emergency and can't make the game or will be late? What if the contest is postponed? Being prepared to handle out-of-the-ordinary circumstances will help you when those unplanned events happen.

If players are late, you may have to adjust your starting lineup. While this may not be a major inconvenience, do stress to your players the importance of being on time for two reasons:

◎ Part of being a member of a team means being committed and responsible to the other members. When players don't show up, or show up late, they break that commitment.

◎ Players need to go through a warm-up to physically prepare for the contest. Skipping the warm-up risks injury.

Consider making a team rule stating that players need to show up 20 minutes before a game and go through the complete team warm-up, or they won't start.

An emergency might cause *you* to be late or miss a game. In such cases, notify your assistant coach, if you have one, or the league coordinator. If notified in advance, a parent of a player or another volunteer might be able to step in for the contest.

Sometimes a game will be postponed because of inclement weather or for other reasons (such as unsafe court conditions). If the postponement takes place before game day, you'll need to call each member of your team to let them know. If it happens while the teams are on the court preparing for the game, gather your team and tell them the news and why the game is being postponed. Make sure all your players have rides home before you leave.

The Warm-Up

Players need to both physically and mentally prepare for a game once they arrive at the gym. Physical preparation involves warming up. We've suggested that players arrive 20 minutes before the game to warm up. Conduct the warm-up similar to practice warm-ups, with some brief games that focus on skill practice and stretching.

Players should prepare to do what they will do in the game: dribble, pass, receive, shoot, defend, and rebound. This doesn't mean they spend extensive time on each skill; you can plan two or three brief practice games that encompass all of those skills.

After playing a few brief games, your players should stretch. You don't need to deliver any big pep talk, but you can help your players mentally prepare as they stretch by reminding them

◎ of the tactics and skills they've been working on in recent practices. Especially focus their attention on what they've been doing well. Focus on their strengths.

◎ of the team tactics you decided on in your previous practice.

45

◎ to focus on performing the tactics and skills to the best of their individual abilities, and to play together as a team.

◎ to play hard, play smart, and have fun!

During the Contest

The bulleted list you just read goes a long way toward defining your focus for coaching during the contest. Throughout the game, you'll keep the game in proper perspective and help your players do the same. You'll observe how your players execute tactics and skills and how well they play together. You'll make tactical decisions in a number of areas. You'll model appropriate behavior on the bench, showing respect for opponents and referees, and demand the same of your athletes. You'll watch out for your athletes' physical safety and psychological welfare, in terms of building their self-esteem and helping them manage stress and anxiety.

Proper Perspective

Winning is the short-term goal, but the "Winners" in YMCA Winners doesn't refer to winning games. It refers to helping your players learn the tactics, skills, and rules of basketball, how to become fit, and how to be good sports in basketball and in life. That's the long-term goal of YMCA Winners Basketball. Your young athletes are winning when they are becoming better human beings through their participation in basketball. Keep that perspective in mind when you coach. *You* have the privilege of setting the tone for how your team approaches the game. Keep winning and all aspects of the competition in proper perspective, and your young charges likely will follow suit.

Tactical Decisions

While you aren't called on to be a great military strategist, you are called on to make tactical decisions in several areas throughout a contest. You'll make decisions about who starts the game and when to enter substitutes, about making slight adjustments to your team's tactics, and about correcting players' performance errors or leaving the correction for the next practice.

Starting and Substituting Players

In considering playing time, remember Pillar One of the Seven Pillars of YMCA Youth Super Sports: Everyone plays at least half of each game. This should be your guiding principle as you consider starting and substitution patterns. We suggest you consider two options in substituting players:

◎ **Substituting Individually.** Replace one player with another. This offers you a lot of latitude in deciding who goes in when, and gives you the greatest mix of players throughout the game, but it can be hard to keep track of playing time (this could be eased by assigning an assistant or a parent to this task). Remember that each player is required to play one half of each game.

◎ **Substituting by Quarters.** The advantage here is that you can easily track playing time, and players know how long they will be in before they might be replaced.

Adjusting Team Tactics

At the 8 to 9 and 10 to 11 age levels, you probably won't adjust your team tactics too significantly during a game; rather, you'll focus on the basic tactics in general and emphasize during breaks which tactics your team needs to work on in particular. However, coaches of 12- to 13-year-olds might have cause to make tactical adjustments to improve their team's chances of performing well and winning. As games progress, assess your opponents' style of play and tactics, and make adjustments that are appropriate—that is, that your players are prepared for. For example, if your opponent likes to run a lot, and is beating your team on fast breaks, you might make sure you have at least a few quick players who can get back on defense.

However, don't stress tactics too much during a game. Doing so can take the fun out of the game for the players. If you don't trust your memory, carry a pen and notepad to note which team tactics and individual skills need attention in the next practice.

Correcting Players' Errors

In chapter 5 you learned about two types of errors: learning errors and performance errors. Learning errors are ones that occur because athletes don't know how to perform a skill. Athletes make performance errors not because they don't know how to do the skill, but because they made a mistake in executing what they do know.

Sometimes it's not easy to tell which type of error athletes are making. Knowing your athletes' capabilities helps you to know whether they know the skill and are simply making mistakes in executing it, or whether they don't really know how to perform the skill. If they are making learning errors—that is, they don't know how to perform the skills—you'll need to make note of this and teach them at the next practice. Game time is not the time to teach skills.

If they are making performance errors, however, you can help players correct those errors during a game. Players who make performance errors often do so because they have a lapse in concentration or motivation—or they are simply demonstrating the human quality of sometimes doing things incorrectly. A word of encouragement to concentrate more may help. If you do correct a performance error during a contest, do so in a quiet, controlled, and positive tone of voice during a break or when the player is on the bench with you.

For those making performance errors, you have to decide if it is just the occasional error anyone makes, or an expected error for a youngster at that stage of development. If that is the case, then the player may appreciate you not commenting on the mistake. The player knows it was a mistake and knows how to correct it. On the other hand, perhaps an encouraging word and a "coaching cue" (such as "Remember to follow through on your shots") may be just what the athlete needs. Knowing the players and what to say is very much a part of the "art" of coaching.

Coach's and Players' Behavior

Another aspect of coaching on game day is managing behavior—both yours and your athletes'. The two are closely connected.

Your Conduct

You very much influence your players' behavior before, during, and after a contest. If you're up, your players are more likely to be up. If you're anxious, they'll notice and the anxiety can be contagious. If you're negative, they'll respond with worry. If you're positive, they'll play with more enjoyment. If you're constantly yelling instructions or commenting on mistakes and errors, it will be difficult for players to concentrate. Let players get into the flow of the game.

Remember that the focus in YMCA Youth Super Sports is on positive competition and on having fun. A coach who overorganizes everything and dominates a game from the sideline is definitely *not* making the contest fun.

So how should you conduct yourself on the bench? Here are a few pointers:

◎ Be calm, in control, and supportive of your players.

◎ Encourage players often, but instruct during play sparingly. Players should be focusing on their performance during a game, not on instructions shouted from the bench.

◎ If you need to instruct a player, do so when you're both on the bench, in an unobtrusive manner.

◎ Never yell at players for making a mistake. Instead, briefly demonstrate or remind them of the correct technique and encourage them.

Remember, you're not playing for a gold medal in the Olympics. YMCA Winners competitions are designed to help players develop their skills and themselves and to have fun. Coach at games in a manner that helps your players do just that.

Players' Conduct

You're responsible for keeping your players under control. Do so by setting a good example and by disciplining when necessary. Set team rules of good behavior consistent with the philosophy of YMCA Youth Super Sports. If players attempt to cheat, fight, argue, badger, yell disparaging remarks, and the like, it is your responsibility to correct the misbehavior. Consider team rules in these areas of game conduct:

◎ Players' language

◎ Players' behavior

◎ Interactions with referees

◎ Discipline for misbehavior

◎ Dress code for competitions

Players' Physical Safety

We have devoted the entire next chapter (chapter 7) to providing for players' safety, but it's worth noting here that safety during contests can be affected by how referees are calling the rules. If they aren't calling rules correctly, and this risks injury to your players, you must intervene. Voice your concern in a way that places the emphasis where it should be: on the athletes' safety. One of the referees' main responsibilities is to provide for athletes' safety; you are not adversaries here. Don't hesitate to address an issue of safety with a referee when the need arises.

Players' Psychological Welfare

Athletes often attach their self-worth to winning and losing. This idea is fueled by coaches, parents, and peers who place great emphasis on winning. Players become anxious when they're uncertain if they can meet the expectations of others or of themselves when meeting these expectations is important to them.

If you place too much importance on the game or cause your athletes to doubt their abilities, they will become anxious about the outcome and their performance. If your players look uptight and anxious during the contest, find ways to reduce both the uncertainties about how their performance will be evaluated and the importance they are attaching to the game. Help athletes focus on realistic personal goals—goals that are reachable and measurable and that will help them improve their performance. Another way to reduce anxiety on game day is to stay away from emotional pre-game pep talks. We provided guidance earlier in what to address before the game.

When coaching during contests, remember that the most important outcome from playing basketball is to build or enhance players' self-worth. Keep that firmly in mind, and strive to make every coaching decision in the best interest of your athletes' self-worth.

Opponents and Referees

Respect opponents and referees. Without them, you wouldn't have a competition. Opponents provide an opportunity for your team to test itself, to improve, and to excel.

You and your team show respect for opponents by giving your best effort. Showing respect doesn't necessarily mean being "nice" to your opponents, though it does mean being civil. You owe your opponents your best effort.

Don't allow your players to "trash talk" or taunt an opponent. That's disrespectful to the spirit of the competition and to the opponent. Immediately remove a player from a contest if he or she disobeys your orders here.

Remember that referees are quite often teenagers—in many cases not much older than the players themselves. The level of officiating should be commensurate to the level of play. In other words, don't expect perfection from referees any more than you do from your own players. And realize that the referees are there to help players learn the rules and skills, too. Especially at younger levels, they *won't* make every call, because to do so would stop the contest every 10 seconds.

After the Contest

When the game is over, join your team in congratulating the coaches and players of the opposing team, and thank the referees. Check on any injuries players sustained and let them know how to care for them. Be prepared to speak with the referees about any problems that occurred during the game. Then hold a brief Team Circle, as explained in a moment, to ensure that your players are on an even keel, whether they won or lost.

Winning With Class, Losing With Dignity

When celebrating a victory, make sure your team does so in a way that doesn't show disrespect for the opponents. It's fine and appropriate to be happy and celebrate a win, but don't allow your players to taunt the opponents or boast about their victory. Keep winning in perspective. Winning and losing are a part of life, not just a part of sports. If players can handle both equally well, they'll be successful in whatever they do.

Athletes are competitors, and competitors will be disappointed in defeat. If your team has made a winning effort, let them know that. After a loss, help them keep their chins up and maintain a positive attitude that will carry over into the next practice and contest.

The Team Circle

If your team has performed well in a game, compliment them and congratulate them immediately afterward. Tell them specifically what they did well, whether they won or lost. This will reinforce their desire to repeat their good performances.

Don't criticize individual players for poor performances in front of teammates. Help a player understand how to improve skills, but do so in the next practice, not immediately after a game.

The post-game Team Circle isn't the time to go over tactical problems and adjustments. The players are either so happy after a win or so dejected after a loss that they won't absorb much tactical information immediately following a game. Your first concern should be your players' attitudes and mental well-being. You don't want them to be too high after a win or too low after a loss. This is the time you can be most influential in keeping the outcome in perspective and keeping them on an even keel.

And last but not least, make sure your players have transportation home.

Safety

One of your players breaks free down the court, dribbling the ball. But a defender catches up and accidentally trips the player, who is going in for a lay-up. Your player is not getting up from the floor and seems to be in pain. What do you do?

No coach wants to see players get hurt. But injury remains a reality of sport participation; consequently, you must be prepared to provide first aid when injuries occur and to protect yourself against unjustified lawsuits. Fortunately, there are many preventive measures coaches can institute to reduce the risk. This chapter will describe how you can

◎ create the safest possible environment for your players,

◎ respond appropriately when players get hurt, and

◎ protect yourself from injury liability.

Providing for Players' Safety

You can't prevent all injuries from happening, but you can take preventive measures that give your players the best possible chance for injury-free participation. In creating the safest possible environment for your athletes, we'll explore what you can do in these six areas:

◎ Preseason physical examinations

◎ Players' fitness

◎ Equipment and facilities inspection

◎ Player match-ups and inherent risks

◎ Proper supervision and record-keeping

◎ Environmental conditions

We'll begin with what should take place *before* the season begins: the preseason physical examination.

Preseason Physical Examination

We recommend that your players have a physical examination before participating in YMCA Winners basketball. The exam should address the most likely areas of medical concern and identify youngsters at high risk. We also suggest that you have players' parents or guardians sign a participation agreement form and a release form to allow their children to be treated in case of an emergency. See appendix B, Preparticipation Screening for YMCA Youth Sports Programs, for specific information on what should take place during the preseason physical examination.

Players' Fitness

Players need to be in, or get in, shape to play the game at the level expected. To do so, they'll need to have adequate *cardiorespiratory fitness* and *muscular fitness*. We'll address fitness issues in detail in chapter 15, but here we'll briefly describe these two types of fitness as they apply to players' safety and injury prevention.

Cardiorespiratory fitness involves the body's ability to store and use fuels efficiently to power muscle contractions. As players get in better shape, their bodies are able to more efficiently deliver oxygen and fuels to muscles and carry off carbon dioxides and other wastes. Basketball involves lots of running; most players will have to be able to move almost continuously and make short bursts throughout a game. Youngsters who aren't as fit as their peers often overextend in trying to make up for their lack of fitness, which could result in lightheadedness and nausea.

An advantage of YMCA Winners basketball is that kids are active during almost the entire practice; there is no standing around in lines or watching teammates take part in drills. Players will be attaining higher levels of cardiorespiratory fitness as the season progresses simply by taking part in practice. However, watch closely for signs of low levels of cardiorespiratory fitness; don't let your athletes do too much until they're fit. You might privately counsel youngsters who appear overly winded, suggesting that they train outside of practice to increase their fitness.

Muscular fitness encompasses strength, muscle endurance, power, speed, and flexibility. This type of fitness is affected by physical maturity, as well as strength training and other types of training. Your players will likely exhibit a relatively wide range of muscular fitness. Those who have greater muscular fitness will be able to run faster and pass harder. They will also sustain fewer muscular injuries, and those injuries will tend to be more minor in nature. And in case of injury, recovery rate is accelerated for those with higher levels of muscular fitness. We'll address the issue of building muscular strength in chapter 15.

Two other components of fitness and injury prevention are the warm-up and the cooldown. Although young bodies are generally very limber, they too can get tight from inactivity. The warm-up should address each muscle group and get the heart rate elevated in preparation for strenuous activity. Therefore, we have built into the practice plans 10 minutes of warming up, which includes playing games and stretching.

As practice winds down, slow players' heart rates with an easy jog or walk. Then, during the Team Circle that concludes the practice, have players stretch for five minutes to help avoid stiff muscles and make them less tight before the next practice or contest.

Equipment and Facilities Inspection

Another way to prevent injuries is to examine regularly the court on which your players practice and play. Remove hazards, report conditions you cannot remedy, and request maintenance as necessary. If unsafe conditions exist, either make adaptations to avoid risk to your players' safety or stop the practice or game until safe conditions have been restored.

Player Match-Ups and Inherent Risks

We recommend you group teams in two-year age ranges if possible. You'll encounter fewer mismatches in physical maturation with narrow age ranges. Even so, two 12-year-old boys might differ by 90 pounds in weight, a foot in height, and three or four years in emotional and intellectual maturity. This presents dangers for the less mature. Whenever possible, match players against opponents of similar size and physical maturity. Such an approach gives smaller, less mature youngsters a better chance to succeed and avoid injury, and provides more mature players with more of a challenge. Closely supervise games so that the more mature do not put the less mature at undue risk.

Matching helps protect you from certain liability concerns. But you also must warn players of the inherent risks involved in playing basketball, because "failure to warn" is one of the most successful arguments in lawsuits against coaches. So, thoroughly explain the inherent risks of basketball, and make sure each player knows, understands, and appreciates those risks.

The preseason parent-orientation meeting is a good opportunity to explain the risks of the sport to parents and players. It is also a good occasion to have both the players and their parents sign waivers releasing you from liability should an injury occur. Such waivers do not relieve you of responsibility for your players' well-being, but they are recommended by lawyers.

Proper Supervision and Record Keeping

To ensure players' safety, you will need to provide both general supervision and specific supervision. *General supervision* is being in the area of activity so that you can see and hear what is happening. You should be

◉ immediately accessible to the activity and able to oversee the entire activity;

◉ alert to conditions that may be dangerous to players and to take action to protect them; and

◉ able to react immediately and appropriately to emergencies.

Specific supervision is direct supervision of an activity at practice. For example, you should provide specific supervision when you teach new skills and continue it until your athletes understand the requirements of the activity, the risks involved, and their own ability to perform in light of these risks. You need to also provide specific supervision when you notice either players breaking rules or a change in the condition of your athletes.

As a general rule, the more dangerous the activity the more specific the supervision required. This suggests that more specific supervision is required with younger and less experienced athletes.

As part of your supervision duty, you are expected to foresee potentially dangerous situations and to be positioned to help prevent them from occurring. This requires that you know basketball well, especially the rules that are intended to provide for safety. Prohibit dangerous horseplay, and hold practices only under safe weather conditions (e.g., cancel practice if severe winter weather is forecast). These specific supervisory activities will make the play environment safer for your players and will help protect you from liability if a mishap does occur.

For further protection, keep records of your season plans, practice plans, and players' injuries. Season and practice plans come in handy when you need evidence that players have been taught certain skills, whereas accurate, detailed injury-report forms offer protection against unfounded lawsuits. Ask for these forms from your YMCA (appendix E has a sample injury-report form), and hold onto these records for several years so that an "old basketball injury" of a former player doesn't come back to haunt you.

Environmental Conditions

Most problems due to environmental factors are related to excessive heat or cold, though you should also consider other environmental factors such as severe weather and pollution. While the risks here for an indoor sport are relatively minimal, a little thought about the potential problems and a little effort to ensure adequate protection for your athletes will eliminate most serious emergencies that are related to environmental conditions.

Heat

On hot, humid days the body has difficulty cooling itself. Because the air is already saturated with water vapor (humidity), sweat doesn't evaporate as

Water, Water Everywhere

Encourage players to drink plenty of water before, during, and after practice. Because water makes up 45 percent to 65 percent of a youngster's body weight and water weighs about a pound per pint, the loss of even a little bit of water can have severe consequences for the body's systems. And it doesn't have to be hot and humid for players to become dehydrated. Nor do players have to feel thirsty; in fact, by the time they are aware of their thirst, they are long overdue for a drink.

easily. Therefore, body sweat is a less effective cooling agent, and the body retains extra heat. Hot, humid environments make athletes prone to heat exhaustion and heatstroke (see more on these in "Serious Injuries" on page 61). And if *you* think it's hot or humid, it's worse on the kids—not just because they're more active, but because youngsters under the age of 12 have a more difficult time than adults regulating their body temperature. To provide for players' safety in hot or humid conditions, take the following preventive measures.

◎ **Monitor weather conditions and adjust practices accordingly.** Figure 7.1 shows the specific air temperatures and humidity percentages that can be hazardous.

◎ **Acclimatize players to exercising in high heat and humidity.** Athletes can make adjustments to high heat and humidity over 7 to 10 days. During this time, hold practices at low to moderate activity levels and give the players water breaks every 20 minutes.

◎ **Switch to light clothing.** Players should wear shorts and white T-shirts.

◎ **Identify and monitor players who are prone to heat illness.** Players who are overweight, heavily muscled, or out of shape will be more prone to heat illness, as are athletes who work excessively hard or who have suffered heat illness before. Closely monitor these athletes and give them water breaks every 15 to 20 minutes.

◎ **Make sure athletes replace water lost through sweat.** Encourage your players to drink one liter of water each day, to drink eight ounces of water every 15 minutes during practice or competition, and to drink four to eight ounces of water 15 minutes before practice or competition.

◎ **Replenish electrolytes lost through sweat.** Sodium (salt) and potassium are lost through sweat. The best way to replace these nutrients is by

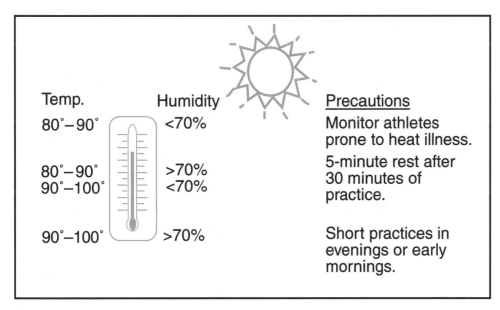

Temp.	Humidity	Precautions
80°–90°	<70%	Monitor athletes prone to heat illness.
80°–90°	>70%	5-minute rest after 30 minutes of practice.
90°–100°	<70%	
90°–100°	>70%	Short practices in evenings or early mornings.

Figure 7.1 Warm-weather precautions.

eating a normal diet that contains fresh fruits and vegetables. Bananas are a good source of potassium. The normal American diet contains plenty of salt, so players don't need to go overboard in salting their food to replace lost sodium.

Severe Weather

Severe weather refers to a host of potential dangers, including lightning storms and the potential for tornadoes. Sometimes basketball practices might be held outside; if you do practice outdoors, you'll need to pay heed to this information.

Lightning is of special concern because it can come up quickly and can cause great harm or even kill. For each five-second count from the flash of lightning to the bang of thunder, lightning is one mile away. A flash-bang of 10 seconds means lightning is two miles away; a flash-bang of 15 seconds indicates lightning is three miles away. A practice or competition should be stopped for the day if lightning is three miles away or less (15 seconds or less from flash to bang).

Safe places to take cover when lightning strikes are: fully enclosed metal vehicles with the windows up, enclosed buildings, and low ground (under cover of bushes, if possible). It's *not* safe to be near metallic objects—flag poles, fences, light poles, metal bleachers, and so on. Also avoid trees, water, and open fields.

Cancel practice when under either a tornado watch or warning. If for some reason you are practicing or competing when a tornado is nearby, you should get inside a building if possible. If not, lie in a ditch or low-lying area, or crouch near a strong building, and use your arms to protect your head and neck.

The keys with severe weather are caution and prudence. Don't try to get that last 10 minutes of practice in if lightning is on the horizon. Don't continue to play in heavy rains. Many storms can strike both quickly and ferociously. Respect the weather and play it safe.

Air Pollution

Poor air quality and smog can present real dangers to your players, even playing indoors. Both short- and long-term lung damage are possible from participating in unsafe air. While it's true that participating in clean air is not possible in many areas, restricting activity is recommended when the air-quality ratings are worse than moderate, or when there is a smog alert. Your local health department or air-quality control board can inform you of the air-quality ratings for your area and when restricting activities is recommended.

 ## Responding to Players' Injuries

No matter how good and thorough your prevention program, injuries may occur. When injury does strike, chances are you will be the one in charge. The severity and nature of the injury will determine how actively involved you'll be in treating the injury. But regardless of how seriously a player is hurt, it is your responsibility to know what steps to take. So let's look at how you should prepare in order to be able to provide basic emergency care to your injured athletes and take the appropriate action when an injury does occur.

Being Prepared

Being prepared to provide basic emergency care involves three steps: being trained in cardiopulmonary resuscitation (CPR) and first aid; having an appropriately stocked first aid kit on hand at practices and games; and having an emergency plan.

CPR and First Aid Training

We recommend that all YMCA Winners coaches receive CPR and first aid training from a nationally recognized organization (the National Safety Council, the American Heart Association, the American Red Cross, or the American Sport Education Program). You should be certified based on a practical and written test of knowledge. CPR training should include pediatric and adult basic life support and obstructed airway.

First Aid Kit

A well-stocked first aid kit should include the following:

◎ List of emergency phone numbers

◎ Change for a pay phone

◎ Face shield (for rescue breathing and CPR)

◎ Bandage scissors

◎ Plastic bags for crushed ice

◎ Three-inch and four-inch elastic wraps

◎ Triangular bandages

◎ Sterile gauze pads—three-inch and four-inch squares

◎ Saline solution for eyes

◎ Contact lens case

◎ Mirror

◎ Penlight

◎ Tongue depressors

◎ Cotton swabs

◎ Butterfly strips

◎ Bandage strips—assorted sizes

◎ Alcohol or peroxide

◎ Antibacterial soap

◎ First aid cream or antibacterial ointment

◎ Petroleum jelly

◎ Tape adherent and tape remover

◎ White athletic tape (1-1/2-inch)

◎ Prewrap

◎ Sterile gauze rolls

◎ Insect sting kit

◎ Safety pins

◎ 1/8-inch, 1/4-inch, and 1/2-inch foam rubber

◎ Disposable surgical gloves

◎ Thermometer

Emergency Plan

An emergency plan is the final step in preparing to take appropriate action for severe or serious injuries. The plan calls for three steps:

1. Evaluate the injured player. Your CPR and first aid training will guide you here.

2. Call the appropriate medical personnel. If possible, delegate the responsibility of seeking medical help to another calm and responsible adult who is on hand for all practices and games. Write out a list of emergency phone numbers and keep it with you at practices and games. Include the following phone numbers:

◎ Rescue unit
◎ Hospital
◎ Physician
◎ Police
◎ Fire department

Take each athlete's emergency information to every practice and game (see appendix C). This information includes who to contact in case of an emergency, what types of medications the athlete is using, what types of drugs he or she is allergic to, and so on.

Give an emergency response card (see appendix D) to the contact person calling for emergency assistance. This provides the information the contact person needs to convey and will help that person keep calm, knowing that everything he or she needs to communicate is on the card. Also complete an injury report form (see appendix E) and keep it on file for any injury that occurs.

3. Provide first aid. If medical personnel are not on hand at the time of the injury, you should provide first aid care to the extent of your qualifications. Again, your CPR and first aid training will guide you here, but the following are important notes:

Emergency Steps

Your emergency plan should follow this sequence:

1. Check the athlete's level of consciousness.
2. Send a contact person to call the appropriate medical personnel and to call the athlete's parents.
3. Send someone to wait for the rescue team and direct them to the injured athlete.
4. Assess the injury.
5. Administer first aid.
6. Assist emergency medical personnel in preparing the athlete for transportation to a medical facility.
7. Appoint someone to go with the athlete if the parents are not available. This person should be responsible, calm, and familiar with the athlete. Assistant coaches or parents are best for this job.
8. Complete an injury report form while the incident is fresh in your mind.

◎ Do not move the injured athlete if the injury is to the head, neck, or back; if a large joint (ankle, knee, elbow, shoulder) is dislocated; or if the pelvis, a rib, or an arm or leg is fractured.

◎ Calm the injured athlete and keep others away from him or her as much as possible.

◎ Evaluate whether the athlete's breathing is stopped or irregular, and if necessary, clear the airway with your fingers.

◎ Administer artificial respiration if breathing is stopped. Administer CPR if the athlete's circulation has stopped.

◎ Remain with the athlete until medical personnel arrive.

Taking Appropriate Action

Proper CPR and first aid training, a well-stocked first aid kit, and an emergency plan help prepare you to take appropriate action when an injury occurs. In the previous section, we spoke about the importance of providing first aid *to the extent of your qualifications.* Don't "play doctor" with injuries; sort out minor injuries that you can treat from those that you need to call for assistance.

Next we'll look at taking the appropriate action for minor injuries and more serious injuries.

Minor Injuries

Although no injury seems minor to the person experiencing it, most injuries are neither life-threatening nor severe enough to restrict participation. When such injuries occur, you can take an active role in their initial treatment.

Scrapes and Cuts. When one of your players has an open wound, the first thing you should do is to put on a pair of disposable surgical gloves or some other effective blood barrier. Then follow these three steps:

1. *Stop the bleeding* by applying direct pressure with a clean dressing to the wound and elevating it. The player may be able to apply this pressure while

you put on your gloves. Do not remove the dressing if it becomes soaked with blood. Instead, place an additional dressing on top of the one already in place. If bleeding continues, elevate the injured area above the heart and maintain pressure.

2. *Cleanse the wound* thoroughly once the bleeding is controlled. A good rinsing with a forceful stream of water, and perhaps light scrubbing with soap, will help prevent infection.

3. *Protect the wound* with sterile gauze or a bandage strip. If the player continues to participate, apply protective padding over the injured area.

4. *Remove and dispose of gloves* carefully to prevent you or anyone else from coming into contact with blood.

For bloody noses not associated with serious facial injury, have the athlete sit and lean slightly forward. Then pinch the player's nostrils shut. If the bleeding continues after several minutes, or if the athlete has a history of nosebleeds, seek medical assistance.

Strains and Sprains.   The physical demands of basketball practices and games often result in injury to the muscles or tendons (strains), or to the ligaments (sprains). When your players suffer minor strains or sprains, immediately apply the PRICE method of injury care:

P Protect the athlete and injured body part from further danger or further trauma.

R Rest the area to avoid further damage and foster healing.

I Ice the area to reduce swelling and pain.

C Compress the area by securing an ice bag in place with an elastic wrap.

E Elevate the injury above heart level to keep the blood from pooling in the area.

Treating Bloody Injuries

You shouldn't let a fear of acquired immune deficiency syndrome (AIDS) stop you from helping a player. You are only at risk if you allow contaminated blood to come in contact with an open wound, so the surgical disposable gloves that you wear will protect you from AIDS should one of your players carry this disease. Check with your director or the YMCA of the USA for more information about protecting yourself and your participants from AIDS.

Bumps and Bruises. Inevitably, basketball players make contact with each other and with the ground. If the force of a body part at impact is great enough, a bump or bruise will result. Many players continue playing with such sore spots, but if the bump or bruise is large and painful, you should act appropriately. Enact the PRICE formula for injury care and monitor the injury. If swelling, discoloration, and pain have lessened, the player may resume participation with protective padding; if not, the player should be examined by a physician.

Serious Injuries

Head, neck, and back injuries; fractures; and injuries that cause a player to lose consciousness are among a class of injuries that you cannot and should not try to treat yourself. In these cases you should follow the emergency plan outlined on page 58. We do want to examine more closely your role, however, in preventing and handling two heat illnesses: heat exhaustion and heatstroke.

Heat Exhaustion. Heat exhaustion is a shock-like condition caused by dehydration and electrolyte depletion. Symptoms include headache, nausea, dizziness, chills, fatigue, and extreme thirst (see figure 7.2 for heat exhaustion and heatstroke symptoms). Signs include pale, cool, and clammy skin; rapid, weak pulse; loss of coordination; dilated pupils; and profuse sweating (this is a key sign).

A player suffering from heat exhaustion should rest in a cool, shaded area, drink cool water, and have ice applied to the neck, back, or abdomen to help cool the body. You may have to administer CPR if necessary, or send for emergency medical assistance if the athlete doesn't recover or his or her condition worsens. Under no conditions should the athlete return to activity that day, or before he or she regains all the weight lost through sweat. If the player had to see a physician, he or she shouldn't return to the team until released by the physician in writing.

Heatstroke. Heatstroke is a life-threatening condition in which the body stops sweating and body temperature rises dangerously high. It occurs when dehydration causes a malfunction in the body's temperature control center in the brain. Symptoms include the feeling of being on fire (extremely hot), nausea, confusion, irritability, and fatigue. Signs include hot, dry, and flushed or red skin (this is a key sign); lack of sweat; rapid pulse; rapid breathing; constricted pupils; vomiting; diarrhea; and possibly seizures, unconsciousness, or respiratory or cardiac arrest. See figure 7.2 for heat exhaustion and heatstroke symptoms.

Send for emergency medical assistance immediately and have the player rest in a cool, shaded area. Remove excess clothing and equipment on the player, and cool his or her body with cool, wet towels or by pouring cool water over him or her. Apply ice packs to the armpits, neck, back, abdomen, and between the legs. Have a conscious athlete drink cool water. Place an unconscious athlete on his or her side to allow fluids and vomit to drain from the mouth.

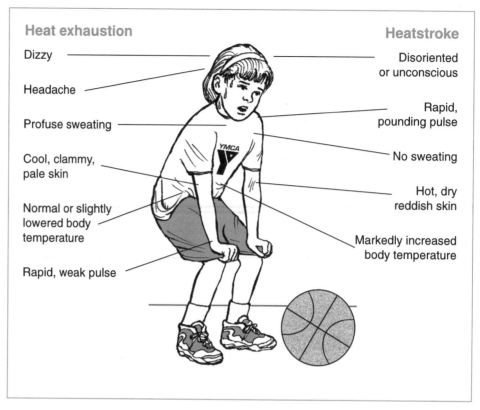

Heat exhaustion

Dizzy

Headache

Profuse sweating

Cool, clammy, pale skin

Normal or slightly lowered body temperature

Rapid, weak pulse

Heatstroke

Disoriented or unconscious

Rapid, pounding pulse

No sweating

Hot, dry reddish skin

Markedly increased body temperature

Figure 7.2 Symptoms of heat exhaustion and heatstroke.

An athlete who has suffered heatstroke can't return to the team until he or she is released by a physician in writing.

 ## Protecting Yourself

When one of your players is injured, naturally your first concern is his or her well-being. Your feelings for youngsters, after all, are what made you decide to coach. Unfortunately, there is something else that you must consider: Can you be held liable for the injury?

From a legal standpoint, a coach has nine duties to fulfill, as listed below. We've discussed all but planning in this chapter. We'll advise you of your duty to properly plan the activity by providing you with appropriate season and practice plans in chapters 9 to 12. Following are your legal duties.

1. Provide a safe environment.

2. Properly plan the activity.

3. Provide adequate and proper equipment.

4. Match or equate athletes.

5. Warn of inherent risks in the sport.

6. Supervise the activity closely.

7. Evaluate athletes for injury or incapacitation.

8. Know emergency procedures and first aid.

9. Keep adequate records.

Keep records of the season plan and practice plans that we provide, and of players' injuries. Season and practice plans come in handy when you need evidence that players have been taught certain skills, and injury reports offer protection against unfounded lawsuits. Hold onto these records for several years so that an "old injury" of a former player doesn't come back to haunt you.

In addition to fulfilling these nine legal duties, you should check your YMCA's insurance coverage and your insurance coverage to make sure your policy will protect you from liability.

Part III

The Instructional Plan

Now that you understand the "coaching essentials"—the principles of communicating, teaching, and coaching 8- to 13-year-olds, as well as safety principles—we'll move on to the next big step: the instructional plan. In part III we try to make the task of coaching easy and enjoyable for you by providing a complete instructional plan that maps out what we want you to teach.

In chapter 8, we'll describe the way we want you to teach basketball to your players. We call it the games approach. It's not the traditional way adults have taught sports to youngsters, but you'll see why it is a better way—the YMCA way. It's essential that you understand this games approach to teaching YMCA Winners basketball because we want you to use it even though you may be more comfortable with a more traditional approach.

In chapter 9 we'll present an overview of what you'll teach the entire season—not just the tactics and skills but the rules and traditions, the fitness concepts, and some key character development concepts. Then in chapters 10, 11, and 12 we'll provide you with practice plans for 8- to 9-year-olds, 10- to 11-year-olds, and 12- to 13-year-olds, respectively. When you want to know more about how to teach a skill, rule, fitness, or character concept listed in the practice plans, then turn to part IV.

The Games Approach to Coaching Basketball

Do you remember how as a kid you were taught by adults to play a sport, either in an organized sports program or physical education class? They probably taught you the basic skills using a series of drills that, if the truth be known, you found very boring. As you began to learn the basic skills, they eventually taught you the tactics of the game, showing you when to use these skills in various game situations. Do you remember how impatient you became during what seemed to be endless instruction, and how much you just wanted to play? Well, forget this traditional approach to teaching sports.

Now can you recall learning a sport by playing with a group of your friends in the neighborhood? You didn't learn the basic skills first; there was no time for that. You began playing immediately. If you didn't know the basic things to do, your friends told you quickly during the game so they could keep playing. Try to remember, because we're going to ask you to use a very similar approach to teaching basketball to young people called the games approach, an approach we think knocks the socks off the traditional approach.

On the surface, it would seem to make sense to introduce basketball by first teaching the basic skills of the sport and then the tactics of the game, but we've discovered that this approach has disadvantages. First, it teaches the skills of the sport out of the context of the game. Kids may learn to pass, dribble, and shoot the ball, but they find it difficult to use these skills in the real game. This is because they do not yet understand the fundamental tactics of basketball and do not appreciate how best to use their newfound skills.

Second, learning skills by doing drills outside of the context of the game is so-o-o-o boring. The single biggest turnoff about adults teaching kids sports is that we overorganize the instruction and deprive kids of their intrinsic desire to play the game.

As a YMCA Winners coach we're asking that you teach basketball the YMCA way, the games approach way. Clear the traditional approach out of your mind. Once you fully understand the games approach, you'll quickly see its superiority in teaching basketball. Not only will kids learn the game better, but you and they will have much more fun. And as a bonus, you'll have far fewer discipline problems.

With the games approach to teaching basketball, we begin with a game. This will be a modified and much smaller game designed to suit the age and ability of the players. As the kids play in these "mini" games, you can begin to help them understand the nature of the game and to appreciate simple concepts of positioning and tactics. When your players understand what they must do in the game, they are then eager to develop the skills to play the game. Now motivated to learn the skills, you can demonstrate the skills of the game, practice using game-like drills, and provide individual instruction by identifying players' errors and helping to correct them.

In the traditional approach to teaching sports, players do this:

Learn the skill → Learn the tactics → Play the game

In the games approach players do this:

Play the game → Learn the tactics → Learn the skill

In the past we have placed too much emphasis on the learning of skills and not enough on learning how to play skillfully—that is, how to use those skills in competition. The games approach, in contrast, emphasizes learning what to do first, then how to do it. Moreover—and this is a really important point— the games approach lets kids discover what to do in the game not by you telling them, but by their experiencing it. What you do as an effective coach is help them discover what they've experienced.

In contrast to the "skill-drill-kill the enthusiasm" approach, the games approach is a guided discovery method of teaching. It empowers your kids to solve the problems that arise in the game, and that's a big part of the fun in learning a game.

Now let's look more closely at the games approach to see the four-step process for teaching basketball:

1. Play a modified basketball game.

2. Help the players discover what they need to do to play the game successfully.

3. Teach the skills of the game.

4. Practice the skills in another game.

Step 1. Play a Modified Basketball Game

Okay, it's the first day of practice; some of the kids are eager to get started, while others are obviously apprehensive. Some have rarely shot a ball, most don't know the rules, and none knows the positions in basketball. What do you do?

If you use the traditional approach, you start with a little warm-up activity, then line the players up for a simple shooting drill and go from there. With the games approach, you begin by playing a modified game which is developmentally appropriate for the level of the players and also designed to focus on learning a specific part of the game.

Don't worry about modifying the game to be developmentally appropriate—we've done it for you. Our practice plans in chapters 10 through 12 are based on three-player teams for 8- to 9-year-olds, four-player teams for 10- to 11-year-olds, and five-player teams for older kids. We've also modified the size of the court, the basket height, the ball, the free-throw line distance, and the rules. We'll tell you more about these changes later.

The second reason to modify the game is to place emphasis on a limited number of situations in the game. This is one way you "guide" your players to discover certain tactics in the game.

For instance, you have your players play a 3 v 3 (three players versus three players) half-court game. The objective of the game is to make three passes before attempting to score. Playing the game this way forces players to think about what they have to do to keep possession of the ball.

Step 2. Help the Players Discover What They Need to Do

As your players are playing the game, look for the right spot to "freeze" the action, step in, and hold a brief question-and-answer session to discuss problems they were having in carrying out the goals of the game. You don't need to pop in on the first miscue, but if they repeat the same types of mental or physical mistakes a few times in a row, step in and ask them questions that relate to the aim of the game and the necessary skills required. The best time to interrupt the game is when you notice that they are having trouble carrying out the main goal, or aim, of the game. By stopping the game, freezing action, and asking questions, you'll help them understand

◎ what is the aim of the game;

◎ what they must do to achieve that aim; and

◎ what skills they must use to achieve that aim.

For example, if your players are playing a game in which the objective is to make three passes before attempting to score, but they are having trouble doing so, interrupt the action and ask the following questions.

Coach: What are you supposed to do in this game?
Athlete: Pass the ball three times before scoring.

Coach: What does your team have to do to keep the ball for three passes in a row?
Athlete: Pass the ball.

Coach: Yes, and what else?
Athlete: You have to be able to get the pass, too.

Coach: OK. You have to be able to pass the ball and catch the ball when it's passed. Why don't we practice passing the ball and catching the pass?

Through the modified game and skillful questioning on your part, your players realize that accurate passing and catching skills are essential to their success in controlling the ball. Just as important, rather than TELLING them that passing and catching skills are critical, you lead them to that discovery through a well-designed modified game and through questions. This questioning that leads to players' discovery is a crucial part of the games approach. Essentially you'll be asking your players—usually literally—"What do you need to do to succeed in this situation?"

Asking the right questions is a very important part of your teaching. We've given you sample questions in each practice plan (see chapters 10 through 12) to help you know where to begin. At first asking questions will be difficult because your players have little or no experience with the game. And if you've learned sports through the traditional approach, you'll be tempted to tell your players how to play the game, and not waste time asking them questions. Resist this powerful temptation to tell them what to do, and especially don't do so before they begin to play the game.

If your players have trouble understanding what to do, phrase your questions to let them choose between one option and another. For example, if you ask them, "What's the fastest way to get the ball down the court?" and get answers such as "Throw it" or "Hit it," then ask, "Is it passing or dribbling?"

Immediately following the question-and-answer session you will begin a skill practice, which is Step 3 of the four-step process.

Sometimes players simply need to have more time playing the game, or you may need to modify the game further so that it is even easier for them to discover what they are to do. It'll take more patience on your part, but it's a powerful way to learn. Don't be reluctant to change the numbers in the teams or some aspect of the structure of the game to aid this discovery. In fact, we advocate playing "lopsided" games (3 v 1, 3 v 2) in the second game of each practice; we'll explain this concept in a moment.

Step 3. Teach the Skills of the Game

Only when your players recognize the skills they need to be successful in the game do you want to teach the specific skills through focused drills. This is when you use the more traditional approach to teaching sports skills, which we described in chapter 5. To refresh your memory, we called it the IDEA approach:

I   Introduce the skill.

D   Demonstrate the skill.

E   Explain the skill.

A   Attend to players practicing the skill.

Step 4. Practice the Skills in Another Game

Once the players have practiced the skill, you then put them in another game situation—this time a lopsided game (e.g., 3 v 1, 3 v 2). Why use lopsided teams? It's simple: As a coach, you want your players to experience success as they're learning skills. The best way to experience success early on is to create an advantage for the players. This makes it more likely that, for instance, in a 3 v 1 game, your three offensive players will be able to make three passes before attempting to score.

When you get to the practice plans in chapters 10 through 12, you'll see that we use even-sided games (e.g., 3 v 3, 4 v 4) in Game 1s, and lopsided games in Game 2s. The reasoning behind this is to introduce players to a situation similar to what they will experience in competition, and to let them discover the challenges they face in performing the necessary skill. Then you teach them the skill, have them practice it, and put them back in another game—this time a lopsided one to give them a greater chance of experiencing success.

As players improve their skills you don't need to use lopsided games. At a certain point having a 3 v 1 or 4 v 2 advantage will be too easy for the kids and won't challenge them to hone their skills. At that point you lessen the advantage to, say, 3 v 2 or 4 v 3, or you may even decide that they're ready to practice the skill in even-sided competition. The key is to set up situations where your athletes experience success, yet are challenged in doing so. This will take careful monitoring on your part, but playing lopsided games as kids are learning skills is a very effective way of helping athletes learn and improve.

And that's the games approach. Your players will get to *play* more in practice, and once they learn how the skill fits into their performance and enjoyment of the game, they'll be more motivated to work on those skills, which will help them to be successful.

Season Plans

The season plan is what you'll teach for the season in the sequence you will teach it. We provide you with a season plan for three age groups—8 to 9, 10 to 11, and 12 to 13. If you have little coaching experience, we recommend you follow our plan closely. If you've coached considerably but have not used the games approach, we request that you try this new approach. It will be a challenge to change, but it really is a better way.

Coaches sometimes make the mistake of teaching advanced tactics and skills before teaching the basics. This makes it more difficult for athletes to learn. We have carefully selected the sequence in which tactics, skills, rules, and fitness concepts are laid out in the season plans to be developmentally appropriate for each age group. Thus, we suggest you follow this sequence your first year of coaching. As you gain experience coaching and you come to know your players better, you should adjust the season plan in future years to optimize their learning.

The season plans we've laid out have five components:

◎ Purpose

◎ Tactics and skills

◎ Rules and traditions

◎ Fitness concepts

◎ Character development concepts

Here's a brief description of each component:

◎ **Purpose.** This is the overall purpose of the particular practice—what you are focusing on for that practice.

◎ **Tactics and Skills.** Tactics are what to do during the game (and when to do it). Tactics are also an understanding of the problems faced by each team during the game and how those problems can be solved. An example of tactics is ways to maintain possession of the ball. Skills are the physical skills traditionally taught, such as dribbling or passing or shooting the ball.

◎ **Rules and Traditions.** Rules of the sport are taught as part of playing games and learning skills. Traditions are those "unwritten rules" that players follow to be courteous and safe, such as raising your hand when you foul someone or playing cooperatively with others on your team.

◎ **Fitness Concepts.** We have woven important fitness concepts (in the form of brief discussions) into each practice plan.

◎ **Character Development Concepts.** The four core values—caring, honesty, respect, and responsibility—can all be related to many situations that arise while playing basketball. For example, playing cooperatively with teammates shows that you care about them. Again, we suggest specific ideas for discussing character development values within each practice.

Youth sports programs traditionally focus on teaching tactics and skills, but they don't have any plans for teaching rules and traditions, fitness concepts, and character development concepts. These elements are part of what make YMCA Youth Super Sports unique and special. With our season plans, we focus not only on skill development but also on the development of the whole youngster in areas that are important not just for the season but for a lifetime.

 ## Season Plan for 8- to 9-Year-Olds

At this age, kids will begin to explore tactics that help them keep possession of the ball, attack the basket, create space, and play good defense. The following grid provides an overview of each component of practice from Week 1 through Week 12. The specific practice plans for 8- to 9-year-olds are found in chapter 10.

8- to 9-Year-Olds

Week	Purpose	Tactics and skills	Rules and traditions	Fitness concepts	Character development concepts
1A	To play a 2 v 2 game, focusing on boundaries and rules	Dribbling, passing, and receiving	Inbounds; double dribble; traveling	**General fitness** Physical activity makes you fit, contributing to cardiorespiratory fitness, muscular strength and endurance, and flexibility.	**Four core values** We'll stress four core values: caring, honesty, respect, responsibility.
1B	To maintain possession of the ball using the triple threat position	Triple threat position; receiving passes	Holding, tripping	**Safety** It's important to notify your coach whenever you hurt yourself, even if you think it's a minor injury.	**Honesty** You need to play by the rules and be honest if you break one.
2A	To attack the basket by receiving a pass, squaring to the basket, and scoring	Shooting	Lane violation	**General fitness** It's important both to warm up and cool down.	**Responsibility** Working and playing as a team works better than playing as a bunch of individuals.
2B	To maintain possession of the ball by support-ing teammates	Creating passing lanes	Jump ball	**Flexibility** Stretch until you feel a pull but no pain; hold for 10 seconds.	**Respect** Respect opponents by shaking or slapping hands at the end of a game.
3	To create space in the attack by creating passing lanes	Using L-cuts and V-cuts to elude the defender	Personal and technical fouls	**Healthy habits** Drink enough water during practice.	**Responsibility** Cheer for your team-mates when you're on the sideline.
4	To attack the basket by using a power dribble	Drop step and drive to the basket; jump stop	Charging and block-ing fouls; raise your hand when you foul	**Safety** Stay in your own space.	**Caring** Compliment players—even opponents—on good plays.
5	To use space in the attack by creating passing lanes and repositioning for a pass	Drop step and drive to the basket; creating passing lanes		**Cardiorespiratory fitness** Aerobic endurance is important for health.	**Caring** Share the ball—don't be a ball hog!

(continued)

8- to 9-Year-Olds *(continued)*

Week	Purpose	Tactics and skills	Rules and traditions	Fitness concepts	Character development concepts
6	To win the ball through on-the-ball defense	Defensive positioning on the ball		**Cardiorespiratory fitness** As your heart beats faster, it pumps blood and delivers oxygen to muscles faster.	**Respect** Celebrate victories in ways that don't embarrass opponents.
7	To win the ball through off-the-ball defense	Defensive positioning on the ball		**Muscular strength and endurance** Muscles adapt to harder work by getting stronger.	**Respect** Respect officials, and thank them at the end of games.
8	To win the ball by rebounding	Boxing out to rebound	Over-the-back fouls	**Training and conditioning** Improve your physical conditioning by practicing/ playing longer.	**Responsibility** Teamwork means helping each other.
9	To attack the basket through the give-and-go	The give-and-go play		**Muscular strength and endurance** The longer you play before your muscles tire, the more muscular endurance you have.	**Caring** Everyone gets a chance to learn and play.
10	To maintain possession of the ball and use space in the attack	Creating passing lanes; Triple threat position; ball fakes and jab steps		**Healthy habits** Check off your healthy habits as you do them.	**Caring** Forgive teammates for mistakes.
11	To win the ball by preventing the offense from scoring	Tight defense		**Training and conditioning** Your body loses conditioning if you stop exercising. Use it or lose it!	**Responsibility** Learn from your mistakes and take responsibility for trying to improve.
12	To create space and attack the basket by using the give-and-go	Creating passing lanes; give-and-go		**Healthy habits** Good eating habits are important for physical activity and for life. Eat healthy and avoid junk foods.	**Respect** Be honest, caring, responsible, and respectful.

Season Plan for 10- to 11-Year-Olds

As youngsters grow, so does the game: the ball grows larger, the basket becomes taller, the free-throw line retreats farther from the basket. Players continue to work on the tactics and skills they developed as 8- to 9-year-olds, but the tactics become a little more complex as they delve deeper into creating and using space to attack. In addition, they learn how to set screens and how to defend against screens, and they hone their skills in maintaining possession and defending space. The following outline provides an overview of each component of practice from Week 1 through Week 12. The specific practice plans for 10- to 11-year-olds are found in chapter 11.

YMCA Winners Basketball Season Plan

10- to 11-Year-Olds

Week	Purpose	Tactics and skills	Rules and traditions	Fitness concepts	Character development concepts
1A	To create space in the attack by creating passing lanes	Creating passing lanes	Inbounds; traveling; double dribble	**General fitness** The difference between physical fitness and physical activity.	**Four core values** We'll stress caring, honesty, respect, responsibility.
1B	To attack the basket by receiving a pass, squaring to the basket, and scoring	Shooting	Lane violation	**General fitness** It's important to warm up before physical activity.	**Caring** Always help both teammates and opponents if they are hurt or if you have fouled them.
2A	To create space in the attack by creating passing lanes	Using L-cuts and V-cuts to elude the defender		**Cardiorespiratory fitness** The heart transports oxygen through the body.	**Responsibility** It's responsible to be ready for practice and games.
2B	To attack the basket by using a power dribble	Drop step and drive to the basket; Jump stop	Charging and blocking fouls; raise your hand when you foul	**Cardiorespiratory fitness** Cardiorespiratory fitness is improved by running.	**Respect** Always show respect for your opponents as well as your teammates.
3	To win the ball through on-the-ball defense	Defensive positioning on the ball	Holding, reaching in, tripping; technical fouls	**General fitness** You need to exercise every day, not just the days you have practice.	**Respect** Respect officials, and thank them at the end of games.
4	To win the ball through off-the-ball defense	Defensive positioning off the ball	Hand-checking, pushing	**Muscular strength and endurance** Different muscles perform different activities.	**Honesty** Strive to be honest and avoid dishonesty.

(continued)

10- to 11-Year-Olds *(continued)*

Week	Purpose	Tactics and skills	Rules and traditions	Fitness concepts	Character development concepts
5	To win the ball by rebounding	Boxing out to rebound	Over-the-back fouls	**Flexibility** Stretching improves flexibility and helps prevent injury.	**Responsibility** It's every player's responsibility to try to get into position to help teammates.
6	To attack the basket through the give-and-go	The give-and-go play		**Safety** It's important to use safety equipment to prevent injury.	**Caring** Compliment your teammates and opponents when they make good plays.
7	To create space in the attack by setting screens	Setting screens; attacking the basket off a screen	Setting moving screens	**Training and conditioning** If you work your body a little harder than last time, it will adapt and become stronger.	**Respect** It's important to respect yourself and your teammates by always playing safely.
8	To defend space against screens	Defending against screens		**Flexibility** You should feel a slight pull but no pain when stretching.	**Caring** It's important to behave in ways that show you care about your teammates.
9	To win the ball on jump balls	Defensive and offensive positioning for jump balls	Jump ball	**Training and conditioning** An emphasis on training the specific muscles you use for your sport is called "specificity training."	**Responsibility** Work to improve your skills.
10	To create space in the attack by using off-the-ball screens	Screening off the ball		**Healthy habits** Try to choose meals from the bottom of the food pyramid.	**Honesty** Good players look honestly at themselves and think of ways to improve.
11	To defend space by communicating and playing good defense	Fighting through screens; communicating on defense		**Healthy habits** You need a balance of good foods for good health.	**Responsibility** We win as a team and we lose as a team.
12	To use space in the attack by rolling off a screen toward the basket	Pick-and-roll		**Training and conditioning** Stay in shape after the season's over.	**Caring** It's important to forgive people for their mistakes.

Season Plan for 12- to 13-Year-Olds

The players build upon the tactics and skills they learned in the previous 2 years. The following outline provides an overview of each component of practice from Week 1 through Week 12. The specific practice plans for 12- to 13-year-olds are found in chapter 12.

YMCA Winners Basketball Season Plan

12- to 13-Year-Olds

Week	Purpose	Tactics and skills	Rules and traditions	Fitness concepts	Character development concepts
1A	To attack the basket by using a power dribble	Drop step and drive to the basket; jump stop; crossover dribble	Charging and blocking fouls; raise your hand when you foul	**General fitness** We'll work to improve our cardiorespiratory fitness, flexibility, and muscular strength and endurance.	**Four core values** We'll stress caring, honesty, respect, responsibility.
1B	To create space in the attack by creating passing lanes	Using L-cuts and V-cuts to elude the defender	Traveling; double dribble; lane violation; inbounds	**General fitness** Work on improving your overall fitness by doing a variety of exercises.	**Respect** Play with respect no matter how your opponents are playing.
2A	To attack the basket through the give-and-go	The give-and-go play	Technical fouls	**Overload principle** FIT stands for Frequency, Intensity, and Time.	**Respect** Show respect for your opponents after the game no matter what happened during the game.
2B	To win the ball through off-the-ball defense	Defensive positioning off the ball	Holding, tripping, hand checking	**Overload principle** Do other physical activities away from practice to improve and maintain your fitness level.	**Responsibility** Remember to bring and use proper equipment.
3	To win the ball by rebounding	Boxing out to rebound	Over-the-back fouls	**Overload principle** Overload the work your body does by increasing intensity.	**Honesty** Be honest even when others don't see what happens.
4	To create space in the attack by setting screens	Setting screens; Attacking the basket off a screen	Setting moving screens	**Flexibility** It's important to stretch and get limber before physical activity.	**Respect** Show opponents respect at the end of the game.

(continued)

12- to 13-Year-Olds *(continued)*

Week	Purpose	Tactics and skills	Rules and traditions	Fitness concepts	Character development concepts
5	To defend space against screens	Defending against screens	Pushing	**Flexibility** Stretch your muscles every day and always before any activity—this will help reduce the chance of injury.	**Responsibility** Always pay attention at practice and don't distract others.
6	To attack the basket by setting screens	Setting and using screens	Setting moving screens	**Muscular strength and endurance** Work on improving each of the three areas of fitness.	**Caring** Encouraging each other with positive comments shows you care about your teammates.
7	To create space in the attack by using off-the-ball screens	Screening off the ball		**Cardiorespiratory fitness** You need to feel a little tired when exercising to improve cardiorespiratory fitness.	**Respect** Respect officials, and thank them at the end of games.
8	To use space in the attack by rolling off a screen toward the basket	Pick-and-roll		**Cardiorespiratory fitness** Use the "talk test" during aerobic exercise to determine how hard you're working.	**Caring** Encourage your teammates rather than getting angry or impatient with them.
9	To defend space by communicating and play good defense	Fighting through screens; communicating on defense		**Healthy habits** Drink water often; drink before you get thirsty.	**Respect** Respect your body by practicing healthy habits.
10	To win the ball and use space in the attack by making a quick transition from defense to offense	Rebound and outlet; transition from defense to offense		**Healthy habits** Choose healthy foods rather than junk foods.	**Responsibility** Each player has responsibility to play together and put the team first.
11	To win the ball by rebounding free throws	Rebounding free throws	Free-throw lane violations	**Healthy habits** Brush your teeth, get enough sleep, and stay away from drugs.	**Caring** Support your teammates.
12	To restart play by running set plays on in-bounds passes	In-bounds pass from offensive end line		**Reversibility principle** If you stop being active, you lose your strength and endurance.	**Respect** Celebrate in a way that doesn't make your opponents feel bad.

chapter 10

Practice Plans for 8- to 9- Year-Olds

This chapter contains the 14 practice plans you'll use with your 8- to 9-year-old YMCA Winners Basketball players. It also contains recommendations for modifying your practices to make them developmentally appropriate for 8- and 9-year-olds. By following these practice plans, you will be presenting the game and coaching in a way that maximizes players' skill development *and* their enjoyment of the game.

Each plan contains the following sections:

◎ Purpose

◎ Equipment

◎ Practice Plan

Purpose focuses on what you want to teach your players during that practice; it is your main "theme" for that day. *Equipment* notes what you'll need on hand for that practice. The *Practice Plan* section outlines what you will do during each practice session. It consists of these elements:

◎ Warm-Up

◎ Fitness Circle

◎ Games

◎ Skill Practices

◎ Team Circle and Wrap-Up

You'll begin each session with about five minutes of warm-up activities. This will be followed by five minutes of a Fitness Circle, during which you lead players in an activity and discussion about an item that relates to their fitness. Then you'll have your players play a modified basketball game. You'll look for your cue to interrupt that game—your cue being when players are having problems with carrying out the basic goal or aim of the game. At this point you'll "freeze" the action, keeping the players where they are, and ask brief questions about the tactical problems the players encountered and what skills they need to "solve" those problems. (Review chapter 8 for more on interrupting a game and holding a question-and-answer session.) We provide discussion questions in each practice plan. In addition, we provide coach's points, when appropriate, with games and skill practices as points of emphasis in most effectively conducting the practice.

Then you'll teach the skill that the players need to successfully execute the tactic. Chapter 13 contains descriptions of all the skills, so a page reference will be given to guide you to the appropriate description. During this skill practice session, you'll use the IDEA approach:

I Introduce the skill.

D Demonstrate the skill.

E Explain the skill.

A Attend to players practicing the skill.

Your introduction, demonstration, and explanation of a skill should take no more than two to three minutes; then you'll attend to players and provide teaching cues or further demonstration as necessary while they practice the skill according to the practice plan.

After the skill practices, you will usually have the athletes play another game or two to let them use the skills they just learned and to understand them in the context of a game. Note that in Game 1 when players are being introduced to a new tactic or skill, they will play an even-sided game (e.g., 3 v 3). This allows them to encounter the challenges they will face in executing the tactic or skill in competition. Then in most Game 2s they should play lopsided games (3 v 1, 3 v 2) to increase their chances of experiencing success and beginning to master the new skill. However, if your players are showing proficiency with the new skill, you can use even-sided games in Game 2. The choice is yours; for more on this issue, see chapter 8.

The Practice Plan section concludes with a Team Circle that focuses on character development. You will talk to your players and lead them in an activity about some aspect of basketball that relates to one of the four core values—caring, honesty, respect, and responsibility. Following this, you'll wrap up the practice with a few summary comments and remind them of the next practice or game day.

A note about Fitness Circles and Team Circles: These times are meant to be true discussions—not lectures where you're doing all the talking and your players are doing all the listening. Ask the questions provided, and wait for your players to respond. Don't immediately feed them the answers that we provide. These answers are meant simply to help you guide the discussion. Your role in Team Circles is as much to ask questions and get players to respond as it is to dole out information.

Making Games Simpler or More Challenging

Here are ways to make practice games simpler or more challenging:

- Equally increase or decrease the number of players suggested (e.g., if we suggest playing 3 v 3, make it simpler by playing 2 v 2, or make it more challenging by playing 4 v 4).

- Add an extra defender to make it harder on the offense (e.g., 3 v 4 instead of 3 v 3) once players have acquired the skills they need to be successful.

- Add an extra offensive player to make it easier for the offense (e.g., 4 v 3 instead of 3 v 3).

- Change the type of defense played. The three types of defenses (see "Scrimmages") are cooperative, active, and competitive. To make a game simpler, have your players play a cooperative defense; to make it more challenging, have them play an active or a competitive defense.

- Begin with *no* defense.

- Perform the skill or game at a slower than normal pace to make it simpler.

- Increase or decrease the number of passes you require before the offense can attempt a shot.

We encourage you to consider these changes during each practice. Whether you make them or not depends on how your players are responding. The more skilled they are, the more likely they'll need greater challenges to continue improving.

Eight- and nine-year-olds don't possess the size, strength, stamina, and skills to play the full-blown adult version of basketball, and attempting to fit them into the adult mold will prove frustrating for all involved. We suggest you incorporate the following modifications into your practices to help your players learn the game, improve their skills, and have fun while they're at it. These suggestions fall into three categories: equipment and court, rules, and scrimmages.

Equipment and Court

Equipment and court should be substantially modified for young players to best learn the game and improve their skills. We recommend the following modifications:

- Size of ball: Junior (#5)

- Height of basket: 7 feet

- Free-throw line distance: 9 feet

- Court size: Short court (baskets on opposite sides of the width of a court)

Rules

You need to strike a balance between calling the players for violations and fouls every time they commit one, while still teaching the appropriate rules and the skills they need to eventually fully comply with the rules. But your players won't learn much in practice if you're blowing the whistle every 10 seconds for another rules violation or foul. Therefore we suggest the following rules modifications during practices:

◎ **Clock rules:** Don't call three-second lane violations, five-second counts, or 10-second backcourt violations. Don't run a shot clock.

◎ **Defense:**
—Use a player-to-player defense only.
—Don't use a full-court press; defense can pick up their players at half court or closer to their own basket.
—Don't allow defenders to touch the ball when it's held by the ball handler. Defenders may steal the ball only when it's passed or dribbled.
—Defenders may not intentionally get in the way of an offensive player in an attempt to draw a charging foul against that player. Don't teach taking a charge.

◎ **Double dribble:** Allow one violation per player possession; gradually eliminate this allowance.

◎ **Traveling:** Give an extra step for starting or stopping.

While the following points are not really rules modifications, they are worth noting here and emphasizing in practice:

◎ Don't allow players to wear jewelry. Doing so is dangerous to them and to other players.

◎ Players should call their own fouls.

◎ Don't allow players to undercut a player shooting a lay-up.

◎ Players should keep control of their body and the ball: no rough play.

◎ Players should be good sports and show respect. Don't tolerate unsporting conduct.

 ## Scrimmages

Besides the obvious changes in court and equipment, a casual observer of a YMCA Winners basketball practice would note another difference in the practice setting: the number of players used in scrimmages and practice games. Using smaller numbers allows players to touch the ball more often and thus practice the skills they need to acquire. It also keeps everyone more active and gives players more experience in a variety of situations that call for different tactics and skills. Here are suggestions for scrimmages and practice games:

◎ Use small-sided games (e.g., 1 v 1, 2 v 1, 2 v 2, 3 v 2, 3 v 3) on half-court play or cross-court playing (short court, see the figure that follows). Remember, using small-sided games means more touches per player, which means players develop skills more quickly. The greatest leaps in skill improvement are made through the use of small-sided games.

◎ Use modified half-court games in which players play 1 v 1 or 2 v 2, taking turns trying to score.

◎ Use "regular" half-court rules: an offensive rebound can be shot again, while a defensive rebound must result in that team or player restarting at the top of the key.

◎ Rotate partners (opponents) and teams often. Play three- to five-minute games, then rotate players. Changing partners changes the game.

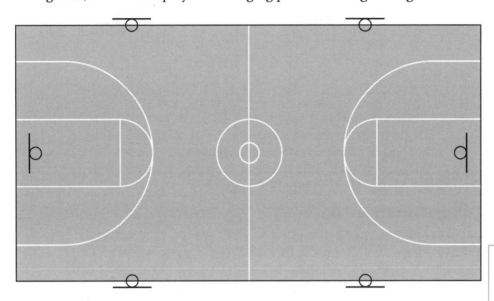

Key to Diagrams

⊕	=	Side basket
⓪	=	Player with ball
O	=	Offensive player
X	=	Defensive player
C	=	Coach
PC	=	Player-coach
- - - ➤	=	Pass
∿∿➤	=	Dribble
——➤	=	Move
===➤	=	Shoot
R	=	Rebounder
P	=	Partner
■	=	Marked spots
⊣	=	Screen or box out
S	=	Shooter

A note regarding defense: At this level, the focus is on offensive skills. Although defensive skills are important, if they are introduced too soon they may prohibit the development of offensive skills, especially if peers play defense aggressively. Introduce defensive skills after players have developed some proficiency with off- and on-the-ball skills. Control defensive play by instituting three levels of involvement:

1. **Cooperative Defense (cold)**—The player assumes a defensive posture two arm lengths from the opponent, is relatively passive, and at times even coaches the opponent.

2. **Active Defense (warm)**—The player assumes a defensive posture about one and a half arm lengths from the opponent, has active hands and feet, but makes no attempts to intercept the ball.

3. **Competitive Defense (hot)**—The player assumes a defensive posture, is positioned appropriately, and attempts to intercept the ball.

Explain how to play a modified half-court game. The games should be more cooperative than they are competitive. Limit your focus to boundaries, starting and restarting game play, and keeping control. Be flexible regarding all violations (double dribble, traveling), but do enforce an "out of control rule." For example, don't allow a player to pick up the ball and run with it without dribbling.

Okay, on to the practice plans themselves. Following are practice plans for the 2 weeks of your preseason and then for the 10 weeks of your competitive season.

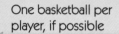 **PURPOSE**

To play a 2 v 2 game, focusing on boundaries and rules.

Equipment

- ☑ One basketball per player, if possible
- ☑ One portable basket per two players, if possible
- ☑ Tape, markers, or cones

Warm-Up (5 minutes)

Begin each practice with 5 to 10 minutes of warm-up activities to get players loosened up and ready to go.

Players travel from one basket to the next dribbling, jump stopping, and shooting short shots (two to three feet).

Fitness Circle (5 minutes)

Following the warm-up, gather the players and demonstrate the stretching protocol (see chapter 15 for stretches for the major muscle groups). Ask a team leader to lead stretches in subsequent practices. After the team is finished stretching, briefly discuss the fitness concept for that practice.

Key Idea: General fitness

Gather players into a group. Have a ball ready. "I want everybody to run in place at a slow pace. Now a bit faster. Now everyone stop." Choose a player to demonstrate a bounce pass. "That was a good pass. Now I need all of you to pass the ball to each other and practice passing and catching." Have kids pass two times each. Next, have them perform a leg stretch. "Those four activities we did are a part of basketball, but they also are ways to improve your fitness. Each activity helps to improve a different area of fitness. Running improves your *cardiorespiratory fitness,* passing helps your *muscular strength* and your *muscular fitness,* and stretching helps your *flexibility.* Throughout the season we'll be learning more about fitness in our fitness circles."

Game 1 (10 minutes)

Following the Fitness Circle, get the kids playing a game. Follow most games with a time of questions and answers—with YOU asking the questions and your PLAYERS providing the answers—about what the goal of the game was and what skills and tactics they needed to perform to succeed in the game. For many games, we provide diagrams or figures showing how the game is begun. We also often provide "coach's points" for you to pass along to your players during the games.

Goal

Players will play as a team making good passes in setting up good shots.

Description

Play 2 v 2 half-court games (see "Play a Modified Basketball Game" on page 63 for general rules). Teams earn a point only when they complete a pass before shooting. Players can dribble three times before passing.

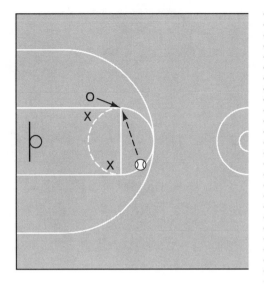

☞ Teach the five-second inbounds rule (see page 278).

Coach: What is the goal of the game?
Players: To make good passes to set up baskets.

Coach: What do you have to do to be successful at passing?
Players: Catch the ball, then pass the ball right to your teammate.

Coach: What types of passes are there?
Players: Overhead, bounce, and chest pass.

Coach: How do you play as a team?
Players: Work together and talk to each other.

Skill Practice 1 (10 minutes)

Follow Game 1 with a Skill Practice. Use the IDEA approach: Introduce, Demonstrate, and Explain a skill or tactic, then Attend to your players as they practice that tactic. The question-and-answer session, in which your PLAYERS tell you what skills and tactics they need to be successful in the game, leads directly to the Skill Practice. We often provide coach's points with the Skill Practices; pass these points along to your players. We also provide "coaching cues"—phrases to help your players focus on the task at hand—during many Skill Practices and Games.

1. Introduce, demonstrate, and explain how to make *overhead, bounce, and chest passes* (see pages 258–260).
2. Practice passing.

Description

Pair up players. Practice the three types of passes.

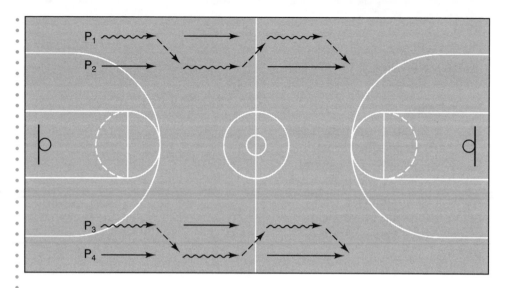

Skill Practice 2 (10 minutes)

1. Introduce, demonstrate, and explain how to *dribble* (see page 252).
2. Practice dribbling and passing.

Description

Pair up players. Partner 1 dribbles 8 to 10 times and then passes to partner 2. Partner 2 starts dribbling forward and then passes over to partner 1, who is moving alongside. Partners continue to move forward, dribbling and passing. Partners should try different types of passes (e.g., bounce, chest).

COACH's cues

Passing

"Step in the direction of the pass!"

"Elbows in!"

"Follow through—fingers pointed to target!"

Catching

"Target hands."

"Eyes on the ball!"

"Reach!"

"Pull it in."

Dribbling

"Dribble to move forward!"

"Pass on the move!"

"Control the ball."

"Lead your partner."

COACH's point

☞ Encourage players to be moving when they are both dribbling and receiving.

☞ Remind passers to pass a little in front of their partner.

Game 2 (15 minutes)

Goal

Players will play as a team, focusing on maintaining possession while passing and dribbling.

Description

Play 3 v 1, 3 v 2, or 2 v 2 half-court games, depending on the skill proficiency of your players (see chapter 8 for help on deciding how to use lopsided games). Rotate players accordingly so that all players have a chance to play offense and defense. Teams earn a point when they complete one pass before they shoot. If a team makes a basket they get the ball again (for the second turn only).

☞ Teach rules on double dribbling and traveling (see page 278).

Team Circle (5 minutes)

Key Idea: Four core values

Gather players into a circle. "Everyone stand side by side in a circle. We're going to keep standing side by side as a group while we try to pass the ball to those across the circle from us. We'll pass slowly, and remember to stay side by side at all times." Repeat for 10 passes. "If you were just catching a pass by yourself and could move to get the ball, it would have been much easier. But when we think of working together as a team, it takes more effort. We need to put just as much effort into being good teammates, with everyone doing their part. We'll talk about four qualities or values that help us be better players—*caring, honesty, respect,* and *responsibility.* These qualities are just as important as shooting, dribbling, and passing. Give me an example of each of the four values." Listen to their responses and discuss.

Wrap-Up

Make summary comments about practice. Remind them of the next practice and give them a sneak preview of its emphasis: receiving passes in the triple threat position.

☞ PURPOSE

To maintain possession of the ball by using the triple threat position.

Equipment

☑ One basketball per two players, if possible

☑ Court space with three or four baskets

☑ Tape or markers

☑ Different colored vests or shirts to differentiate teams

Warm-Up (10 minutes)

On your signal, players begin dribbling without losing control. Players stop and hold the ball quickly on your signal. Dribble three times: 20, 30, 45 seconds.

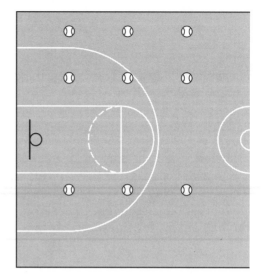

Fitness Circle (5 minutes)

Key Idea: Safety

Gather players into a group. Choose one player to act out being injured (limping) and have a second player get a coach to report the injury. "What did you see happening?" Listen to their responses. "When you get injured, it will probably look like what was acted out. If it hurts, you should stop and let me know right away. Don't pretend it doesn't hurt. Most times injuries are not bad, but sometimes they can be serious. If you get hurt even a little, I need to come over and check your injury. If you see a player who looks hurt or in pain or if you saw her get injured, let me know. Telling me if you're hurt helps me keep you safe during games and practices."

Week 1, Practice 2

Game 1
(10 minutes)

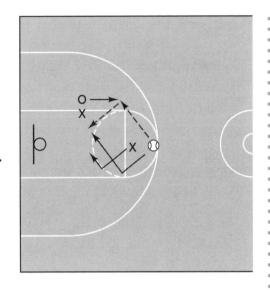

Goal

Players will move to open positions on the court and be prepared to shoot, pass, or dribble when they have the ball.

Description:

Play 2 v 2 half-court games. Teams must pass at least twice before shooting. Players cannot dribble. All restarts are made at half court.

☞ Teach rules on holding and tripping (see page 277).

Coach: What was the goal of the game?
Players: To get open, be prepared to shoot, pass, or dribble.

Coach: What did you and your teammates have to do to be successful?
Players: Make quick and accurate passes. Catch the ball under control. Move to an open space.

Coach: What did you do to keep the defense from stealing the ball or blocking your shot?
Players: Protected the ball by keeping body between the defense and the ball. Held the ball firmly with two hands; used the body to protect the ball. Used quick passes.

Coach: Once you received the ball, what was the best way to hold it so the defense didn't know whether you were going to shoot or pass?
Players: Holding the ball as if you're going to shoot (triple threat Players), with one hand behind the ball and the other at its side.

Skill Practice 1
(15 minutes)

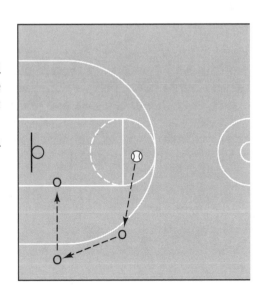

1. Introduce, demonstrate, and explain how to receive the ball in *triple threat position* (see page 262).

2. Practice receiving passes in triple threat position.

Description

Players in fours practice passing from point to wing, to baseline, to a high or low post. Mark positions with tape or markers.

Players pass, then move to another position. Players receiving the ball must

- present a target for the passer;
- receive ball in the triple threat position and jump stop;
- give a ball fake with a jab step before passing; and
- perform a quick, accurate pass to a partner.

(To simplify this practice, have players focus on presenting a target to the passer, receiving the ball in triple threat position, and making quick, accurate passes, but don't have them perform a jab step and ball fake.)

COACH's cues

"Target hands!"

"Triple threat!"

"Ready position." (Be ready to fake out opponent with the option to shoot, pass, or dribble.)

"Hand position." (Hands in shooting position on the ball.)

"Holding position." (Hold the ball to the side of the hip.)

"Fake a pass, then make a pass."

"Step toward your target."

"Elbows in."

"Fingers pointed at your target."

Game 2 (15 minutes)

Goal

Players will provide a target for the passer, receiving the ball in triple threat position using a jump stop.

Description

Play 3 v 1, 3 v 2, or 2 v 2 half-court games, depending on the skill proficiency of your players. Rotate players accordingly so that all players have a chance to play offense and defense. Once players receive a pass, they should ball fake and jab step, then focus on making a quick, accurate pass to a teammate. Players shoot when they're open after their team has completed at least two consecutive passes. (See figure at the top of page 91.)

Team Circle
(5 minutes)

Key Idea: Honesty

Gather players into a group. "Think about the rules in basketball. I am going to tell you a rule. Raise your hand if you think it's something you should let the official know happened." Examples: traveling, tripping another player, dribbling the ball out of bounds. "You should let the official know about all of those rules being broken, even if the official does not see it. Raising a hand or telling officials is an honest thing to do when you break a rule, even if it is an accident. It's important to be honest when you break a rule in practice and in games. It is a quality that makes you a better player."

Wrap-Up

Make summary comments about practice. Remind them of the next practice, and give them a sneak preview: the emphasis will be on shooting.

Week 2, Practice 1

👉 PURPOSE

To attack the basket by receiving a pass, squaring to the basket, and scoring.

Equipment

- ☑ One basketball per two players, if possible
- ☑ Court space with three or four baskets
- ☑ Tape or markers
- ☑ Different colored vests or shirts to differentiate teams

Warm-Up
(10 minutes)

Players in pairs play "Around the Key"—one player shoots; the partner rebounds and returns the ball. The shooter tries to make five different shots around the free-throw lane in 30 seconds. Players receive one point for each shot made.

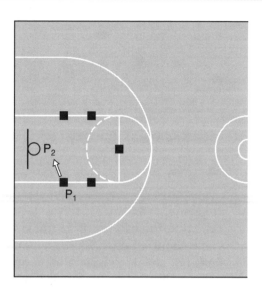

Fitness Circle
(5 minutes)

Key Idea: General fitness

Gather players into a group. "Everyone think of a hill. Get a picture of a hill in your mind. Close your eyes and see it in your mind. You see it? Now pretend we're all bicycling up that hill. We start at the bottom and slowly climb. We have to work harder and harder as we make it to the top. Then we gradually start pedaling back down the hill, which is not as hard as going up. That hill is the way your body will move every practice. We start slow with a *warm-up*. As you ride up the hill, this is how we move in the middle of practice. Toward the end of our practice, we gradually start to come back down the hill, slowing our bodies down. This is called the *cool-down*. A warm-up and cool-down are important parts of healthy fitness."

Game 1 (10 minutes)

Goal

Players will score as often as possible. The focus is on using the triple threat and using ball fakes and jab steps.

Description:

Play 3 v 3 half-court games. Players must complete two or more consecutive passes before attempting a shot. Encourage players to make quick passes, to use target hands, and to call for the ball. They cannot dribble. All restarts are at half-court. Players earn one point for each shot attempted and two points for each basket scored.

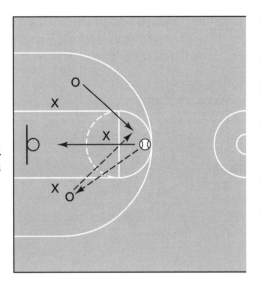

☞ Teach the rule on lane violations (see page 278).

Coach: What was the goal of the game?
Players: To score following two consecutive passes.

Coach: From where on the court did you score most of your points?
Players: Close to the basket.

Coach: Why is it better to shoot from a position close to the basket, rather than far from the basket?
Players: More likely to score when closer—higher percentage shot.

Coach: Besides shooting from a close range, what else did you do to successfully perform a shot?
Players: Squared shoulders to the basket; elbow under ball and close to body, one hand behind the ball and the other at the side of the ball; staggered stance with knees slightly bent; followed through, aimed.

Skill Practice 1 (15 minutes)

1. Introduce, demonstrate, and explain how to *shoot* (see pages 262–264).
2. Practice shooting.

Description

Players in pairs shoot three shots from each of five spots marked around the basket (about six to eight feet away). Partners rebound the ball and pass accurately to shooters, who provide a target, receive the ball in triple threat, square up, and shoot. The goal is to score on two out of three shots at each spot.

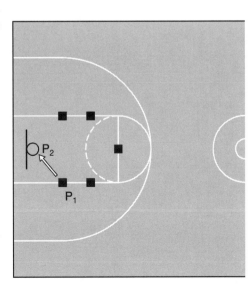

To simplify, change the shooting goal from making two of every three shots to shooting from two different spots for 30 seconds, or simply shooting three shots from each spot.

COACH's cues

"Square up!"

"BEEF!"

"**B**ase firm."

"**E**lbow under ball."

"**E**xtend arm."

"**F**ollow through or flip wrist."

Game 2 (15 minutes)

Goal

Players will score as many field goals as possible.

Description

Play 3 v 1, 3 v 2, or 3 v 3 half-court games, depending on the skill proficiency of your players. Rotate players accordingly so that all players have a chance to play offense and defense. Players must complete two or more consecutive passes before attempting a shot. (See figure at the top of page 95.)

COACH's point

☞ Limit your focus to one or two shooting cues at a time (e.g., keep your base firm, elbow under the ball).

Team Circle
(5 minutes)

Key Idea: Responsibility

Gather players into groups of two partners. "Everyone stand and balance on one foot." Wait while everyone gets his or her balance. "Now one of you offer your shoulder for your teammate to lean on. If you're leaning on your partner's shoulder, now try to balance on one foot again. . . . Change places. If you were leaning before, now let your partner lean on your shoulder and stand on one foot." Wait until everyone has balanced with the help of a partner. "Now come back here. Wasn't it easier to balance when you were leaning on your partner? It works that way in basketball, too. When you help each other during practices and games, we work better as a team. Each of you can contribute. Your teammates count on you to contribute to the team. That is being responsible to your team."

Wrap-Up

Make summary comments about practice. Remind them of the next practice and give them a sneak preview: The focus will be on supporting teammates with the ball by creating passing lanes.

Week 2, Practice 2

☞ PURPOSE

To maintain possession of the ball by supporting teammates.

Equipment

☑ One basketball per two players, if possible

☑ Court space with three or four baskets

☑ Tape or markers

☑ Different colored vests or shirts to differentiate teams

Warm-Up (10 minutes)

Players in pairs play "Around the Key"—one player shoots; the partner rebounds and returns the ball. The shooter tries to make five different shots around the free-throw lane in 30 seconds. Players receive one point for each shot made.

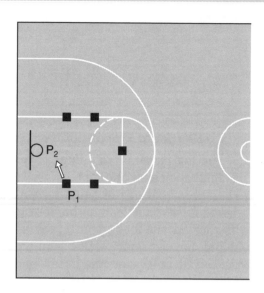

Fitness Circle (5 minutes)

Key Idea: Flexibility

Gather players into a circle sitting down with their legs stretched in front of them. "Think of stretching a rubber band as far as you can. What happens if you stretch the band too far?" Listen to their responses. "That's right. It breaks. Muscles work in sort of the same way. Stretching your muscles too far can tear and injure them. But it's important to stretch your muscles for them to be flexible. Everyone reach forward and try to touch your toes, but stretch only until you feel a slight pulling in your leg muscle—make sure it doesn't hurt." Tell them to hold the stretch for 10 counts without bouncing. "Stretching your muscles is important to keep them flexible, but you shouldn't feel pain. The main basketball muscles to stretch are the front of your thighs (quadriceps), the back of your thighs (hamstrings), the back of your lower legs (calves), your shoulders (deltoids), and your arms (biceps, triceps)." Demonstrate stretching each muscle group.

Game 1
(10 minutes)

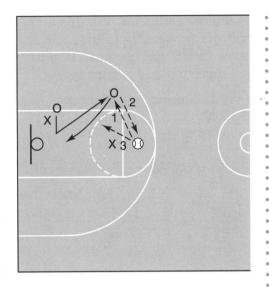

Goal

Players will support their teammate with the ball.

Description

Play 2 v 2 half-court games. Players must complete at least three passes before shooting. They receive one point for three consecutive passes, and two points for every field goal.

☞ Teach rules on the jump ball (see page 244).

Coach: What was the goal of the game?
Players: To support the player with the ball.

Coach: What did you have to do to provide support?
Players: Move to an open space; get away from our defender.

Coach: How were you able to get away from your defender?
Players: Using cuts and fakes.

Coach: Was it easier to get away from defenders when you were moving quickly or at just a normal speed?
Players: Quickly.

Coach: When you were trying to get away from defenders, was your first quick step or jab step toward them or away from them?
Players: Toward them.

Skill Practice 1 (15 minutes)

1. Introduce, demonstrate, and explain *creating passing lanes* (see page 238).
2. Practice providing support for teammates by creating passing lanes.

Description

Play 3 v 1 games. Offensive players move to open space. Defenders play cooperative to active defense. Use offensive positions on one or both sides of the basket. Players pass, then move to an offensive

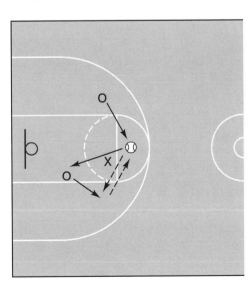

99

☞ Freeze Skill Practice 1 and Game 2 occasionally to show players where good supporting positions are.

☞ Make sure that players don't get too close to their teammate with the ball when they are trying to provide support.

position (point, wing, baseline, or high or low post) adjacent to the ball. Players should provide a target for receiving the ball, receive it in triple threat, and use a ball fake before passing. Emphasize using quick jab steps to create passing lanes.

"Quick cuts!"

"Fake a pass, make a pass!"

Game 2
(15 minutes)

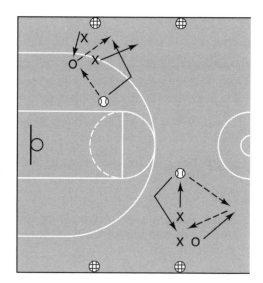

Goal

Players will support their teammate with the ball.

Description

Play 3 v 1, 3 v 2, or 2 v 2 short-court games, depending on the skill proficiency of your players. Rotate players accordingly so that all players have a chance to play offense and defense. Players must complete at least three passes before shooting. They receive one point for three consecutive passes, and two points for every field goal.

Team Circle
(5 minutes)

Key Idea: Respect

Gather players into two lines standing opposite each other about five feet apart. "I want each line to walk toward the other and give each person in the other line a high-five. Imagine that the other line is your opponent for a game. Show me how you would act toward an opponent and what you would say if it was the end of the game and we lost the game. Start." Assist kids if necessary. Listen to responses some players provide to each other. "At the end of each game it is important to show respect for your opponent. We do this by slapping hands and saying something like 'good game,' even if we lose the game."

Wrap-Up

Make summary comments about practice, and remind them of the next practice: Its emphasis is on creating passing lanes by using different types of cuts.

Week 3

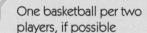 PURPOSE

To create space in the attack by creating passing lanes.

Equipment

- ☑ One basketball per two players, if possible
- ☑ Court space with three or four baskets
- ☑ Tape or markers
- ☑ Different colored vests or shirts to differentiate teams

Warm-Up
(10 minutes)

Players in pairs play "Around the World." Spots are marked in an arc about five feet from the basket. Shooters follow a set pattern. The first player shoots from spot #1; if the shot is good, the player moves to spot #2. The player continues until he or she misses a shot. On a missed shot, the shooter may elect to stay there until his or her next turn, or "chance it." This gives the player another shot immediately, but if the shooter misses, he or she goes back to the beginning. A made chance allows the shooter to skip the next spot.

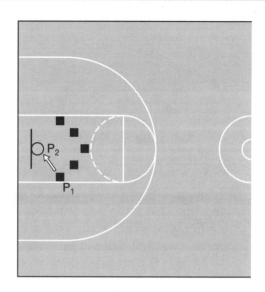

Fitness Circle
(5 minutes)

Key Idea: Healthy habits

Gather players into a group. "Everyone run in place for 15 seconds. Ready? Go! . . . Now stop! Whenever we run and dribble during our practice, our body starts to get warm. When our bodies get really warm, what do you think happens to cool them off?" Wait for their responses. "Our bodies start to sweat. Sweat is the water that comes out of all the pores in your skin. Then the sweat evaporates into the air. Since your body sweats to cool off, what do you think we need to put back into our bodies?" Wait for someone to say "water." "That's right. Drinking enough water every day is an important healthy habit. You'll need to drink more water if you're running and playing a lot. I want to challenge all of you to drink one glass of water a day for every year of your age. How many is that? . . . Eight? Nine? I know you can drink that many glasses a day!"

Week 3

Game 1 (10 minutes)

Goal

Players will provide support for their teammate with the ball.

Description

Play 2 v 2 half-court games. Players must complete at least three passes before shooting. They receive one point for three consecutive passes, and two points for every field goal. (See figure at the top of page 99.)

Coach: What was the goal of the game?
Players: To support the player with the ball.

Coach: How were you able to support the player with the ball?
Players: Using a ball fake and a jab step, move quickly.

Coach: Is a zigzag or curved pathway better when performing a cut?
Players: Zigzag.

Coach: Can you describe the angle of these cuts using letters of the alphabet?
Players: V and L.

Coach: Why would V- or L-cuts be better than curved?
Players: It's harder for the defender to stay with you.

Coach: What did you do if your defender was closely guarding you?
Players: Used a cut to get away.

Coach: When would a V-cut be most effective, close to the lane or away from the lane?
Players: Away from the lane by 10 to 12 feet.

Coach: When would the L-cut be most effective?
Players: Close to the lane near the baseline.

Skill Practice 1 (15 minutes)

1. Introduce, demonstrate, and explain how to execute *V-cuts* and *L-cuts* (see pages 249–250).
2. Practice V-cuts and L-cuts.

Description

Play 2 v 2 games with the focus on players using V-cuts and L-cuts, receiving passes, and using jump stops and the triple threat position. Sequence:

- O_1 ball fakes, jab steps, and passes to O_2, who V-cuts as O_1 is ball faking.
- O_2 catches the ball in a triple threat position using a jump stop.
- Repeat three times and rotate.
- When all four players in a group have practiced the V-cut three times, go through the rotation again, this time practicing the V-cut on the opposite side of the basket.

☞ The only difference between V- and L-cuts is the angle from which the offense moves into the defense, then toward the pass.

☞ Emphasize making "razor-sharp" cuts.

☞ Teaching off-the-ball movements is important—as we know, good players know how to get open to receive a pass.

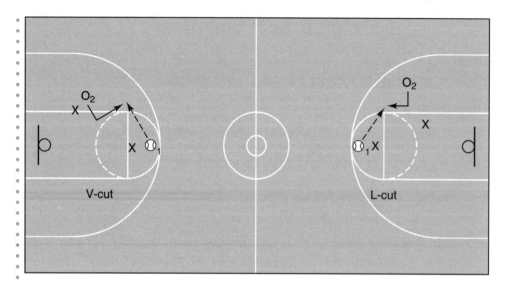

V-cut   L-cut

- When all four players have practiced the V-cut on both sides of the basket, go through the rotation again, using the same sequence to practice L-cuts on both sides of the basket.

The defense should play passive, cooperative defense. (To simplify, begin with no defense.)

Game 2 (15 minutes)

Goal

Players will provide support to their teammate with the ball, using V-cuts and L-cuts to get open.

Description

Play 3 v 1, 3 v 2, or 2 v 2 short-court games, depending on the skill proficiency of your players. Rotate players accordingly so that all players have a chance to play offense and defense. Players must complete at least three passes before shooting. They receive one point for three consecutive passes, and two points for every field goal. (See figure on page 100.)

Team Circle
(5 minutes)

Key Idea: Responsibility

Gather players into two groups; one group will spread out and pass to each other. The other group will be to one side, as if on the bench during a game; they should be silent for the first 30 seconds of the activity. Then have them cheer and encourage on-court players; continue this activity for 30 more seconds. "When players are on the bench during a game, they should be encouraging their teammates, no matter what's happening in the game. This is being responsible to your team. It helps players to keep trying hard even if they are losing or have made some mistakes. How did it feel when you were playing and the bench players didn't encourage you? How about when they did encourage you?" Listen to both responses and have players compare feelings.

Wrap-Up

Make summary comments about practice and give reminders for the first game.

Week 4

PURPOSE

To attack the basket by using a power dribble.

Equipment

☑ One basketball per two players, if possible

☑ Court space with three or four baskets

☑ Tape or markers

☑ Different colored vests or shirts to differentiate teams

Warm-Up (10 minutes)

Players in pairs play "Around the World." Spots are marked in an arc about five feet from the basket. Shooters follow a set pattern. The first player shoots from spot #1; if the shot is good, the player moves to spot #2. The player continues until he or she misses a shot. On a missed shot, the shooter may select to stay there until his or her next turn, or "chance it." This gives the player another shot immediately, but if the shooter misses, he or she goes back to the beginning. A made chance allows the shooter to skip the next spot. (See figure on page 102.)

Fitness Circle (5 minutes)

Key Idea: Safety

Gather players into a group. "Pretend you're a 'player in a bubble.' Walk around and work at not bumping into your teammates to make sure their bubbles don't break." Keep kids in a confined area. Time them for one minute. "Now we'll do the same thing while jogging." Time for 30 seconds. "It's important not to run into other players—that is a foul, even if it's an accident. It's important to play as safely as you can. Thinking about the other players' bubbles will help you stay in your own space during practices and games."

Game 1 (10 minutes)

Goal

Players will score in the lane.

Description

Play 3 v 3 half-court games. All shots must be in the lane, on drives. (See figure on the top of page 95.)

Coach: What was the goal of the game?
Players: Score in the lane.

Coach: What's an effective way to drive to the basket?
Players: Drop step and dribble.

Coach: What should you do on a drive when it's congested in the lane?
Players: Stop and shoot if open, or pass off.

Skill Practice 1 (10 minutes)

1. Introduce, demonstrate, and explain how to use a *jump stop* prior to shooting.
2. Practice shooting off of jump stops.

Description

Play 1 v 1; defenders play cooperative defense. Players with the ball use a ball fake, jab step, and drive to the basket. They jump stop about two feet from the basket and shoot. (To simplify, begin with no defense.)

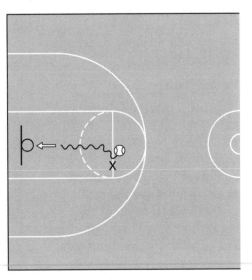

COACH's cues

"Arm should look like a yo-yo."

"Ball down, eyes up."

"Two-foot jump stop."

"Eyes on target."

"In the square, in the basket."

COACH's point

☞ Briefly describe charging fouls and blocking fouls (which often occur when a player drives to the basket). See page 277.

☞ Instruct players to raise their hand when they foul.

☞ Use examples from the Skill Practice or Games to illustrate how driving to the basket can create passing lanes.

Coach: How should your dribble change when someone is guarding you?
Players: Keep the ball closer to your body and keep the ball between yourself and the defender.

Game 2 (10 minutes)

Goal

Players will attempt to score in 15 seconds or less.

Description

Play 1 v 1 games. The player with the ball starts at the foul line. Check the ball (the defensive player starts with the ball and gives it to the offensive player when they are ready to play). The offensive player begins in triple threat position. The offensive player gets two points for every basket scored off a jump stop, and one point for every basket scored otherwise.

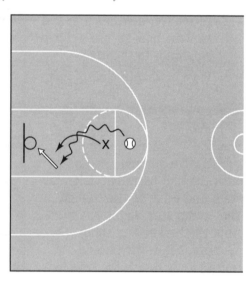

Game 3 (10 minutes)

Goal

Players will shoot as often as possible off of a dribble and drive.

Description

Play 3 v 1, 3 v 2, or 3 v 3 games, depending on the skill proficiency of your players. Rotate players accordingly so that all players have a chance to play offense and defense. Players can't dribble—except to drive to the basket. (See figure at the top of page 95.)

Week 4

Team Circle
(5 minutes)

Key Idea: Caring

Gather players into groups of two and give each group one ball. Players should dribble and pass the ball to each other, making sure to distribute the ball to their partners. "Each of you should say two good things about your partner's skills. Then come back to me in a group. Begin." Wait for them to regroup. "What were some of the comments your teammates told you?" Listen to their responses. "What kind of value or quality is it when you go out of your way to say something good about a teammate's playing?" Listen to responses and encourage discussion as needed. "Caring is one of our core values. You show you care about your teammates when you encourage them. It's also appropriate to compliment your opponents on their good plays."

Wrap-Up

Make summary comments about the practice and reminders for the next game.

Week 5

PURPOSE

To use space in the attack by creating passing lanes and repositioning for a pass.

Equipment

☑ One basketball per two players, if possible

☑ Court space with three or four baskets

☑ Tape or markers

☑ Different colored vests or shirts to differentiate teams

Warm-Up
(10 minutes)

Play 1 v 1 games, starting at foul line. Defense checks the ball and offense begins in a triple threat position. (See figure on page 108.)

Fitness Circle
(5 minutes)

Key Idea: Cardiorespiratory fitness

Gather the players into a circle. "Remember the hill we imagined we bicycled up a few practices ago? We start slow going up, then go faster toward the top and come slowly back down. Let's start up that hill by running in place slowly, getting a little faster, faster, and now really fast. Now start to slow down. A little slower. Slower. And stop." Run with players to model. "That was a short version of moving during our practice. We run faster to make our heart and lungs stronger; this is called *cardiorespiratory fitness*. We start slowly and then gradually slow down at the end of the practice to help our hearts pump blood and carry oxygen from our lungs to our muscles."

Game 1 (10 minutes)

Goal

Players will attempt to score on drives to the basket.

Description

Play 3 v 3 half-court games. Teams must make three consecutive passes before shooting. Players are allowed to dribble when needed. (See figure at the top of page 95.)

Coach: What was the goal of the game?
Players: To score on drives.

Coach: When should you drive?
Players: When you have an open lane to the basket and no teammate is open for a good shot.

Coach: Players off the ball, what was happening when you weren't able to create a passing lane to support the ball handler?
Players: Couldn't get away from defense; couldn't get a good angle to cut; ball handler too far away; too many players in one place.

Coach: What should ball handlers do under these circumstances?
Players: Dribble to reposition themselves to create an open passing lane or move closer to the basket.

Coach: Should you dribble toward your teammates or away from your teammates?
Players: Away.

Coach: Why should you dribble away and not toward?
Players: Opens up more space for teammates to move.

Skill Practice 1 (15 minutes)

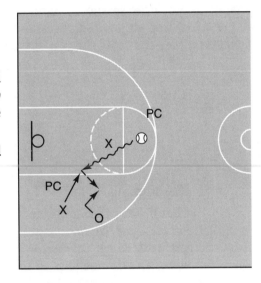

1. Introduce, demonstrate, and explain how to use a *drop step* and drive to the basket (see page 252).
2. Practice the drop step and drive.

Description

Play 2 v 2 games with a cooperative defense. Players with the ball will ball fake, jab step, then drop step and drive to the basket. Passive defenders try to shut down passing lanes. Offense off the ball use various cuts to create a passing lane. For each 2 v 2 game, two other players will coach. One will coach the cooperative defenders to close down the lane; the other will coach the offense to reposition themselves to create open passing lanes. Switch roles after three attempts.

111

COACH's point

☞ Have players perform in "slow motion" so all players can understand and perform the skills.

☞ Stop play as needed to reinforce the goal of the game—take advantage of "teachable moments."

COACH's cues

"Quick cuts!"

"Drop and drive!"

"Watch the belly button of the player attempting to fake."

"Anticipate!"

Game 2 (15 minutes)

Goal

Players will use drop steps and drive to the basket.

Description

Play 3 v 1, 3 v 2, or 3 v 3 games, depending on the skill proficiency of your players. Rotate players accordingly so that all players have a chance to play offense and defense. Give two points for every basket scored off a drop step and drive, and one point for every basket scored otherwise. (See figure at the top of page 95.)

Team Circle (5 minutes)

Key Idea: Caring

Gather players into a group and choose two to demonstrate with you. You will dribble the ball and have the two players work to get in position to receive a pass. Keep dribbling, and do not pass to them. "Were the other players in good position to get a pass? . . . Why didn't they get the ball? . . . I didn't pass the ball. Sharing the ball so all players get a chance shows you care about your teammates." Have players get into groups of three and dribble and pass the "caring" way. Bring players back together. "Raise your hand if you think that caring is an important quality or value on this team. It is important!"

Wrap-Up

Make summary comments about practice and give reminders for the next game.

Week 6

Warm-Up (10 minutes)

Play 1 v 1 games, starting at the foul line. Defense checks the ball and offense begins in a triple threat position. (See figure on page 108.)

Fitness Circle (5 minutes)

Key Idea: Cardiorespiratory fitness

Gather players into a circle and give one child a ball to hold. "What does the heart pump to the whole body?" Listen to responses until someone says "blood." "What does the blood carry to the muscles?" Listen until someone says "oxygen." "We're going to pretend that the ball is oxygen and that you're big blood vessels or tubes that carry the blood. Pass the ball to the person next to you." Each player should touch the ball until the ball completes the circle. "The oxygen in your blood starts at your heart and travels to your lungs, legs, arms, and brain." Try assigning a part of the body to each player. "Playing basketball helps your heart and lungs get better at getting oxygen to your muscles—this is called *cardiorespiratory fitness*."

PURPOSE

To win the ball through on-the-ball defense.

Equipment

- ☑ One basketball per two players, if possible
- ☑ Court space with three or four baskets
- ☑ Tape or markers
- ☑ Different colored vests or shirts to differentiate teams
- ☑ Two cones

Game 1 (10 minutes)

Goal

Defenders will keep the opposing team from scoring.

Description

Play 3 v 3 half-court games. Use a competitive defense. The offensive team can't dribble and must complete at least three consecutive passes before shooting. The defensive team scores one point if the offensive team does not complete three passes. (See figure at the top of page 95.)

☞ Emphasize that defense is attitude.

Coach: What did you do to keep the opposing team from scoring?
Players: Closely guarded opponent, rebounded so they wouldn't get a second shot.

Coach: What defensive position or actions interfered most and kept your opponent from scoring?
Players: Keeping your body between opponent and goal. Being sure you can always see the ball. Guarding opponent closely. Keeping hands and feet moving; playing active defense.

Skill Practice 1 (10 minutes)

1. Introduce, demonstrate, and explain proper *on-the-ball positioning* (see pages 269–271).
2. Practice on-the-ball defensive positioning.

Description

Pair up players. The player with the ball dribbles forward in a zigzag pattern. The defensive player maintains proper defensive posture and attempts to block the offensive player's forward progress. The defender tries to steal the ball without fouling or cause a turnover. 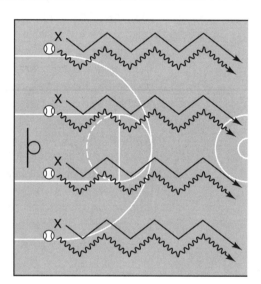 Players switch roles after one length of the court.

Game 2 (10 minutes)

Goal

Defenders will play good on-the-ball defense.

Description

Play 1 v 1 games with active to competitive defense. Offensive players can dribble, but as soon as they pick up the dribble, defensive players move closer and use active hands and feet. (See figure on page 108.)

Week 6

COACH's cues

"Medium body posture."
"Active hands and active feet!"
"See the ball!"

Game 3 (10 minutes)

Goal

Defenders will keep the opposing team from scoring.

Description

Same as Game 1, except play 2 v 3 half-court games. Rotate players accordingly so that all players have a chance to play offense and defense.

Team Circle (5 minutes)

Key Idea: Respect

Gather players in a group near two cones 10 feet apart. Act out two examples of celebrating for good play or a win. One should be exaggerated and obviously inappropriate, the other modeling the kind of celebrating you'd like to see from your team. "If you think the first example I showed you is the way to celebrate a good play, stand by this cone. If you think the second is the best way to celebrate, stand by this one." All players should vote. After all players have voted, ask why they voted the way they did. "The second example is the kind of celebrating that shows respect for your opponents."

Wrap-Up

Make summary comments about practice and reminders for the next game.

PURPOSE

To win the ball through off-the-ball defense.

Equipment

☑ One basketball per two players, if possible

☑ Court space with three or four baskets

☑ Tape, cones, or markers

☑ Different colored vests or shirts to differentiate teams

Warm-Up (10 minutes)

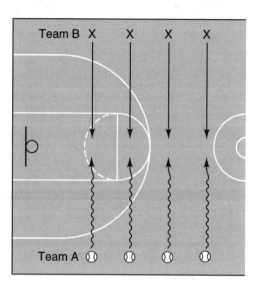

Players play "Now you have it, now you don't." Divide players into two teams. Each team stands on opposite sidelines of the gym facing each other. Each member of team A has a ball; team B doesn't. On signal, team A players begin dribbling toward the opposite sideline. Team B approaches, trying to take away the balls. If a team B player gains possession of a ball, that player dribbles toward the opposite sideline. When players from team A or team B make it over their "goal" line (the opposing sideline), they stay there until all balls are behind the sidelines. Team B is now given the balls and the game begins again.

Fitness Circle (5 minutes)

Key Idea: Muscular strength and endurance

Gather players into a group in their own space. "We're going to move different directions in our own space. I will point to a direction and the whole group should jog slowly in that direction. When I put my hand up, everyone stop." Point to directions of: forward, one side, the other side, and backward. "When you jog in different directions, you use different muscles. It's important to improve your muscular strength and endurance in all your muscles in your body. We can do that by running, passing and dribbling the ball, and spreading out on the court."

Week 7

Game 1 (10 minutes)

Goal

Defenders will prevent the offensive team from passing, receiving passes, and scoring.

Description

Play 3 v 3 half-court or short-court games. Players can't dribble and must make at least three consecutive passes before shooting. Defensive team receives one point for each turnover and two points for each steal without fouling. Treat fouls like violations—the other team gets the ball. (See figure at the top of page 95.)

Coach: How did you position yourself to prevent the offensive team from passing?
Players: Overplayed toward potential passing lanes; closely guarded player with the ball.

Coach: How did you position yourself to deny a pass?
Players: Overplayed toward the ball; kept hand in passing lane.

Skill Practice 1 (10 minutes)

1. Introduce, demonstrate, and explain proper *off-the-ball positioning* (see pages 271–272).
2. Practice off-the-ball defensive positioning.

Description

Paired-up players practice off-the-ball defensive positioning (partners can also coach each other). As an option, you can have a player with the ball waiting to pass to his or her offensive teammate.

☞ Remind players to stay focused on defense.

Game 2 (10 minutes)

Goal

Defenders try to deny offense from making successful passes; offense tries to make six consecutive passes.

Description

Play 2 v 2 games using a competitive defense. For each 2 v 2 game, two other players serve as coaches. One offensive player begins at the point, the other at a wing position. The ball starts at the point. From a triple threat position, the ball handler uses a ball fake to give his or her teammate a chance

to get open; or the ball handler dribbles to open a passing lane if necessary. Rotate after a turnover or after six consecutive passes. One player-coach gives feedback for the on-the-ball defense; the other player-coach gives feedback for the off-the-ball defense.

COACH's cues

"Medium body posture."
"Active hands and active feet!"
"See the ball!"
"Anticipate!"

Game 3 (10 minutes)

Repeat first game, except play 2 v 3, with players focusing on off-the-ball defensive positioning. Rotate players accordingly so that all players have a chance to play offense and defense.

Week 7

Team Circle
(5 minutes)

Key Idea: Respect

Gather children together in a group and choose one child to help demonstrate. The child will pretend to be an official; you will be a player. Dribble the ball and pass out of bounds. Direct the child to blow a whistle or make a sound to stop play when this occurs. Stop and bring the ball back to the child. "What did I do when the whistle sounded?" Listen to responses—discuss stopping on hearing the whistle, bringing the ball over, and not arguing about the call. "You need to respect the official and their decisions at all times. It also shows respect to the official when you thank them at the end of the game."

Wrap-Up

Make summary comments about practice and give reminders for the next game.

PURPOSE

To win the ball by rebounding.

Equipment

☑ One basketball per two players, if possible

☑ Court space with three or four baskets

☑ Tape or markers

☑ Different colored vests or shirts to differentiate teams

Warm-Up (10 minutes)

Players take and follow their shots. Players with the ball shoot for 20, 30, or 45 seconds. They shoot, rebound, and shoot again. Players are limited to three dribbles before their next shot. They keep track of how many shots they make during the timed interval.

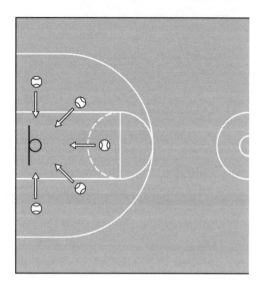

Fitness Circle (5 minutes)

Key Idea: Training and conditioning

Gather players into a circle. "Everyone run in place for 10 seconds. . . . Now stop. Now run in place for 20 seconds. . . . Stop. Next we'll run for 30 seconds. . . . Stop. When you run, you're improving your body's physical conditioning in your heart, lungs, and muscles. Every time you play basketball a little bit longer and let your body get a little more tired, your body improves its physical conditioning. When your body has better conditioning you can keep up with opponents and play longer without getting too tired."

Week 8

Game 1 (10 minutes)

Goal

Defenders try to prevent the offensive team from scoring—and from rebounding missed shots.

Description

Play 3 v 3 half-court games. Players can't dribble and must make at least three consecutive passes before shooting. The defensive team receives one point for winning or rebounding the ball after only one shot. (See figure at the top of page 95.)

Coach: What was the goal of the game?
Players: To prevent scoring and prevent a second shot.

Coach: What did you do to prevent a second shot?
Players: Got the rebound after the first shot.

Coach: How did you position yourself to get the rebound?
Players: Moved between offensive player and basket.

(You could repeat this game with an offensive focus. In this case, the offensive team would earn a point for each shot attempt and rebound. You'd want to instruct your offensive rebounders to protect the ball, and to tip the ball to the basket or assume a shooting position as quickly as possible, like a pogo stick.)

Skill Practice 1 (15 minutes)

1. Introduce, demonstrate, and explain how to *box out* to rebound (see page 268).
2. Practice boxing out and rebounding.

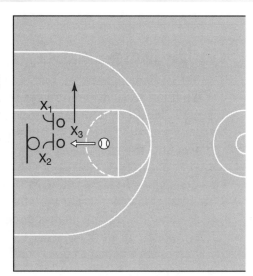

Description

Play 3 v 3 games with 2 v 2 under the boards and a shooter and an outlet. The shooter shoots the ball. On the release, X_1 and X_2 turn and box out their offensive players. X_3 (the outlet) moves right or left, depending on which side of the basket the rebound occurs. The player rebounding the ball turns and passes to X_3. Repeat three times, then rotate teams. Also consider rotating duties within the teams—for example, the outlet person and the shooter become rebounders. The defenders try to successfully outlet three times in a row.

☞ Talk about the possible fouls that can occur (e.g., over the back; see page 277).

COACH's cues

"Create a stable wall between opponent and ball."
"Elbows out—palms wide, feel for opponent."
"Put buttocks under opponents."

Game 2 (15 min)

Goal

Defenders try to prevent the offensive team from scoring—and from rebounding missed shots.

Description

Play 2 v 3 or 3 v 3 short-court games, depending on the skill proficiency of your players. Rotate players accordingly so that all players have a chance to play offense and defense. Players can't dribble and must make at least three consecutive passes before shooting. The defensive team receives one point for winning or rebounding the ball after only one shot. (See figure at the top of page 95.)

Team Circle (5 minutes)

Key Idea: Responsibility

Gather players between two cones about 10 feet apart. "What are some different ways you can move the ball and score?" Listen to their responses. Provide the example of players working together to move the ball and score as one choice. Give the example of one player working without any other teammates as the other choice. "Which of the two is the best example of teamwork? If you vote for the first example, stand at this cone; if you vote for the second example, stand at this cone. If everyone makes good teamwork their responsibility, we can all work together to be successful. When you're responsible to your team, you become a better player."

Wrap-Up

Make summary comments about practice and give reminders for the next game.

Week 9

Warm-Up (5 minutes)

Players take and follow their shots. Players with the ball shoot for 20, 30, or 45 seconds. They shoot, rebound, and shoot again. Players are limited to three dribbles before their next shot. They keep track of how many shots they make during the timed interval. (See figure on page 120.)

Fitness Circle (5 minutes)

Key Idea: Muscular endurance

Gather players into a group. "Stand with your arms straight out from your sides. Give enough space so you don't bump your neighbor. Circle your arms like this." Demonstrate. "Keep going until you get very tired, then stop." Wait until the last player stops. "Do your arms feel tired? That is called muscle fatigue. Muscles can keep moving and tightening only for so long before tiring out. The longer you can play before your muscles tire out, the more *muscular endurance* you have. You can improve your muscular endurance by playing basketball."

☞ **PURPOSE**

To attack the basket through the give-and-go.

Equipment

☑ One basketball per two players, if possible

☑ Court space with three or four baskets

☑ Tape or markers

☑ Different colored vests or shirts to differentiate teams

Game 1 (10 minutes)

Goal

Players will pass and cut to the basket, looking for return passes and good shots.

Description

Play 3 v 3 half-court or short-court games. Teams must make at least two passes before taking a shot. Shots must be within five feet of the basket. Offensive players pass and cut to the basket, presenting a target if they're open. If they receive the ball as they're cutting to the basket, they shoot.

Coach: What was the goal of the game?
Players: To pass and cut; to present target if open.

Coach: What happened when you were able to get open?
Players: Ball was returned and shot was attempted.

Coach: How did you get open?
Players: Used a ball fake, ran ahead of defender, kept body between defender and ball on way to basket.

Coach: What did the other offensive player do to create an open lane for you to attack the basket?
Players: Moved out of the lane.

Skill Practice 1 (10 minutes)

1. Introduce, demonstrate, and explain how to execute a *give-and-go* (see pages 240–241).
2. Practice the give-and-go.

Description

Play 3 v 1, 2 v 1, 3 v 2, or 3 v 3 half-court games, depending on the skill proficiency of your players. Rotate players accordingly so that all players have a chance to play offense and

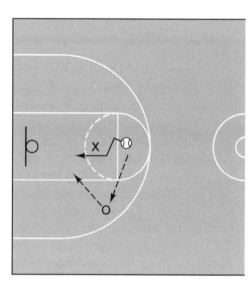

defense. Defenders should play cooperative to active defense. Another player serves as coach. The offense practices the give-and-go three times, using L-cuts or V-cuts toward the basket.

Skill Practice 2 (10 minutes)

Description

Play 2 v 2 games with active to competitive defenders. Two other players serve as coaches. The offense practices the give-and-go three times; then players rotate. (The offense becomes the defense; the defense becomes the coaches; the coaches become the offense.)

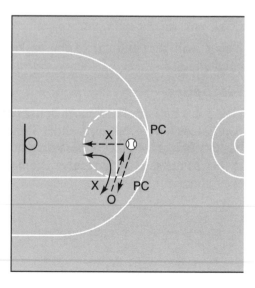

COACH's point

☞ Emphasize that a give-and-go works from all positions on the court.

Week 9

"Pass and cut!"

"Target hand!"

"Keep the defender behind you!"

Coach: What did you do to complete the give-and-go when there was competitive defense?

Players: Used more fakes. Dribbled to create passing lanes. Got open to support player with the ball.

Game 2 (10 minutes)

Same as Game 1, except play 3 v 1, 3 v 2, or 3 v 3 games, depending on the skill proficiency of your players. Rotate players accordingly so that all players have a chance to play offense and defense.

Team Circle (5 minutes)

Key Idea: Caring

Gather players into a group and choose three players to demonstrate. These three will dribble and pass down the court about 20 feet and then back to the group. Set up another group to do the same activity. Rotate players into the two groups until they all get a turn. Bring team back together to discuss. "What was happening every time a new person came into the passing group?" Listen to their responses. Discuss many players getting playing time. "When we share playing time, it shows that you care about your teammates. Players who care about each other want the whole team to get a chance to play. That way everyone can contribute to the team."

Wrap-Up

Make summary comments about practice and give reminders for the next game.

Week 10

Warm-Up (10 minutes)

Players play 1 v 1, starting at the foul line. Defense checks the ball and offense begins in a triple threat position. The offensive player's first movement should be either a ball fake or a jab step. (See figure on page 107.)

Fitness Circle (5 minutes)

Key Idea: Healthy habits

Gather players into a group. "What are healthy habits?" Listen to their responses. "Why do you need to practice healthy habits?" Listen to their responses and encourage discussion of how healthy bodies and minds are important to sports. "Practice healthy habits every day to take care of your bodies—the same way you practice basketball to improve your skills and get to be better players. Keep the list of healthy habits in your mind." Have a list of examples written on a piece of paper clipped to a clipboard, including brushing your teeth; no smoking, alcohol, or drugs; eating healthy foods; and getting plenty of sleep. "Check each item off when you have done that habit during the day." Have a pen to actually check an item off the list. "Every day start your list over again. Doing all the habits daily keeps you healthy."

Game 1 (10 minutes)

Goal

Players will shoot as often as possible and focus on creating passing lanes.

Description

Play 3 v 3 half-court, 5-minute scoring games. One team plays offense for five minutes, then teams switch roles.

Coach: **What was the goal of the game?**
Players: To support the player with the ball.

Coach: **What do you do to provide support?**
Players: Move to get open; get away from your defender.

Coach: **How do you get open?**
Players: Using cuts and fakes.

Skill Practice 1 (15 minutes)

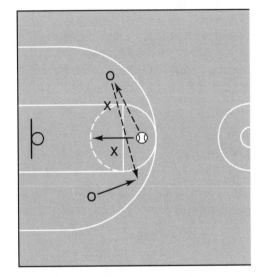

Description

Players play 3 v 2 games; the defense is active to competitive. Offensive players focus on moving to open space. Players pass, then move to an offensive position (point, wing, baseline, or high or low post) adjacent to the ball. Players should provide a target for receiving the ball, receive the ball in triple threat position, and use a ball fake before passing. To create passing lanes, they should use quick jab steps and fake-and-replace movements.

COACH's cues

"Quick cuts!"
"Fake a pass, make a pass!"

COACH's point

☞ Re-teach skills when necessary.

Game 2 (15 minutes)

Goal

Shoot as often as possible and create passing lanes.

Description

Play 3 v 1, 3 v 2, or 3 v 3 short-court games, depending on the skill proficiency of your players. Rotate players accordingly so that all players have a chance to play offense and defense. The offensive team must make at least two passes before taking a shot. All shots must be within five feet of the basket.

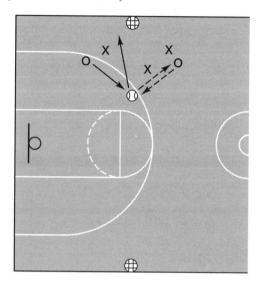

Team Circle (5 minutes)

Key Idea: Caring

Gather players into a group. "Let's imagine we're playing in a game and one of your teammates passes to you. The pass is thrown too far away from you, and you can't get to the ball. Pretend you say, 'What a terrible pass! Get out of here until you learn how to play basketball!' How would you change your comment to sound more positive and make the person feel better?" Listen to their responses. "It is important to make positive comments and not get upset when your teammates make mistakes. This shows you care about your teammates."

Wrap-Up

Make summary comments about practice and reminders for the next game.

Week 11

Warm-Up (10 minutes)

Play 1 v 1 games, starting at the foul line. Defense checks the ball and offense begins in a triple threat position. The offensive player's first movement should be either a ball fake or a jab step. (See figure on page 107.)

Fitness Circle (5 minutes)

Key Idea: Training and conditioning

Split children into two or three groups. Give each group a ball. Instruct them to make a circle, then dribble and pass to others in their group. Continue for one minute, then bring everyone together. "Let's say that activity finished our practice. Now you're finished with practice for the week. What could you do tomorrow to stay active and practice skills that are similar to or the same type of thing we do in practice?" Listen to their responses. Discuss running, dribbling, and other ball-handling skills. "Your body loses its conditioning when you stop using it! It's important to stay active outside of basketball practices. This helps keep you fit for basketball."

> **PURPOSE**
>
> To win the ball by preventing the offense from scoring.
>
> ### Equipment
>
> ☑ One basketball per two players, if possible
>
> ☑ Court space with three or four baskets
>
> ☑ Tape or markers
>
> ☑ Different colored vests or shirts to differentiate teams

Game 1 (10 minutes)

Goal

Defenders will try to keep the opposing team from scoring.

Description

Play 3 v 3 half-court, five-minute scoring games. One team plays offense for five minutes, then teams switch roles. (See figure at the top of page 95.)

Coach: What was the goal of the game?
Players: To keep the offensive team from scoring.

Coach: How did you do that?
Players: Closely guarded opponent, rebounded so they wouldn't get a second shot.

Skill Practice 1
(10 minutes)

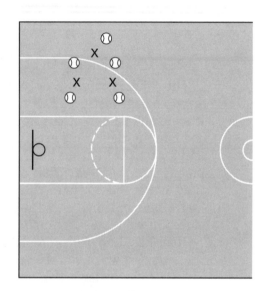

Description

Divide players into a dribblers group and a defenders group. The dribblers group has more players. Confine space; 9 players would need about one-quarter of the court. On signal, the dribblers begin dribbling; the defenders try to steal the ball. Defenders who steal the ball begin dribbling. Go for about 45 seconds, then regroup and switch roles as needed.

COACH's cues

"Ready position! Bend your knees, keep your body low."
"Active hands and feet!"
"Watch your player, watch!"
"Anticipate!"

Game 2 (15 minutes)

Goal

Defenders will try to keep the opposing team from scoring.

Description

Play 2 v 3 short-court games. Offensive players must make at least three passes before taking a shot. The defensive team earns a point if the offensive team does not complete three passes. Switch teams halfway through the game, with the two offensive players joining one defender on defense, and two defenders switching to offense. (See figure on page 128.)

Team Circle (5 minutes)

Key Idea: Responsibility

Gather players into a group. Choose one player to demonstrate with you. Let the player know you'll be passing the ball and that he or she should pretend to be in position to make a basket. Make a bad pass to the player. Identify that the bad pass was your mistake. "Raise your hand if you think it's a part of learning when you make a bad pass." Give them time to raise their hands. "Now raise your hand if you think a bad pass means you are not a good player." Give them time to raise their hands. "Everyone makes mistakes, and when you make one it does not mean you're not a good player. Taking responsibility for your play, even when you can improve, is an important quality for good players."

Wrap-Up

Make summary comments about practice and give reminders for the next game.

Week 12

PURPOSE

To create space and attack the basket by using the give-and-go.

Equipment

☑ One basketball per two players, if possible

☑ Court space with three or four baskets

☑ Tape or markers

☑ Different colored vests or shirts to differentiate teams

Warm-Up (10 minutes)

Players in pairs play "Around the World". Spots are marked in an arc around the basket, about five feet to eight feet out. Shooters follow a set pattern. The first player shoots from spot #1; if the shot is good, the player moves to spot #2. The player continues until he or she misses a shot. On a missed shot, the shooter may select to stay there until his or her next turn, or "chance it." This gives the player another shot immediately, but if the shooter misses, he or she goes back to the beginning. A made chance allows the shooter to skip the next spot. (See figure on page 102.)

Fitness Circle (5 minutes)

Key Idea: Healthy habits

Gather the players into a group. "What kinds of food do you think are the best to eat when you play basketball?" Listen to their responses. Encourage discussion to talk about the difference between healthy foods and unhealthy foods. Healthy choices include fruits, vegetables, grains or cereals, lean meats, plant proteins, and nut butters. Discourage soda, high-sugar foods, fatty meats, chips, and fried foods. "Your body needs all types of food to be healthy. Let's think of three healthy snacks you could eat that would give you energy to practice." Listen to responses and encourage everyone to contribute. Vote on whether the foods they name are the best choice or not. "Eating healthy snacks that give you extra energy to play basketball is a healthy habit you should be practicing every day."

Game 1 (10 minutes)

Goal

Players will pass and cut to the basket.

Description

Play 3 v 3 short-court games. Offensive players must make at least three passes before taking a shot. All shots must be within five feet of the basket. (See figure on page 128.)

Week 12

Coach: What was the goal of the game?
Players: To pass and cut; to present a target.

Coach: How did you get open?
Players: Used a fake, a razor-sharp cut; ran ahead of defender; kept body between defender and ball.

Coach: What did you do to complete the give-and-go when there was competitive defense?
Players: Used more fakes. Dribbled to create passing lanes. Got open to support player with the ball.

Skill Practice 1 (15 minutes)

Description

Play 2 v 2 games with active to competitive defenders. Two other players serve as coaches. Each offensive player practices the give-and-go three times, then rotates. Players move to the other side of the basket and repeat. Then practice the give-and-go three times with a competitive defense (use either side of basket). (See figure at the bottom of page 124.)

COACH's cues

"Pass and cut!"

"Target hand!"

"Get and stay between defender and ball."

Game 2
(15 minutes)

Goal

Players will pass and cut to the basket.

Description

Play 3 v 1, 3 v 2, or 3 v 3 short-court games, depending on the skill proficiency of your players. Rotate players accordingly so that all players have a chance to play offense and defense. Offensive players must make at least three passes before taking a shot. All shots must be within five feet of the basket.

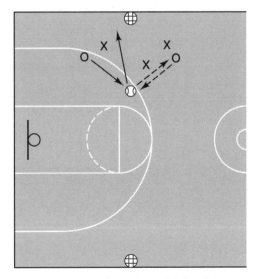

Team Circle
(5 minutes)

Key Idea: Respect

Gather players into groups of two. "Each of you tell your partner two or three ways you saw other players show respect this season. I'll give you two minutes." After two minutes, group all players together again. "Tell us what some of the examples were." Listen to examples and discuss. "It's important to notice respect being practiced and to talk about what we saw. All season we have been working on both basketball skills and being good teammates. Improving both of those areas tells me you have respect for yourselves and your teammates."

Wrap-Up

Make summary comments about practice and give reminders about the final game.

Practice Plans for 10- to 11-Year-Olds

This chapter contains the 14 practice plans you'll use with your 10- and 11-year-old YMCA Winners basketball players. It also contains recommendations for modifying your practices to make them developmentally appropriate for 10- and 11-year-olds. By following these practice plans, you will be presenting the game and coaching in a way that maximizes players' skill development *and* their enjoyment of the game.

Each plan contains the following sections:

◎ Purpose

◎ Equipment

◎ Practice Plan

Purpose focuses on what you want to teach your players during that practice; it is your main "theme" for that day. *Equipment* notes what you'll need on hand for that practice. The *Practice Plan* section outlines what you will do during each practice session. It consists of these elements:

◎ Warm-Up

◎ Fitness Circle

◎ Game

◎ Skill Practice

◎ Team Circle and Wrap-Up

You'll begin each session with about five minutes of warm-up activities. This will be followed by five minutes of a Fitness Circle, during which you lead players through a series of stretches as you briefly discuss an item that relates to their fitness. Then you'll have your players play a modified basketball game. You'll look for your cue to interrupt that game—your cue being when players are having problems with carrying out the basic goal or aim of the game. At this point you'll "freeze" the action, keeping the players where they are, and ask brief questions about the tactical problems the players encountered and what skills they need to "solve" those problems. (Review chapter 8 for more on interrupting a game and holding a question-and-answer session.) We provide discussion questions in each practice plan. In addition, we provide coaching points, when appropriate, with games and skill practices as points of emphasis in most effectively conducting the practice.

Then you'll teach the skill that the players need to acquire to successfully execute the tactic. Chapter 13 contains descriptions of all the skills, so a page reference will be given to guide you to the appropriate description. During this skill practice session, you'll use the IDEA approach:

I   Introduce the skill.

D   Demonstrate the skill.

E   Explain the skill.

A   Attend to players practicing the skill.

Your introduction, demonstration, and explanation of a skill should take no more than two to three minutes; then you'll attend to players and provide teaching cues or further demonstration as necessary while they practice the skill according to the practice plan.

After the skill practices, you will usually have the athletes play another game or two to let them use the skills they just learned and to understand them in the context of a game. Note that in Game 1 when players are being introduced to a new tactic or skill, they will play an even-sided game (3 v 3). This allows them to encounter the challenges they will face in executing the tactic or skill in competition. Then in most Game 2s they should play lopsided games (3 v 1, 3 v 2) to increase their chances of experiencing success and beginning to master the new skill. However, if your players are showing proficiency with the new skill, you can use even-sided games in Game 2. The choice is yours; for more on this issue, see chapter 8.

The Practice Plan section concludes with a Team Circle that focuses on character development. As your players cool down and stretch, you will talk to them about some aspect of basketball that relates to one of the four core values—caring, honesty, respect, and responsibility. Following this, you'll wrap up the practice with a few summary comments and remind them of the next practice or game day.

A note about Fitness and Team Circles: These times are meant to be true discussions—not lectures where you're doing all the talking and your players are doing all the listening. Ask the questions provided, and wait for your players to respond. Don't immediately feed them the answers that we provide. These answers are meant simply to help you guide the discussion. Your role in Team Circles is as much to ask questions and get players to respond as it is to dole out information.

Ten- and 11-year-olds don't possess the size, strength, stamina, and skills to play the full-blown adult version of basketball, and attempting to fit them into the adult mold will prove frustrating for all involved. We suggest you incorporate the following modifications into your practices to help your players learn the game, improve their skills, and have fun while they're at it. These suggestions fall into three categories: equipment and court, rules, and scrimmages.

 # Equipment and Court

Equipment and court should be substantially modified for young players to best learn the game and improve their skills. We recommend the following modifications:

◎ Size of ball: Women's ball (#6)

◎ Height of basket: 8 feet

◎ Free-throw line distance: 9 feet

◎ Court size: Half court or short court

Making Games Simpler or More Challenging

Here are ways to make practice games simpler or more challenging:

- Equally increase or decrease the number of players suggested (e.g., if we suggest playing 3 v 3, make it simpler by playing 2 v 2, or make it more challenging by playing 4 v 4).

- Add an extra defender to make it harder on the offense (e.g., 3 v 4 instead of 3 v 3), once players have acquired the skills they need to be successful.

- Add an extra offensive player to make it easier for the offense (e.g., 4 v 3 instead of 3 v 3).

- Change the type of defense played. The three types of defenses (see "Scrimmages") are cooperative, active, and competitive. To

make a game simpler, have your players play a cooperative defense; to make it more challenging, have them play an active or a competitive defense.

- Begin with *no* defense.

- Perform the skill or game at a slower than normal pace to make it simpler.

- Increase or decrease the number of passes you require before the offense can attempt a shot.

We encourage you to consider these changes during each practice. Whether you make them or not depends on how your players are responding. The more skilled they are, the more likely they'll need greater challenges to continue improving.

Rules

You need to strike a balance between calling the players for violations and fouls every time they commit one, while still teaching the appropriate rules and the skills they need to learn and comply with fully in the long run. But your players won't learn much in practice if you're blowing the whistle every 10 seconds for another rules violation or foul. Therefore, we suggest the following rules modifications during practices:

- **Clock rules:** Don't call 3-second lane violations, 5-second counts, or 10-second backcourt violations. Don't run a shot clock.
- **Defense:**
  —Use a player-to-player defense only.
  —Don't use a full-court press; defense can pick up their players at half court or closer to their own basket.
  —Defenders may not intentionally get in the way of an offensive player in an attempt to draw a charging foul against that player. Don't teach taking a charge.
- **Double dribble:** Allow one violation per player possession; gradually eliminate this allowance.
- **Traveling:** Give an extra step for starting or stopping.

While the following points are not really rules modifications, they are worth noting here and emphasizing in practice:

- Don't allow players to wear jewelry. Doing so is dangerous to them and to other players.
- Players should call their own fouls.
- Don't allow players to undercut a player shooting a lay-up.
- Players should keep control of their body and the ball: no rough play.
- Players should be good sports and show respect. Don't tolerate unsporting conduct.

Scrimmages

Besides the obvious changes in court and equipment, a casual observer of a YMCA Winners basketball practice would note another difference in the practice setting: the number of players used in scrimmages and practice games. Using smaller numbers allows players to touch the ball more often and thus practice the skills they need to acquire. It also keeps everyone more active and gives players more experience in a variety of situations that call for different tactics and skills. Here are suggestions for scrimmages and practice games:

- Use small-sided games (e.g., 1 v 1, 2 v 1, 2 v 2, 3 v 2, 3 v 3, 4 v 4) on half-court play or cross-court playing (short court, see figure on page 85). Remember, using small-sided games means more touches per player, which means players develop skills more quickly. The greatest leaps in skill improvement are made through the use of small-sided games.

◎ Use modified half-court games in which players play 1 v 1 or 2 v 2, taking turns trying to score.

◎ Use "regular" half-court rules: an offensive rebound can be shot again, while a defensive rebound must result in that team or player restarting at the top of the key.

◎ Rotate partners (opponents) and teams often. Play three- to five-minute games, then rotate players. Changing partners changes the game.

A note regarding defense: At this level, the focus is on offensive skills. Although defensive skills are important, if they are introduced too soon they may prohibit the development of offensive skills, especially if peers play defense aggressively. Introduce defensive skills after players have developed some proficiency with off- and on-the-ball skills. Control defensive play by instituting three levels of involvement:

1. **Cooperative Defense (cold)**—The player assumes a defensive posture two arm lengths from the opponent, is relatively passive, and at times even coaches the opponent.

2. **Active Defense (warm)**—The player assumes a defensive posture about one and a half arm lengths from the opponent, has active hands and feet, but makes no attempts to intercept the ball.

3. **Competitive Defense (hot)**—The player assumes a defensive posture, is positioned appropriately, and attempts to intercept the ball.

Explain how to play a modified half-court game. The games should be more cooperative than they are competitive. Limit your focus to boundaries, starting and restarting game play, and keeping control. Be flexible regarding all violations (double dribble, traveling), but do enforce an "out of control rule." For example, don't allow a player to pick up the ball and run with it without dribbling.

Okay, on to the practice plans themselves. Following are practice plans for the 2 weeks of your preseason and then for the 10 weeks of your competitive season.

Key to Diagrams

⊕	=	Side basket
⓪	=	Player with ball
O	=	Offensive player
X	=	Defensive player
C	=	Coach
PC	=	Player-coach
- - - ➤	=	Pass
〜➤	=	Dribble
⟶	=	Move
⟹	=	Shoot
R	=	Rebounder
P	=	Partner
■	=	Marked spots
⊣	=	Screen or box out
S	=	Shooter

Week 1, Practice 1

PURPOSE

To create space in the attack by creating passing lanes.

Equipment

- ☑ One basketball per two players, if possible
- ☑ Court space with three or four baskets
- ☑ Tape or markers
- ☑ Different colored vests or shirts to differentiate teams
- ☑ Two cones

COACH's point

☞ Teach the five-second inbounds rule (see page 278).

Warm-Up (10 minutes)

Begin each practice with five to 10 minutes of warm-up activities to get players loosened up and ready to go.

Players dribble, jump stop, and shoot, traveling from one basket to the next. All shooting should be two to four feet from the basket.

Fitness Circle (5 minutes)

Following the warm-up, gather the players and demonstrate the stretching protocol (see chapter 15 for stretches for the major muscle groups). Ask a team leader to lead stretches in subsequent practices. After the team is finished stretching, briefly discuss the fitness concept for that practice.

Key Idea: General fitness

Gather the team into a group between two cones about 20 feet apart. "Do you think there's a difference between physical activity and physical fitness?" Listen to their responses. "Physical *activity* is any body movement you use while performing a skill or task. Physical *fitness* is a condition of the body. The more fit your body is, the better you can perform some skills and tasks. I will give you some activities. Run to this cone if you think it is regular physical activity. Run to the other cone other if you think it is an activity done for fitness." Examples of physical activity are walking to school or walking stairs to bed; examples of physical fitness are walking to school for exercise, jogging to improve sport performance, or walking stairs to strengthen leg muscles. "All season we will talk and learn about the different areas of fitness during our fitness circles. We'll also work on improving your body's fitness for basketball."

Game 1 (10 minutes)

Following the Fitness Circle, get the kids playing a game. Follow most games with a time of questions and answers—with YOU asking the questions and your PLAYERS providing the answers—about what the goal of the game was and what skills and tactics they needed to perform to succeed in the game. For many games, we provide diagrams or figures (or refer to diagrams and figures on previous pages) showing how the game is begun. We also often provide coach's points for you to pass along to your players during the games.

Week 1, Practice 1

Goal

Shoot as often as possible and create passing lanes.

Description

Play 3 v 3 half-court games. Offensive teams must complete two or more consecutive passes before shooting. Players cannot dribble; all restarts occur at half court. (See figure at the top of page 95.)

Coach: What was the goal of the game?
Players: To shoot as often as possible following two consecutive passes.

Coach: What do you and your teammates do to be successful?
Players: Make quick and accurate passes. Catch the ball under control. Move to an open space. Support player with the ball.

Coach: What do you do to provide support?
Players: Move to get open; get away from your defender.

Coach: How do you get open?
Players: Use cuts and fakes.

Coach: What do you do to keep the defense from stealing the ball or blocking your shot?
Players: Protect the ball by keeping your body between the defense and the ball. Hold the ball firmly with two hands; use body to protect the ball. Use quick passes.

Coach: Once you receive the ball, what is the best way to hold it so the defense doesn't know whether you are going to shoot or pass?
Players: Hold the ball as if you're going to shoot (triple threat position), with one hand behind the ball and the other at its side.

Skill Practice 1 (15 minutes)

Follow Game 1 with a Skill Practice. Use the IDEA approach: Introduce, Demonstrate, and Explain a skill or tactic, then Attend to your players as they practice that tactic. The question-and-answer session, in which your PLAYERS tell you what skills and tactics they need to be successful in the game, leads directly to the Skill Practice. We often provide coaching points with the Skill Practices; pass these points along to your players. We also provide coach's cues—phrases to help your players focus on the task at hand—during many Skill Practices and Games.

1. Introduce, demonstrate, and explain *creating passing lanes* (see page 238).
2. Practice providing support for teammates by creating passing lanes.

Description

Play 3 v 1 games. Offensive players move to open space. Defenders play cooperative to active defense. Use offensive positions on one or both sides of the basket. Players pass, then move to an offensive position (point, wing, baseline, or high or low post) adjacent to the ball. Players should provide a target for receiving the ball, receive it in triple threat, and use a ball fake before passing. Emphasize using quick jab steps to create passing lanes.

Stop Skill Practice 1 and Game 2 occasionally to show players where good supporting positions are.

Reteach when necessary.

Emphasize that players shouldn't get too close to teammates who have the ball.

COACH's cues

"Target hands!"
"Fake a pass, make a pass."
"Throwing action!"
"Elbows!"
"Finish!"
"Quick cuts!"

Game 2 (15 minutes)

Goal

Shoot as often as possible and create passing lanes.

Description

Same as Game 1, except choose either 3 v 1, 3 v 2, or 3 v 3, depending on the skill proficiency of your players (see chapter 8 for help on deciding how to use lopsided games). Rotate players accordingly so that all players have a chance to play offense and defense.

Teach rules on traveling and double dribble (see page 278).

142

Team Circle
(5 minutes)

Key Idea: Four core values

Gather the team into a group. Have four cones set up five feet apart. "We are going to talk about four main values or qualities that good players include in their games and practices. What are the four?" Have players stand at a cone when they provide a value. Have another player provide an example of the value, then have that player join the other player at the cone. Assist players if they cannot think of all four (caring, honesty, respect, responsibility). "We will work to improve our basketball skills and physical fitness but these four values are just as important to learn and practice to help you become good players. We will learn about these values during our team circles."

Wrap-Up

Make summary comments about practice. Remind them of the next practice and give them a sneak preview: The focus will be on receiving a pass, squaring to the basket, and scoring.

Warm-Up (10 minutes)

PURPOSE

To attack the basket by receiving a pass, squaring to the basket, and scoring.

Equipment

- ☑ One basketball per two players, if possible
- ☑ Court space with three or four baskets
- ☑ Tape or markers
- ☑ Different colored vests or shirts to differentiate teams

Warm-Up (10 minutes)

Players in pairs play "Around the Key"—one player shoots; the partner rebounds and returns the ball. The shooter tries to make five different shots around the free-throw lane in 30 seconds. Players receive two points for each shot made. (See figure on page 94.)

Fitness Circle (5 minutes)

Key Idea: General fitness

Gather the team into a group. "Who can tell me what 'warm up' means?" Listen to their responses. They might mention getting the body ready to do more strenuous activity, increasing blood circulation, and moving muscles so they are more flexible and will help prevent injuries. Discuss their responses and other possible responses. "Raise your hand if you think the muscles actually get warmer during warm-up activities?" Listen to their responses. "They do get warmer from the blood circulating and your moving. Give me some examples of good warm-up activities." Choose one for the team to try. "The warm-up is an important part of a good basketball fitness program. We will do a warm-up activity every practice."

Game 1 (10 minutes)

Goal

Players will score as often as possible. The focus is on using the triple threat and using ball fakes and jab steps.

Description

Play 3 v 3 half-court games. Players must complete two or more consecutive passes before attempting a shot. Encourage players to make quick passes, to use target hands, and to call for the ball. They cannot dribble. All restarts are at half court. Players earn one point for each shot attempted and two points for each basket scored. (See figure at the top of page 95.)

COACH's point

☞ Teach the three-second lane violation (see page 278).

Coach: **What was the goal of the game?**
Players: To score following two consecutive passes.

Coach: **From where on the court did you score most of your points?**
Players: Close to the basket.

Coach: **Why is it better to shoot from a position close to the basket, rather than far from the basket?**
Players: More likely to score when closer—higher percentage shot.

Coach: **Besides shooting from a close range, what else did you do to successfully perform a shot?**
Players: Squared shoulders to basket; elbow under ball and close to body; one hand behind the ball and the other at the side of the ball; staggered stance with knees slightly bent; followed through, aimed.

Skill Practice 1 (15 minutes)

1. Introduce, demonstrate, and explain how to *shoot* (see pages 262–264).
2. Practice shooting.

Description

Players in pairs shoot three shots from each of five spots marked around the basket (about six to eight feet away). Partners rebound the ball and pass accurately to shooters, who provide a target, receive the ball in triple threat, square up, and shoot. The goal is to score on two out of three shots at each spot.

(You could simplify the shooting goal from making two of every three shots, to shooting from two different spots for 30 seconds, or simply shooting three shots from each spot.) (See figure at the bottom of page 95.)

☞Give only one or two shooting cues at a time (e.g., keep your base firm, elbow under the ball).

COACH's cues

"Square up!"
"BEEF!"
"**B**ase firm."
"**E**lbow under ball."
"**E**xtend arm."
"**F**ollow through or flip wrist."

Game 2 (15 minutes)

Goal

Players will score as many field goals as possible.

Description

Play 3 v 1, 3 v 2, or 3 v 3 half-court games, depending on the skill proficiency of your players. Rotate players accordingly so that all players have a chance to play offense and defense. Players must complete two or more consecutive passes before attempting a shot. (See figure at the top of page 89.)

Team Circle
(5 minutes)

Key Idea: Caring

Gather the team into a circle. Have two cones set up 10 feet apart. Ask one player to demonstrate with you. Have the player accidentally trip you. Fall down as if you are hurt. "Anna accidentally tripped me; what should she do? If you think she should apologize and help the player up, then raise her hand for a foul, stand at this cone. If you think she should keep playing and raise her hand for committing a foul, stand at this cone." Encourage all players to vote. Discuss why they voted the way they did. Tactfully explain the "caring action" so players don't feel foolish for not realizing they should help. "When you accidentally trip or hurt another player, an opponent or teammate, it is important to help them up or see if they are OK. That shows that you care about other players."

Wrap-Up

Make summary comments about practice. Remind them of the next practice and give them a sneak preview: The focus will be on creating passing lanes.

Week 2, Practice 1

Warm-Up (10 minutes)

Players in pairs play "Around the World." Spots are marked in an arc around the basket, about 5 to 8 feet from the basket. Shooters follow a set pattern. The first player shoots from spot #1; if the shot is good, the player moves to spot #2. The player continues until he or she misses a shot. On a missed shot, the shooter may elect to stay there until his or her next turn, or "chance it." This gives the player another shot immediately, but if the shooter misses, he or she goes back to the beginning. A made chance allows the shooter to skip the next spot. (See figure on page 102.)

Fitness Circle (5 minutes)

Key Idea: Cardiorespiratory fitness

Gather the team into a group. "Who can tell me what *cardiorespiratory fitness* is? When you have good cardiorespiratory fitness, your heart picks up oxygen from your lungs and takes it all over your body." Ask three players to demonstrate. Have one ball ready. The players should be spread out in a line; the ball will be passed zigzag down the line. Stagger players so the ball is passed across to each other, one side then the other side, in the line. "Let's set up our own blood vessel to carry oxygen to the muscles." Set up and perform the activity, with player 1 being the heart, player 2 the lungs, and player 3 the legs. "We need to run more to improve our body's ability to get oxygen to our muscles. That is improving our cardiorespiratory fitness."

PURPOSE

To create space in the attack by creating passing lanes.

Equipment

- ☑ One basketball per two players, if possible
- ☑ Court space with three or four baskets
- ☑ Tape or markers
- ☑ Different colored vests or shirts to differentiate teams

Game 1 (10 minutes)

Goal

Players will provide support for their teammate with the ball.

Description

Play 2 v 2 half-court games. Players must complete at least three passes before shooting. They receive one point for three consecutive passes, and two points for every field goal. (See figure at the top of page 91.)

Coach: What was the goal of the game?
Players: To support the player with the ball.

Coach: How were you able to support the player with the ball?
Players: Using a ball fake and replace, jab step; moving quickly.

Coach: Is a zigzag or curved pathway better when performing a cut?
Players: Zigzag.

Coach: Can you describe the angle of these cuts using letters of the alphabet?
Players: V and L.

Coach: Why would V- or L-cuts be better than curved?
Players: It's harder for the defender to stay with you.

Coach: What did you do if your defender was closely guarding you?
Players: Used a cut to get away.

Coach: When would a V-cut be most effective, close to the lane or away from the lane?
Players: Away from the lane 10 to 12 feet.

Coach: When would the L-cut be most effective?
Players: Close to the lane near the baseline.

COACH's point

☞ The only difference between V- and L-cuts is the angle from which the offense moves into the defense, then toward the pass.

☞ Emphasize making "razor sharp" cuts.

☞ Teaching off-the-ball movements is important—as we know, good players know how to get open.

Skill Practice 1 (15 minutes)

1. Introduce, demonstrate, and explain how to execute *V-cuts* and *L-cuts* (see page 250).
2. Practice V-cuts and L-cuts.

Description

Play 2 v 2 games with the focus on players using V-cuts and L-cuts, receiving passes, and using jump stops and the triple threat position. Sequence:

- O_1 ball fakes, jab steps, and passes to O_2, who V-cuts as O_1 is ball faking.
- O_2 catches the ball in a triple threat position using a jump stop.
- Repeat three times and rotate.
- When all four players in a group have practiced the V-cut three times, go through the rotation again, this time practicing the V-cut on the opposite side of the basket.
- When all four players have practiced the V-cut on both sides of the basket, go through the rotation again, using the same sequence to practice L-cuts on both sides of the basket. The defense should play passive, cooperative defense.

Game 2 (15 minutes)

Goal

Players will provide support to their teammate with the ball, using V-cuts and L-cuts to get open.

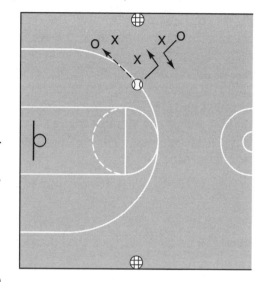

Description

Play 3 v 1, 3 v 2, or 3 v 3 short-court games, depending on the skill proficiency of your players. Rotate players accordingly so that all players have a chance to play offense and defense. Players must complete at least three passes before shooting. They receive one point for three consecutive passes, and two points for every field goal.

Team Circle (5 minutes)

Key Idea: Responsibility

Gather players into a group. Have a clipboard and act as if you are writing or working. Do not pay attention to the group. Continue for one minute. "Hello, everybody. Now I am ready to talk about our team circle for today. How did you feel having to wait for me to get ready to talk to you?" Listen to responses. "Waiting for someone to be ready during practice wastes time. Even if it is a coach. I demonstrated how time is wasted if someone isn't prepared for practice. I read and prepare before practice so I am ready. I want you to do the same. You have a responsibility to the team to be ready when it is time for every practice to start. What do you do at home to get ready for practice?" Discuss responses.

Wrap-Up

Make summary comments about practice. Remind them of the next practice and give them a sneak preview: The focus will be on using a power dribble to drive and score.

149

Week 2, Practice 2

Warm-Up (10 minutes)

Players in pairs play "Around the World." Spots are marked in an arc around the basket, about 5 to 8 feet away. Shooters follow a set pattern. The first player shoots from spot #1; if the shot is good, the player moves to spot #2. The player continues until he or she misses a shot. On a missed shot, the shooter may elect to stay there until his or her next turn, or "chance it." This gives the player another shot immediately, but if the shooter misses, he or she goes back to the beginning. A made chance allows the shooter to skip the next spot. (See figure on page 102.)

Fitness Circle (5 minutes)

Key Idea: Cardiorespiratory fitness

Gather the team into a circle. "What fitness area improves when we run more and strengthen our heart and lungs? *Cardiorespiratory fitness.* When we run more during practice to improve our cardiorespiratory fitness, what will start to happen?" Listen to their responses. Discuss getting fatigued if they run too fast early in the practice. "If you don't want to tire early in the practice, we can use a special test to help you judge how fast to run. It's called a talk test. A talk test can tell you if you're running too fast for your body and need to slow down. Everyone jog to the goal and back with your partner saying 'two points.' You should not be out of breath while you're talking; if you are, slow down!"

Game 1 (10 minutes)

Goal

Players will drive hard to the basket and shoot.

Description

Play 3 v 3 half-court games. Give two points for scores off of drives, and one point for other baskets. Instruct defenders not to clog the lane so that players can drive. Defenders should play "warm" defense.

Week 2, Practice 2

Coach: What was the goal of the game?
Players: Drive and score.

Coach: What's a good way to drive?
Players: Drop step and dribble.

Coach: What should you do if it's congested in the lane?
Players: Stop and shoot if open, or pass off.

Skill Practice 1 (10 minutes)

COACH's point

1. Introduce, demonstrate, and explain how to use a *jump stop* (see pages 251–252) prior to shooting.
2. Practice shooting off of jump stops.

Description

Play 1 v 1; defenders play cooperative defense. Players with the ball use a ball fake, jab step, and drive to the basket. They jump stop and shoot two to four feet from the basket. Watch for good form on the jump stops and shots; players should use the square on the backboard. Alternate players quickly so that there are not a lot of players standing around.

☞ Briefly describe charging fouls and blocking fouls (which often occur when a player drives to the basket). See page 277.

☞ Instruct players to raise their hand when they foul.

COACH's cues

"Arm should look like a yo-yo."

"Ball down, eyes up."

"Two-foot jump stop."

"Eyes on target."

"In the square, in the basket."

☞ Use examples from the Skill Practice or Games to illustrate how driving to the basket can create passing lanes.

Coach: How should your dribble change when someone is guarding you?
Players: Keep the ball closer to the body and keep the ball between yourself and the defender.

Game 2 (10 minutes)

Goal

Players will attempt to score in 15 seconds or less.

Description

Play 1 v 1 games. The player with the ball starts at the foul line. Check the ball: the defensive player starts with the ball and gives it to the offensive player when they are ready to play. The offensive player begins in triple threat position and gets two points for every basket scored off a jump stop, and one point for every basket scored otherwise. (See figure on page 108.)

Game 3 (10 minutes)

Goal

Players will shoot as often as possible off of a dribble and drive.

Description

Play 3 v 1, 3 v 2, or 3 v 3 games, depending on the skill proficiency of your players. Rotate players accordingly so that all players have a chance to play offense and defense. Players can't dribble—except to drive to the basket. (See figure on page 108.)

Team Circle (5 minutes)

Key Idea: Respect

Gather the team into a group. Set two cones up 10 feet apart. "What is one important thing you can do at the end of every game to show you have respect for your opponent?" Listen to responses—discuss shaking or slapping hands, saying "good game." "Let's say some kids on the other team start walking away following a game. What should you do? If you think you should let them walk away without saying anything or trying to shake hands, stand at this cone. If you think you should say 'good game' and hold your hand out anyway, stand at this cone." All players should vote. Ask why players voted the way they did. "You should shake hands and/or say 'good game' following every game; it shows respect for your opponent. If the other team turns away and doesn't participate, you shouldn't change your behavior."

Wrap-Up

Make summary comments about practice and give a preview of the next practice—on-the-ball defense.

Week 3

Warm-Up (10 minutes)

Play 1 v 1 games, starting at the foul line. Defense checks the ball and offense begins in a triple threat position. (See figure on page 108.)

Fitness Circle (5 minutes)

Key Idea: General fitness

Gather the team into a group. "If you participate in basketball practice every week, do you think that's enough to keep your body's fitness to play basketball? Do you think you'll improve your body's fitness in the different areas?" Listen to their responses. "You need to be active outside basketball practice to keep your overall fitness at a level that helps your basketball. What are some activities you could do outside of practice?" Listen to their responses. Discuss practicing skills such as dribbling or shooting alone or with a partner. Ask one player to demonstrate using one ball. Have all players try.

☞ **PURPOSE**

To win the ball through on-the-ball defense.

Equipment

☑ One basketball per two players, if possible

☑ Court space with three or four baskets

☑ Tape or markers

☑ Different colored vests or shirts to differentiate teams

☑ Two cones

COACH's point

☞ Teach rules on holding, tripping, and reaching in (see page 277).

Game 1 (10 minutes)

Goal

Defenders will keep the opposing team from scoring.

Description

Play 3 v 3 half-court games. Use a competitive defense. The offensive team can't dribble and must complete at least three consecutive passes before shooting. The defensive team scores one point if the offensive team does not complete three passes. (See figure at the top of page 95.)

Coach: What do you do to keep the opposing team from scoring?
Players: Closely guard, rebound so they wouldn't get a second shot.

Coach: What defensive position or actions interfere most and kept your opponent from scoring?
Players: Keeping your body between the opponent and the goal. Being sure you can always see the ball. Guarding the opponent closely. Keeping hands and feet moving; playing active defense.

Skill Practice 1 (10 minutes)

1. Introduce, demonstrate, and explain proper *on-the-ball positioning* (see pages 269–271.
2. Practice on-the-ball defensive positioning.

Description

Pair up players. The player with the ball dribbles forward in a zigzag pattern. The defensive player maintains proper defensive posture and attempts to block the offensive player's forward progress. The defender tries to either steal the ball without fouling or cause a turnover. Players switch roles after one length of the court. (See figure on page 114.)

Game 2 (10 minutes)

Goal

Defenders will play good on-the-ball defense.

Description

Play 1 v 1 games with active to competitive defense. Offensive players can dribble, but as soon as they pick up the dribble, defensive players move closer and use active hands and feet.

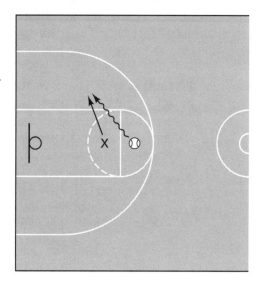

COACH's cues

"Medium body posture."
"Active hands and active feet!"
"See the ball!"
"Anticipate!"

Game 3 (10 minutes)

Goal

Defenders will keep the opposing team from scoring.

Description

Same as Game 1, except play 2 v 3 or 2 v 4. Rotate players accordingly so that all players have a chance to play offense and defense.

Team Circle
(5 minutes)

Key Idea: Respect

Gather the team into a group. Set up two cones 10 feet apart. "What are some of the official's duties during a game?" Listen to and discuss responses. "Who makes the calls during the game? Can you disagree if you think an official's call is not right or do you accept the official's call even if you think it is wrong? If you think you can discuss the call with the official, stand at this cone. If you think the official makes the call and you accept it, stand at this cone." All players should vote. "You need to have respect for the officials at all times. They are in charge on the court during a game. Don't argue with them; accept their calls and decisions. But, if you have a question, ask the official or me during a break."

Wrap-Up

Make summary comments about practice and give reminders for the first game.

Week 4

PURPOSE

To win the ball through off-the-ball defense.

Equipment

☑ One basketball per two players, if possible

☑ Court space with three or four baskets

☑ Tape or markers

☑ Different colored vests or shirts to differentiate teams

Warm-Up (10 minutes)

Players play "Now you have it, now you don't." Divide players into two teams. Each team stands on opposite sidelines of the gym facing each other. Each member of team A has a ball; team B doesn't. On signal, team A players begin dribbling toward the opposite sideline. Team B approaches, trying to take away the balls. If a team B player gains possession of a ball, that player dribbles toward the opposite sideline. When players from team A or team B make it over their "goal" line (the opposing sideline), they stay there until all balls are behind the sidelines. Team B is now given the balls and the game begins again. (See figure on page 116.)

Fitness Circle (5 minutes)

Key Idea: Muscular strength and endurance

Gather the players into a group in a small area. "I want everyone to find a partner and balance back to back while sitting like a chair. I'll time you for one minute." Model the action for the group. "What muscles did you use to hold yourselves up?" Touch the different areas with your hand to show players the muscle groups of their legs, front and back. "You use different muscles to perform different activities. Practicing using specific muscles improves your muscular strength and endurance—that is, how hard you can dribble the ball and how long you can keep going before your muscles get tired."

Game 1 (10 minutes)

Goal

Defenders will prevent the offensive team from passing, receiving passes, and scoring.

Description

Play 3 v 3 half-court games. Players can't dribble except to drive to the basket or reposition to make a pass. They must make at least three consecutive passes before shooting. The defensive team receives one point for each turnover and two points for each steal without fouling. Treat fouls like violations—the other team gets the ball. (See figure at the top of page 95.)

COACH's point

☞ Teach rules on hand-checking and pushing (see page 277).

Week 4

Coach: How do you position yourself to prevent the offensive team from passing?

Players: Overplay toward potential passing lanes; closely guard player with the ball.

Coach: How do you position yourself to deny a pass?

Players: Overplay toward the ball; keep hand in passing lane.

Skill Practice 1 (10 minutes)

- Introduce, demonstrate, and explain proper *off-the-ball positioning* (see pages 271–272).
- Practice off-the-ball defensive positioning.

Description

Paired-up players practice off-the-ball defensive positioning (partners can also coach each other). As an option, you can have a player with the ball waiting to pass to his or her offensive teammate. (See figure on page 117.)

Game 2 (10 minutes)

Goal

Defenders try to deny offense from making successful passes; offense tries to make six consecutive passes.

Description

Play 2 v 2 games using a competitive defense. For each 2 v 2 game, two other players serve as coaches. One offensive player begins at the point, the other at a wing position. The ball starts at the point. From a triple threat position, the ball handler uses a ball fake to give his or her teammate a chance to get open; or the ball handler dribbles to open a passing lane if necessary. Rotate after a turnover or after six consecutive passes. One player-coach gives feedback for the on-the-ball defense; the other player-coach gives feedback for the off-the-ball defense. (See figure on page 118.)

COACH's point

☞ Remind players to stay focused on defense.

COACH's cues

"Medium body posture."

"Active hands and active feet!"

"See the ball!"

"Anticipate!"

157

Game 3 (10 minutes)

Repeat first game, except play 2 v 3 or 2 v 4. Players should focus on off-the-ball defensive positioning. Rotate players accordingly so that all players have a chance to play offense and defense.

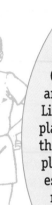

Team Circle (5 minutes)

Key Idea: Honesty

Gather the team into a group. "Give me some examples of being dishonest in practices and games." Listen to responses. After each response, have the players change the examples into acts of honesty. Take three examples. "Honesty is an important value that all players should be practicing every practice and game, especially if a coach isn't there to help you make the right decision, or if an official doesn't see the play."

Wrap-Up

Make summary comments about the practice and give reminders for the next game.

Week 5

Warm-Up (10 minutes)

Players take and follow their shots. Players with the ball shoot for 20, 30, or 45 seconds. They shoot, rebound, and shoot again. Players are limited to three dribbles before their next shot. They keep track of how many shots they make during the timed interval. (See figure on page 120.)

Fitness Circle (5 minutes)

Key Idea: Flexibility

Gather the team into a circle. "Is there such a thing as stretching your muscles too far, or should you stretch as far as you can to improve your flexibility?" Listen to their responses. "Muscles should stretch only until you feel a slight pulling. You should never feel pain stretching. If you do, you're stretching too far." Choose a stretch for the team to try. "I want you to stretch until you feel the slight pulling. Everyone will have different levels of flexibility, but all of you need to stretch properly to stay flexible and prevent injuries."

☞ **PURPOSE**

To win the ball by rebounding.

Equipment

☑ One basketball per two players, if possible

☑ Court space with three or four baskets

☑ Tape or markers

☑ Different colored vests or shirts to differentiate teams

Game 1 (10 minutes)

Goal

Defenders try to prevent the offensive team from scoring—and from rebounding missed shots.

Description

Play 3 v 3 half-court games. Use a competitive defense. Players can't dribble, except to drive to the basket or to reposition to make a pass, and must make at least three consecutive passes before shooting. The defensive team receives one point for winning or rebounding the ball after only one shot. Treat fouls like violations—the other team gets the ball. (See figure at the top of page 95.)

Coach: **What was the goal of the game?**
Players: To prevent scoring and to prevent a second shot.

Coach: **What did you do to prevent a second shot?**
Players: Got the rebound after the first shot.

Coach: **How did you position yourself to get the rebound?**
Players: Moved between offensive player and basket.

You could repeat this game with an offensive focus. In this case, the offensive team would earn a point for each shot attempt and rebound. You'd want to instruct your offensive rebounders to protect the ball, and to tip the ball to the basket or assume a shooting position as quickly as possible, like a pogo stick.

Skill Practice 1 (15 minutes)

1. Introduce, demonstrate, and explain how to *box out* to rebound (see page 268).
2. Practice boxing out and rebounding.

Description

Play 3 v 3 games with 2 v 2 under the boards and a shooter and an outlet. The shooter shoots the ball. On the release, X_1 and X_2 turn and box out their offensive players. X_3 (the outlet) moves right or left, depending on which side of the basket the rebound occurs. The player rebounding the ball turns and passes to X_3. Repeat three times, then rotate offense to defense. The defenders try to outlet successfully three times in a row. (See figure on page 121.)

COACH's cues

"Create a stable wall between opponent and ball."
"Elbows out—palms wide, feel for opponent."
"Put buttocks under opponents."

Talk about the possible fouls that can occur (e.g., over the back; see page 277).

Game 2 (15 minutes)

Goal

Defenders try to prevent the offensive team from scoring—and from rebounding missed shots.

Description

Play 2 v 3 or 3 v 3 short-court games, depending on the skill proficiency of your players. Rotate players accordingly so that all players have a chance to play offense and defense. Players can't dribble and must make at least three consecutive passes before shooting. The defensive team receives one point for winning or rebounding the ball after only one shot. (See figure on page 128.)

Team Circle (5 minutes)

Key Idea: Responsibility

Gather the team into a group. Choose two players to demonstrate with you. Have one player be a defender, using a "cold" defense. You and the other player will pass to each other. You concentrate on demonstrating getting into good position for a pass. "What was I working on during this drill?" Listen to responses; lead discussion to getting into good position for a pass. "It is your responsibility to work hard to get into good position for a pass. When you do that, you're being responsible to your team."

Wrap-Up

Make summary comments about practice and give reminders for the next game.

Week 6

Warm-Up (5 minutes)

Players take and follow their shots. Players with the ball shoot for 20, 30, or 45 seconds. They shoot, rebound, and shoot again. Players are limited to three dribbles before their next shot. They keep track of how many shots they make during the timed interval. (See figure on page 120.)

Fitness Circle (5 minutes)

Key Idea: Safety

Gather the team into a group. Gently tap your head with your fist. "Is my head hard or soft? Right—it's hard because my skull is hard. It's made out of bone. Raise your hand if you think bones can break. Right—we all know that bones can break. That's why we want to control our bodies and protect ourselves when we're playing basketball."

PURPOSE

To attack the basket through the give-and-go.

Equipment

- ✓ One basketball per two players, if possible
- ✓ Court space with three or four baskets
- ✓ Tape or markers
- ✓ Different colored vests or shirts to differentiate teams
- ✓ Two cones

Game 1 (10 minutes)

Goal

Players will pass and cut to the basket, looking for return passes and good shots.

Description

Play 3 v 3 half-court games. Teams must make at least two passes before taking a shot. Shots must be within five feet of the basket. Offensive players pass and cut to the basket, presenting a target if they're open. If they receive the ball as they're cutting to the basket, they shoot.

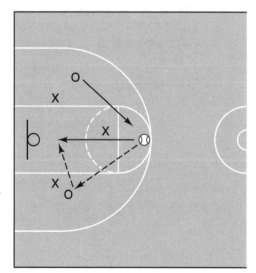

Coach: What was the goal of the game?

Players: To pass and cut; to present target if open.

Coach: What happened when you were able to get open?

Players: Ball was returned and shot was attempted.

Coach: How did you get open?

Players: Used a ball fake, ran ahead of defender, kept body between defender and ball on way to basket.

Coach: What did the other offensive player do to create an open lane for you to attack the basket?

Players: Moved out of the lane.

Skill Practice 1 (10 minutes)

1. Introduce, demonstrate, and explain how to execute a *give-and-go* (see pages 240–241).
2. Practice the give-and-go.

Description

Play 2 v 1 half-court games with cooperative to active defenders. Another player serves as coach. The offense practices the give-and-go three times, using L-cuts or V-cuts toward the basket; then players rotate. (The defender goes to offense; one of the offensive players becomes the coach.)

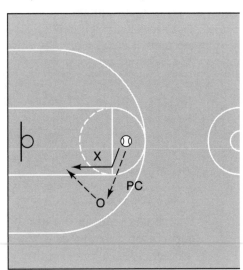

Skill Practice 2 (10 minutes)

Description

Play 2 v 2 games with active to competitive defenders. Two other players serve as coaches. The offense practices the give-and-go three times; then players rotate. (The offense becomes the defense; the defense becomes the coaches; the coaches become the offense.) (See figure at the bottom of page 124.)

COACH's cues

"Pass and cut!"

"Target hand!"

"Keep the defender behind you!"

COACH's point

☞Emphasize that a give-and-go works from all positions on the court.

☞Make sure players cut away from the ball and *toward* the basket.

Coach: What did you do to complete the give-and-go when there was competitive defense?

Players: Used more fakes. Dribbled to create passing lanes. Got open to support player with the ball.

Game 2 (10 minutes)

Same as Game 1, except play 3 v 1, 3 v 2, or 3 v 3 games, depending on the skill proficiency of your players. Rotate players accordingly so that all players have a chance to play offense and defense.

Team Circle (5 minutes)

Key Idea: Caring

Gather the team into a group near two cones 10 feet apart. Discuss examples of good play during a game. Have the players assist in providing examples. "We talked about some examples of good plays. Raise your hand if you think it's a good idea to tell other players they made a good play. Do you think it's a good idea to tell opponents they have made a good play? If you think it is, stand at this cone. If you think you should tell just your teammates they made a good play, stand at this cone." All players should vote. Ask why players voted the way they did. "Telling other players, both teammates and opponents, that they have made a good play shows you care. It is an important value to show others."

Wrap-Up

Make summary comments about practice and give reminders for the next game.

Week 7

Warm-Up (10 minutes)

Players in pairs play "Around the World." Spots are marked in an arc around the basket, about 5 to 8 feet out. Shooters follow a set pattern. The first player shoots from spot #1; if the shot is good, the player moves to spot #2. The player continues until he or she misses a shot. On a missed shot, the shooter may elect to stay there until his or her next turn, or "chance it." This gives the player another shot immediately, but if the shooter misses, he or she goes back to the beginning. A made chance allows the shooter to skip the next spot. (See figure on page 102.)

Fitness Circle (5 minutes)

Key Idea: Training and conditioning

Gather the team into a single-file line. Players will run two distances, one longer than the other. Have the team run the shorter distance first and come back to the starting spot. Then have the team run the longer distance. "Do your muscles feel tired? Running farther, especially if you're a little bit tired, is called *overloading* the muscles. Running a longer distance adds more for the muscles to do. It's training the muscles to make them stronger and able to move longer before getting tired the next time you play. You'll get stronger and have more endurance every time you overload the muscles."

PURPOSE

To create space in the attack by setting screens.

Equipment

- ☑ One basketball per two players, if possible
- ☑ Court space with three or four baskets
- ☑ Tape or markers
- ☑ Different colored vests or shirts to differentiate teams

Game 1 (10 minutes)

Goal

The ball handler tries to use teammates' positioning to lose his or her opponent and attack the basket.

Description

Play 3 v 3 half-court games. Have different players restart plays. Give one extra point for a basket scored off a screen. Players call their own fouls.

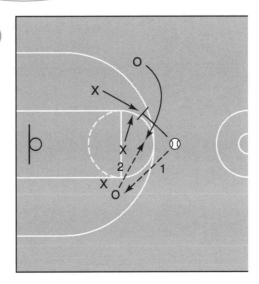

Coach:. What were you trying to do in the game?
Players: Use teammates' positioning to lose opponent and attack the basket.

Coach: Why is the teammates' positioning important?
Players: To create an open shot for the player with the ball.

Coach: What would be a good body position for the player trying to free his or her teammate?
Players: Wide base, bent knees, arms across body to protect self.

Skill Practice 1 (15 minutes)

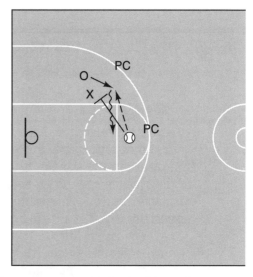

1. Introduce, demonstrate, and explain how to *set screens* (see page 238).
2. Practice setting screens.

Description

Play 2 v 1 games with two other players acting as coaches. Offensive players execute screens. The defensive player plays active defense. One coach will watch to see if the screen is set correctly; the other coach will watch to see if the ball handler uses the screen correctly. The goal is to execute a screen successfully three times in a row.

COACH's point

☞Teach rules on traveling and double dribble (see page 278).

COACH's cues

"Stand firm, straddle feet."
"Hands across chest ready to take impact."
"Roll toward basket or roll to a passing lane."

Week 7

Game 2 (15 minutes)

Goal

The offense attempts to screen the on-the-ball defender so the player with the ball can attack the basket.

Description

Play 3 v 1, 3 v 2, or 3 v 3 half-court games, depending on the skill proficiency of your players. Rotate players accordingly so that all players have a chance to play offense and defense. Have a different player restart the play each possession. Give one extra point for a basket scored off a screen. Players call their own fouls. (See figure on page 166.)

Team Circle (5 minutes)

Key Idea: Respect

Gather the team into a group. "What are some examples of dangerous play for yourself or teammates during a practice or game?" Listen to responses—assess responses to identify whether they are or are not dangerous; discuss responses. Ask players to agree or disagree with responses—are they a good practice or not? They can raise their hand to agree. Discuss three examples. "It is important to have respect for your body and your teammates' bodies. Practicing safe play is a way to do that."

Wrap-Up

Make summary comments about practice and give reminders for the next game.

Week 8

PURPOSE

To defend space against screens.

Equipment

- ☑ One basketball per two players, if possible
- ☑ Court space with three or four baskets
- ☑ Tape or markers
- ☑ Different colored vests or shirts to differentiate teams

Warm-Up (10 minutes)

Players play "21." Two or more players are at the free-throw line. The first player shoots a free throw; a made free throw is worth two points. Players who make a free throw can then shoot a lay-up. A made lay-up is worth one point. If they make both the free throw and the lay-up they get to shoot again. Lay-ups cannot be shot until the first free throw is made. Once players have made one free throw, they always get to shoot the lay-up. Shooters who miss a free throw shoot a lay-up, and then the next player shoots. The winner is the first person to reach 21.

Fitness Circle (5 minutes)

Key Idea: Flexibility

Gather the team into a circle and choose a stretch for them to try. "When we're stretching, should we feel anything?" Listen to their responses. "When I feel the slight pulling, what should I do? Bounce or hold the stretch? Raise your hand if you think bounce. Now raise your hand if you think hold. To get a good stretch, you should hold the stretch for 10 counts, then relax. If you feel the slight pulling go away, you can stretch a bit further. That tells you your muscles are getting more flexible. Be sure to practice proper stretching to improve your flexibility."

Game 1 (10 minutes)

Goal

Offensive players will screen on-the-ball defenders so the player with the ball can attack the goal; defenders will effectively defend against the screen.

Description

Play 3 v 3 half-court games. The offense must make at least two passes before taking a shot. All shots must be within 5 feet of the basket. Have different players restart the play on each possession. Give an extra point for a basket scored off a screen. Give the defense a point for not allowing a shot. Players call their own fouls. (See figure on page 165.)

Week 8

Coach: What is the purpose of an on-the-ball screen?
Players: It allows the player with the ball to drive past the screener and lose the defender to set up a shot or a drive.

Coach: How can you get around the screen once it is set?
Players: Fight over the top (slide between the player setting the screen and the player you're guarding); duck behind the screener.

Skill Practice 1 (10 minutes)

1. Introduce, demonstrate, and explain how to *fight over the top of a screen* (see page 245).
2. Practice fighting over the top of screens.

Description

Play 2 v 2 games with a competitive defense. Offensive players execute screens; defenders being screened must fight over the top of screens, trying to keep the offense from shooting. Two player-coaches evaluate defenders' abilities to fight through screens.

Skill Practice 2 (10 minutes)

1. Introduce, demonstrate, and explain how to *slide behind a screen* (see page 245).
2. Practice sliding behind screens.

Description

Play 2 v 2 games with a competitive defense. Offensive players execute screens; defenders being screened must duck behind the screens and stay with their opponents, trying to keep them from shooting. Two player-coaches evaluate defenders' abilities to slide behind screens.

COACH's point

☞ Perform the Skill Practice in slower motion, if necessary, to help players understand and perform the task.

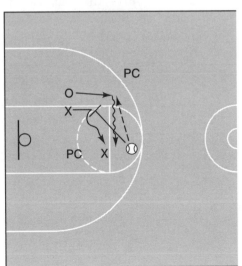

169

Week 8 (cont'd)

COACH's point

☞ Stop play and take advantage of "teachable moments."

"Stay with your opponent!"

"Talk! Let teammates know the screen is there."

"Stand away from the person setting the screen to allow your teammate to move around the pick."

Game 2 (10 minutes)

Repeat Game 1. Rotate players accordingly so that all players have a chance to play offense and defense.

Team Circle (5 minutes)

Key Idea: Caring

Gather the team into a group. "What are some examples of showing you care about your teammates?" Listen to responses. After each response, ask for an example of the same sign of caring that players could do outside of practice. Discuss the on-court and off-court examples at the same time, then ask for another response. "Those were all great ideas to show caring to your teammates. Have you seen someone else show an 'act of kindness' toward another teammate?" Discuss their responses. "It's important to show caring both on and off the court—that means during practice and outside of practice. Teams that show caring to each other play better together."

Wrap-Up

Make summary comments about practice and give reminders for the next game.

Week 9

Warm-Up (10 minutes)

Players play "21." Two or more players are at the free-throw line. The first player shoots a free throw; a made free throw is worth two points. Players who make a free throw then shoot a lay-up. A made lay-up is worth one point. If they make both the free throw and the lay-up they get to shoot again. Lay-ups cannot be shot until the first free throw is made. Once players have made one free throw, they always get to shoot the lay-up. Shooters who miss a free throw shoot a lay-up, and then the next player shoots. The winner is the first person to reach 21.

☞ **PURPOSE**

To win the ball on jump balls.

Equipment

✓ One basketball per two players, if possible

✓ Court space with three or four baskets

✓ Tape or markers

✓ Different colored vests or shirts to differentiate teams

Fitness Circle (5 minutes)

Key Idea: Training and conditioning

Gather the team into a group. "Do you think you should swim to get ready for basketball season? Raise your hand if you think swimming is a good way to prepare for basketball. Swimming is a good way to keep active in the off-season or other times when you don't have basketball practice. To improve your basketball conditioning either before or during basketball season, it's best to participate in skills you use in basketball. That is called *specificity training* because it is specific to the sport. What are some of the training skills we should be using for basketball?" Listen to their responses. "Running, shooting, and dribbling would be the best."

Game 1 (10 minutes)

Goal

Players will gain possession of the ball off the jump ball.

Description

Play 4 v 4 half-court games. After every basket use a jump ball to restart play. Players rotate, allowing each to jump. The team gaining possession of the jump ball continues offensive play until they score or the other team wins the ball. Players call their own fouls.

COACH's point

☞ Teach jump ball rules.

Coach: What did you and your teammates do to gain possession of the ball off the jump ball?

Players: Matched up with opponent on the jump ball circle.

Coach: If you knew your team would win the jump ball, how did you line up on the circle?

Players: Close to the basket so we could turn and score.

Coach: If you knew your team would lose the jump ball, how did you line up on the circle?

Players: Between opponents and their basket so we could defend the goal.

Skill Practice 1 (10 minutes)

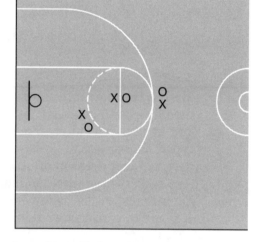

1. Introduce, demonstrate, and explain how to maintain *defensive and offensive positioning for jump balls* (see page 244).

2. Practice positioning for jump balls.

Description

Play 3 v 3 half-court games using a tosser and a player-coach. The jump occurs in the offensive team's circle at the free-throw line; if the offense wins the jump, they try to score. Rotate offense and defenses after each jump ball. The defense tries to win the jump; barring that, they try to force the offense to make at least five passes before shooting.

COACH's cues

"Match up!"

"Position for defensive jump ball!"

"Drop back quickly!"

"Protect the basket!"

"Anticipate!"

Game 2 (10 minutes)

Repeat Game 1, except use either a short or full court.

Team Circle
(5 minutes)

Key Idea: Responsibility

Gather the team into a circle. "I want everyone to think of one thing that you, personally, can improve in your basketball play that can make you a better player. I will go around the circle; when it is your turn tell everyone what you think you can work on." Go to each player one at a time; assist them, if necessary. Allow players the option to pass their turn. "It is important to look at your own game to see where you can improve. Improving your own game is your responsibility. We can't get better as a team unless each individual tries to improve."

Wrap-Up

Make summary comments about practice and give reminders for the next game.

Week 10

PURPOSE

To create space in the attack by using off-the-ball screens.

Equipment

- ☑ One basketball per two players, if possible
- ☑ Court space with three or four baskets
- ☑ Tape or markers
- ☑ Different colored vests or shirts to differentiate teams
- ☑ Two cones

Warm-Up (10 minutes)

Players play "5 × 4 Shooting"—a game that focuses on form shooting and footwork. Players must make five shots of each of the following:

- Feet square to the basket, one to two feet from the basket, right and left side of the basket (five shots total here)
- Shoulders at 90 degrees to the basket; pivot off the left foot, square shoulders to basket, and shoot
- Same as above but pivot off the right foot
- Toss the ball from the free-throw line, use a two-foot jump stop about 5 to 8 feet from the basket, and shoot

COACH's cue

"Toes of pivot foot nailed to the floor!"

Fitness Circle (5 minutes)

Key Idea: Healthy habits

Gather the team into a group near two cones about 10 feet apart. Show a pyramid shape with your hands and fingers put together. "This is a pyramid. Does anyone know what the food pyramid is? We use the food pyramid to remind us how to eat well. The bottom of the pyramid has foods like carbohydrates (breads, cereals, rice) and fruits and vegetables; these should be eaten in greater amounts. The top of the pyramid has high-fat and sweeter foods such as fried foods, cake, and chips; these we should eat in smaller amounts. Tell me a snack and run to this cone if it is a bottom-of-the-pyramid snack or to the other cone if it is a top-of-the-pyramid snack. It's important to eat foods that give you energy for playing basketball. Bottom-of-the-pyramid foods give you more energy to play basketball and are much healthier."

Week 10

Game 1 (10 minutes)

Goal

The offense attempts to screen off-the-ball defenders so their offensive teammates can move to support the ball handler.

Description

Play 4 v 4 half-court games. Have different team members restart the play on each possession. Give an extra point for each basket scored off a screen. Players call their own fouls.

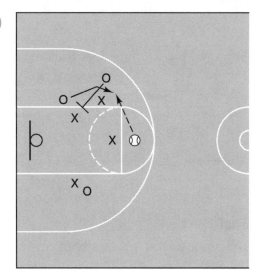

Coach: How did you use the off-the-ball screen to free up your teammate?
Players: By setting a pick or screen on the defender, same as on-the-ball.

Coach: How did you know where to set the screen?
Players: By setting screen so teammate can get open to receive a pass, depending on where a passing lane can be opened; facing away from the direction teammate needs to run.

Coach: How should you move to best use the screen?
Players: Cut toward the screen, brushing or nearly brushing shoulders as you pass the pick or screen.

Skill Practice 1 (15 minutes)

Description

Play 3 v 3 half-court games; two players act as coaches, one watching the offense, the other, the defense. The offensive screens off the ball.

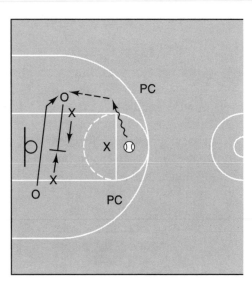

COACH's cues

"Anticipate ball movement!"

"Screen so the player can move *to* the ball or *to* the basket."

"Brush shoulders so the defender can't get through the screen."

Game 2 (15 minutes)

Goal

The offense attempts to screen off-the-ball defenders so their offensive teammates can move to support the ball handler.

Description

Play 4 v 1, 4 v 2, 4 v 3, or 4 v 4 games, depending on the skill level of your players. Rotate players accordingly so that all players have a chance to play offense and defense. Have different team members restart the play on each possession. Give an extra point for each basket scored off a screen. Players call their own fouls. (See figure at the top of page 175.)

Team Circle (5 minutes)

Key Idea: Honesty

Gather the team into a circle. "I want you to think back to our last practice. Remember talking about improving our games? Each player said one thing they could improve on in their game. Tell me how many of you feel you have tried to improve your game from the last practice." Call on players to tell what they did to try to improve. "All good players look honestly at themselves and how they are playing to see where they can improve their game. It's important to be honest with yourself about how you're playing; you don't need to feel bad about needing to improve your skills. The more you improve individually, the more you contribute to the team."

Wrap-Up

Make summary comments about practice and give reminders for the next game.

Week 11

Warm-Up (10 minutes)

Players play "5 × 4 Shooting"—a game that focuses players on form shooting and footwork. Players must make five shots of each of the following:

- Feet square to the basket, one to two feet from the basket, right and left side of the basket (five shots total here)
- Shoulders at 90 degrees to the basket; pivot off the left foot, square shoulders to basket, and shoot
- Same as above but pivot off the right foot
- Toss the ball from the free-throw line, use a two-foot jump stop about 5 to 8 feet from the basket, and shoot

Fitness Circle (5 minutes)

Key Idea: Healthy habits

Gather the team into a group near two cones about 10 feet apart. Tell team that one cone represents good health habits and the other poor health habits. "Give me examples of some daily habits. If you think it's a healthy habit, stand at this cone. If you think it's a poor health habit, stand at this cone." Ask all players to participate. "It's important to have all our habits be healthy habits every day. This helps your body stay healthy and helps you perform better in basketball."

To defend space by communicating and playing good defense.

Equipment

- ☑ One basketball per two players, if possible
- ☑ Court space with three or four baskets
- ☑ Tape or markers
- ☑ Different colored vests or shirts to differentiate teams
- ☑ Two cones

Game 1 (10 minutes)

Goal

The defense will play effective player-to-player, competitive defense to keep the offense from scoring.

Description

Play 4 v 4 half-court games. Players call their own fouls. Players can dribble only to drive to the basket. The offense uses screens to score and create passing lanes in the attack. (See figure at the top of page 175.)

Coach: How did you defend the offensive team?
Players: With player-to-player defense.

Coach: What are the advantages of player-to-player defense?
Players: All players are closely guarded, which increases the chance to win the ball; all defensive members know their responsibility.

Coach: What are the disadvantages of player-to-player defense?
Players: Defense can get spread out too far away from the basket; it's difficult to match players of equal ability.

Coach: How can you help your teammates while in player-to-player defense?
Players: Let them know when a screen is being set; pick up the player when there's a scoring threat.

Skill Practice 1 (10 minutes)

Description

Play 3 v 3 games, using two player-coaches. Begin by playing in slower motion, using a cooperative to active defense. Offensive players execute on-the-ball screens. Defensive players must fight through the screen and stay with their opponents; they transition into playing competitive defense. They attempt to keep the offense from getting a good shot. The player-coaches evaluate defenders' abilities in getting around screens.

Skill Practice 2 (10 minutes)

Description

The same as Skill Practice 1, except the emphasis here is on off-the-ball screens.

"Call 'screen left' or 'screen right.'"

"Quick movements, jab steps and fakes."

"Stay between your player and the basket."

☞ Solid player-to-player defense is the foundation for all other facets of defense.

Game 2 (10 minutes)

Goal

The defense will try to keep the offense from scoring in 30 seconds.

Description

Play 2 v 3, 3 v 4, or 3 v 3 half-court games with two player-coaches. The offense sets both on-the-ball and off-the-ball screens. The player-coaches evaluate defenders' abilities in getting around screens. Rotate the coaches into the game after two minutes (four 30-second periods). (See figure on page 178.)

Team Circle (5 minutes)

Key Idea: Responsibility

Gather the team into a circle. Create two imaginary situations for the players. One is a game that they win and two players score the majority of the points. In the other situation the team loses in a shot given up by a player who has a defensive lapse. "In the first game, we won. Even though Kyle and Andrew scored most of the points, did you all contribute?" "Yes, we all contributed and won as a team." "In the next game, Willie let a player slip by him to score the winning basket. Is he responsible for the team's loss?" "No. We all are responsible for wins and losses. We win and lose as a team."

Wrap-Up

Make summary comments about practice and give reminders for the next game.

Week 12

PURPOSE

To use space in the attack by rolling off a screen toward the basket.

Equipment

- ✓ One basketball per two players, if possible
- ✓ Court space with three or four baskets
- ✓ Tape or markers
- ✓ Different colored vests or shirts to differentiate teams

Warm-Up (10 minutes)

Players play "5 × 4 Shooting"—a game that focuses players on form shooting and footwork. Players must make five shots of each of the following:

- Feet square to the basket, one to two feet from the basket, right and left side of the basket (five shots total here)
- Shoulders at 90 degrees to the basket; pivot off the left foot, square shoulders to basket, and shoot
- Same as above but pivot off the right foot
- Toss the ball from the free-throw line, use a two-foot jump stop about 5 to 8 feet from the basket, and shoot

Fitness Circle (5 minutes)

Key Idea: Training and conditioning

Gather the team into a group. "Everyone jog to the opposite basket and back. Do you remember your first days of practice and how you felt after running that distance?" Discuss their responses. "Think about running an even longer distance during the beginning of the season. Compare how you feel now that it's the end of the season. Your bodies are conditioned from playing all season. Remember to stay active during the off-season. Play other sports or participate in other physical activities. If you don't participate in physical activity after the season, all the training you did for your body will be lost. Your body will reverse its conditioning. This is called the *reversibility principle*—you use it or lose it!"

Week 12

Game 1 (10 minutes)

Goal

The offensive player who sets a screen, either on or off the ball, cuts toward the basket.

Description

Play 4 v 4 half-court games. Have a different team member restart the play on each possession. Give an extra point for each basket scored off a screen. Players call their own fouls. The defense attempts to get around the screen and stay with the player cutting to the basket.

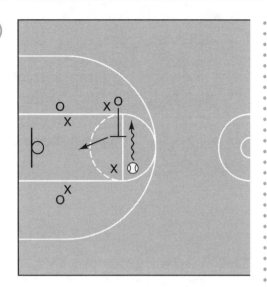

Coach: After you set the screen, what do you do?
Players: Move toward the basket.

Coach: How did this movement create space in your attack?
Players: Created a passing lane, set up a potential high percentage shot (lay-up).

Coach: Which picks—high or low—provided more opportunities to shoot?
Players: High, because they allowed the player to roll away from defense and kept the defensive player from getting between offense and the basket.

Skill Practice 1 (15 minutes)

1. Introduce, demonstrate, and explain how to execute a *pick-and-roll* (see page 242).
2. Practice pick-and-rolls.

Description

Play 3 v 3 half-court games with two player-coaches evaluating the effectiveness of the offensive players. The offense tries to score twice off a pick-and-roll and then switches to defense.

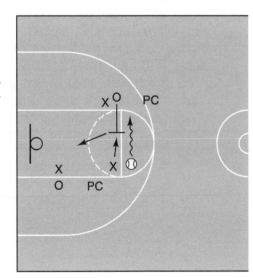

Week 12

☞ Focus on the offensive performance.

COACH's cues

"Open up to the ball when rolling to the basket!"
"Watch for the ball!"
"Show target hands!"
"Attack the basket quickly!"

Game 2 (15 minutes)

Same as Game 1, except play 4 v 1, 4 v 2, 4 v 3, or 4 v 4 games, depending on the skill proficiency of your players. Rotate players accordingly so that all players have a chance to play offense and defense.

Team Circle (5 minutes)

Key Idea: Caring

Gather the team in groups of four or five players. Give each group a scenario in which one player makes a mistake. Direct them to problem-solve and decide as a group what would be a good response. Give them two minutes to discuss. Bring each group back as a team and discuss each group's decision. Have players agree or disagree with each group's response by raising their hands. "All of you have done a good job in problem solving. It is important to show you care about your teammates. You can do this by forgiving their mistakes."

Wrap-Up

Make summary comments about practice and give reminders about the final game.

Practice Plans for 12- to 13- Year-Olds

This chapter contains the 14 practice plans you'll use with your 12- and 13-year-old YMCA Winners basketball players. It also contains recommendations for modifying your practices to make them developmentally appropriate for 12- and 13-year-olds. By following these practice plans, you will be presenting the game and coaching in a way that maximizes players' skill development *and* their enjoyment of the game.

Each plan contains the following sections:

◎ Purpose

◎ Equipment

◎ Practice Plan

Purpose focuses on what you want to teach your players during that practice; it is your main "theme" for that day. *Equipment* notes what you'll need on hand for that practice. The *Practice Plan* section outlines what you will do during each practice session. It consists of these elements:

◎ Warm-Up

◎ Fitness Circle

◎ Games

◎ Skill Practices

◎ Team Circle and Wrap-Up

You'll begin each session with about five minutes of warm-up activities. This will be followed by five minutes of a Fitness Circle, during which you lead players through a series of stretches as you briefly discuss an item that relates to their fitness. Then you'll have your players play a modified basketball game. You'll look for your cue to interrupt that game—your cue being when players are having problems with carrying out the basic goal or aim of the game. At this point you'll "freeze" the action, keeping the players where they are, and ask brief questions about the tactical problems the players encountered and what skills they need to "solve" those problems. (Review chapter 8 for more on interrupting a game and holding a question-and-answer session.) We provide discussion questions in each practice plan. In addition, we provide coaching points, when appropriate, with games and skill practices as points of emphasis in most effectively conducting the practice.

Then you'll teach the skill that the players need to acquire to successfully execute the tactic. Chapter 13 contains descriptions of all the skills, so a page reference will be given to guide you to the appropriate description. During this skill practice session, you'll use the IDEA approach:

I   Introduce the skill.

D   Demonstrate the skill.

E   Explain the skill.

A   Attend to players practicing the skill.

Your introduction, demonstration, and explanation of a skill should take no more than two to three minutes; then you'll attend to players and provide teaching cues or further demonstration as necessary as they practice the skill according to the practice plan.

After the skill practices, you will usually have the athletes play another game or two to let them use the skills they just learned and to understand them in the context of a game. Note that in Game 1 when players are being introduced to a new tactic or skill, they will play an even-sided game (4 v 4). This allows them to encounter the challenges they will face in executing the tactic or skill in competition. Then in most Game 2s they should play lopsided games (4 v 1, 4 v 2) to increase their chances of experiencing success and beginning to master the new skill. However, if your players are showing proficiency with the new skill, you can use even-sided games in Game 2. The choice is yours; for more on this issue, see chapter 8.

The Practice Plan section concludes with a Team Circle that focuses on character development. As players cool down and stretch, you will talk to your players about some aspect of basketball that relates to one of the four core values—caring, honesty, respect, and responsibility. Following this, you'll wrap up the practice with a few summary comments and remind them of the next practice or game day.

A note about Fitness and Team Circles: These times are meant to be true discussions—not lectures where you're doing all the talking and your players are doing all the listening. Ask the questions provided, and wait for your players to respond. Don't immediately feed them the answers that we provide. These answers are meant simply to help you guide the discussion. Your role in Team Circles is as much to ask questions and get players to respond as it is to dole out information.

Twelve- and 13-year-olds don't possess the size, strength, stamina, and skills to play the full-blown adult version of basketball, and attempting to fit them into the adult mold will prove frustrating for all involved. We suggest you incorporate the following modifications into your practices to help your players learn the game, improve their skills, and have fun while they're at it. These suggestions fall into three categories: equipment and court, rules, and scrimmages.

Equipment and Court

Equipment and court should be substantially modified for young players to best learn the game and improve their skills. We recommend the following guidelines:

- ◎ Size of ball: regulation ball (#7)
- ◎ Height of basket: 9 to 10 feet
- ◎ Free-throw line distance: 12 to 15 feet
- ◎ Court size: Half court, short court, full court

We encourage you to consider these changes during each practice. Whether you make them or not depends on how your players are responding. The more skilled they are, the more likely they'll need greater challenges to continue improving.

Making Games Simpler or More Challenging

Here are ways to make practice games simpler or more challenging:

- Equally increase or decrease the number of players suggested (e.g., if we suggest playing 3 v 3, make it simpler by playing 2 v 2, or make it more challenging by playing 4 v 4).
- Add an extra defender to make it harder on the offense (e.g., 3 v 4 instead of 3 v 3) once players have acquired the skills they need to be successful.
- Add an extra offensive player to make it easier for the offense (e.g., 4 v 3 instead of 3 v 3).

- Change the type of defense played. The three types of defenses (see "Scrimmages") are cooperative, active, and competitive. To make a game simpler, have your players play a cooperative defense; to make it more challenging, have them play an active or a competitive defense.
- Begin with *no* defense.
- Perform the skill or game at a slower than normal pace to make it simpler.
- Increase or decrease the number of passes you require before the offense can attempt a shot.

Rules

You need to strike a balance between calling the players for violations and fouls every time they commit one, while still teaching the appropriate rules and the skills they need to comply with the rules fully in the long run. In the previous two levels of YMCA Winners basketball, we have recommended that you allow players an extra step before calling traveling, and allow one double dribble violation per player possession before calling double dribble. As players mature to the 12 to 13 age level, we recommend you do call these violations now, to help players refine their ballhandling skills. We also recommend that you teach and call the over-and-back violation and most clock violations: the 3-second lane violation; the 5-second inbounds violation; and the 10-second backcourt violation. We still recommend the following modifications, though, for this level:

- **Clock rules:** Don't run a shot clock.
- **Defense:**
  —Use a player-to-player defense.
  —Do not use a full-court press; in most cases, the defense can pick up their players at half court or closer to their own basket.

While the following points are not really rules modifications, they are worth noting here and emphasizing in practice:

- Don't allow players to wear jewelry. Doing so is dangerous to them and to other players.
- Players should call their own fouls.
- Don't allow players to undercut a player shooting a lay-up.
- Players should keep control of their body and the ball: no rough play.
- Players should be good sports and show respect. Don't tolerate unsporting conduct.

Scrimmages

Besides the obvious changes in court and equipment, a casual observer of a YMCA Winners basketball practice would note another difference in the practice setting: the number of players used in scrimmages and practice games. Using smaller numbers allows players to touch the ball more often and thus practice the skills they need to acquire. It also keeps everyone more active and gives players more experience in a variety of situations that call for different tactics and skills. Here are suggestions for scrimmages and practice games:

- Use small-sided games (e.g., 1 v 1, 2 v 1, 2 v 2, 3 v 2, 3 v 3, 4 v 4) on half-court play or cross-court playing (short court, see figure on page 85). Remember, using small-sided games means more touches per player, which means players develop skills more quickly. The greatest leaps in skill improvement are made through the use of small-sided games.

◎ Use modified half-court games in which players play 1 v 1 or 2 v 2, taking turns trying to score.

◎ Use "regular" half-court rules: an offensive rebound can be shot again, while a defensive rebound must result in that team or player restarting at the top of the key.

◎ Rotate partners (opponents) and teams often. Play three- to five-minute games, then rotate players. Changing partners changes the game.

A note regarding defense: Control defensive play by instituting three levels of involvement:

1. Cooperative Defense (cold)—The player assumes a defensive posture two arm lengths from the opponent, is relatively passive, and at times even coaches the opponent.

2. Active Defense (warm)—The player assumes a defensive posture about one and a half arm lengths from the opponent, has active hands and feet, but makes no attempts to intercept the ball.

3. Competitive Defense (hot)—The player assumes a defensive posture, is positioned appropriately, and attempts to intercept the ball.

Okay, on to the practice plans themselves. Following are practice plans for the 2 weeks of your preseason and then for the 10 weeks of your competitive season.

Key to Diagrams

⊕	=	Side basket
Ⓞ	=	Player with ball
O	=	Offensive player
X	=	Defensive player
C	=	Coach
PC	=	Player-coach
- - - →	=	Pass
～～→	=	Dribble
—→	=	Move
⟹	=	Shoot
R	=	Rebounder
P	=	Partner
■	=	Marked spots
⊣	=	Screen or box out
S	=	Shooter

PURPOSE

To attack the basket by using a power dribble.

Equipment

- [x] One basketball per two players, if possible
- [x] Court space with three or four baskets
- [x] Tape or markers
- [x] Different colored vests or shirts to differentiate teams

Warm-Up (10 minutes)

Begin each practice with 5 to 10 minutes of warm-up activities to get players loosened up and ready to go.

Players dribble, jump stop, and shoot, traveling from one basket to the next. All shooting should be 2 to 4 feet from the basket.

Fitness Circle (5 minutes)

Following the warm-up, gather the players and demonstrate the stretching protocol (see chapter 15 for stretches for the major muscle groups). Ask a team leader to lead stretches in subsequent practices. After the team is finished stretching, briefly discuss the fitness concept for that practice.

Key Idea: General fitness

Gather team into a group. "Do we play basketball to get in shape or do we get in shape to play basketball? Let's talk about both sides. What do you think?" Discuss for two or three minutes. "We should improve our fitness—cardiorespiratory, flexibility, and muscular strength and endurance—in order to play better basketball. By playing basketball we gets lots of opportunities to improve our fitness. All season we'll be talking more about the different areas of fitness and ways to improve those abilities."

Game 1 (10 minutes)

Following the Fitness Circle, get the kids playing a game. Follow most games with a time of questions and answers—with YOU asking the questions and your PLAYERS providing the answers—about what the goal of the game was and what skills and tactics they needed to perform to succeed in the game. For many games, we provide diagrams or figures (or refer to diagrams and figures on previous pages) showing how the game is begun. We also often provide coach's points for you to pass along to your players during the games.

Week 1, Practice 1

Goal

Players will drive hard to the basket and shoot.

Description

Play 3 v 3 half-court games. Give two points for scores off of drive, and one point for other baskets. Instruct defenders not to clog the lane so that players can drive. Defenders should play "warm" defense.

Coach: What was the goal of the game?
Players: Drive and score.

Coach: What's a good way to drive?
Players: Drop step and dribble.

Coach: What should you do if it's congested in the lane?
Players: Stop and shoot if open, or pass off.

Skill Practice 1 (10 minutes)

Follow Game 1 with a Skill Practice. Introduce, demonstrate, and explain a skill or tactic, and then attend to your players as they practice that tactic. The question-and-answer session, in which your PLAYERS tell you what skills and tactics they need to be successful in the game, leads directly to the Skill Practice. We often provide coaching points with the Skill Practices; pass these points along to your players. We also provide coach's cues—phrases to help your players focus on the task at hand—during many Skill Practices and Games.

1. Introduce, demonstrate, and explain how to use a *jump stop* prior to shooting.
2. Practice shooting off of jump stops.

Description

Play 1 v 1; defenders play cooperative defense. Players with the ball use a ball fake, jab step, and drive to the basket. They jump stop and shoot two to four feet from the basket. Watch for good form on the jump stops and the shots; players should use the square on the backboard. (See figure on page 108.)

COACH's point

☞ Briefly describe charging fouls and blocking fouls (which often occur when a player drives to the basket). See page 277.

☞ Instruct players to raise their hand when they foul.

COACH's cues

"Triple threat!"

"Ready position!"

"Hand position!"

"Hold the ball on the side of the hip!"

Driving to basket

"Jab step and ball fake!"

"Arm should look like a yo-yo!"

"Ball down, eyes up!"

"Two-foot jump stop!"

"Eyes on the target."

"In the square, in the basket!"

Coach: How should your dribble change when someone is guarding you?

Players: Keep the ball closer to your body and keep the ball between yourself and the defender.

Skill Practice 2 (10 minutes)

1. Introduce, demonstrate, and explain how to do a *crossover dribble* (see pages 254–255).
2. Practice the crossover dribble.

Description

Play 1 v 1; defenders play cooperative defense. Players with the ball perform crossover dribbles going down or across the court. Players switch roles after one time down the court.

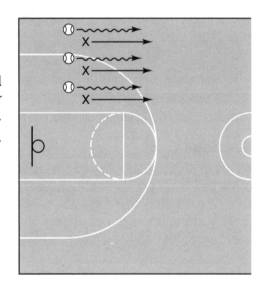

Game 2 (10 minutes)

COACH's point

Goal

Players will use a crossover dribble to drive and score.

Description

Play 3 v 1, 3 v 2, or 3 v 3 games, depending on the skill proficiency of your players (see chapter 8 for help on deciding how to use lopsided games). Rotate players accordingly so that all players have a chance to play offense and defense. Players can't dribble—except to drive to the basket.

Switch teams halfway through the game, with the two defenders joining one offensive player on the offensive team, and two offensive players switching to defense. (See figure at the top of page 95.)

☞ Use examples illustrating how driving to the basket can create passing lanes.

Team Circle (5 minutes)

Conclude practice by gathering your players and leading them through the same stretches you led them through in the Fitness Circle. As you are stretching, discuss a character development concept. These aren't lectures; you want your players' active participation in these discussions.

Key Idea: Four core values

Gather the players into a single-file line. "Everyone turn to your right so the person to the side of you is now in front of you. Put your arms on their shoulders. We are going to walk forward, as a group, using first the right foot and then the left. We will walk slowly, so take your time so we all move together. Get ready with your right foot, now step; get ready with your left foot, now step." Repeat for four steps. "Let go of your teammates. Did we have to work together to walk as a group? We did. All season we will need to work together, with everyone doing their part. We will talk about four values that all players should have—caring, honesty, respect, and responsibility. We need to understand and use these values or qualities every practice and game."

Wrap-Up

Make summary comments about practice. Remind them of the next practice and give them a sneak preview of its emphasis: using cuts to elude defenders and create space in the attack.

191

Week 1, Practice 2

🖙 PURPOSE

PURPOSE

To create space in the attack by creating passing lanes.

Equipment

☑ One basketball per two players, if possible

☑ Court space with three or four baskets

☑ Tape or markers

☑ Different colored vests or shirts to differentiate teams

☑ Two cones

Warm-Up (10 minutes)

Play 1 v 1 games, starting at the foul line. Defense checks the ball and offense begins in a triple threat position. (See figure on page 102.)

Fitness Circle (5 minutes)

Key Idea: General fitness

Gather the team into a group. "Last practice we talked about different kinds of fitness. Can you tell me what they were?" Listen to responses until they say *cardiorespiratory, flexibility,* and *muscular strength and endurance.* "What are some examples of physical activities to improve cardiorespiratory fitness?" Discuss examples (walking, running, swimming, and so on). "Muscular strength and endurance?" Discuss examples (ballhandling skills and drills, dribbling, passing, etc.). "Flexibility?" Discuss examples (leg and arm stretches). "By working hard at all the practices and outside of practice you can help attain the overall fitness you need for basketball."

Game 1 (10 minutes)

Goal

Players will provide support for their teammate with the ball.

Description

Play 2 v 2 half-court games. Players must complete at least three passes before shooting. They receive one point for three consecutive passes, and two points for every field goal. (See figure at the top of page 91.)

COACH's point

🖙 Teach rules on traveling and double dribbling (see page 278).

Week 1, Practice 2

Coach: What was the goal of the game?
Players: To support the player with the ball.

Coach: How were you able to support the player with the ball?
Players: Using a ball fake and replace, jab step, moving quickly.

Coach: What did you do if your defender was closely guarding you?
Players: Used a cut to get away.

Coach: When would a V-cut be most effective, close to the lane or away from the lane?
Players: Away from the lane, 10 to 12 feet.

Coach: When would the L-cut be most effective?
Players: Close to the lane near the baseline.

Skill Practice 1 (15 minutes)

1. Introduce, demonstrate, and explain how to execute *V-cuts* and *L-cuts* (see page 250).
2. Practice V-cuts and L-cuts.

Description

Play 2 v 2 games with the focus on players using V-cuts and L-cuts, receiving passes, and using jump stops and the triple threat position. Sequence:

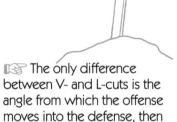

- O_1 ball fakes, jab steps, and passes to O_2, who V-cuts as O_1 is ball faking.
- O_2 catches the ball in a triple threat position using a jump stop.
- Repeat three times and rotate.
- When all four players in a group have practiced the V-cut three times, go through the rotation again, this time practicing the V-cut on the opposite side of the basket.
- When all four players have practiced the V-cut on both sides of the basket, go through the rotation again, using the same sequence to practice L-cuts on both sides of the basket.

The defense should play passive, cooperative defense.

COACH's point

☞ The only difference between V- and L-cuts is the angle from which the offense moves into the defense, then toward the pass.

☞ Emphasize making "razor-sharp" cuts.

☞ Teaching off-the-ball movements is important—as we know, good players know how to get open.

☞ Teach the five-second inbounds rule and lane violations (see page 278).

Game 2
(15 minutes)

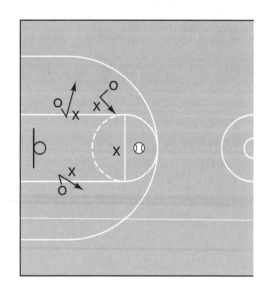

Goal

Players will provide support to their teammate with the ball, using V-cuts and L-cuts to get open.

Description

Play 4 v 2, 4 v 3, or 4 v 4 games, depending on the skill proficiency of your players. Rotate players accordingly so that all players have a chance to play offense and defense.

Players must complete at least three passes before shooting, and they can't dribble except to reposition. They receive one point for three consecutive passes, and two points for every field goal.

Team Circle
(5 minutes)

Key Idea: Respect

Gather the team into a circle near two cones about 10 feet apart. "What should you do if your opponents are committing fouls, complaining to the officials, and doing things that are not fair?" Listen to their responses. "Stand at this cone if you should continue to play your game and not try to commit fouls. Stand at this cone if you should get back at the other team by playing the same way and complain to the officials." All players should vote. Ask players why they voted the way they did. Have players at the "complaining" cone think of other options instead of complaining. "You should not change the way you play your game or stop showing respect to your opponents or the officials. It's important to show respect even if the other team is not."

Wrap-Up

Make summary comments about practice. Remind them of the next practice and give them a preview of the next practice's emphasis: attacking the basket through the give-and-go.

Week 2, Practice 1

Warm-Up (10 minutes)

Players pair up and practice shooting off of various offensive moves. The shooter shoots 25 consecutive shots; the rebounder quickly returns the ball. After 25 shots they switch roles. The shooter follows this pattern:

- First 10 shots—no dribble
- Next 5 shots—dribble once
- Next 5 shots—dribble twice
- Last 5 shots—use a crossover dribble

The shooter keeps moving around the perimeter during all 25 shots.

COACH's cues

Crossover dribble

"Plant same-side foot as hand that's dribbling."

"V-cut in opposite direction."

"Change hands with the dribble."

"Cross the ball over in front."

"Keep the ball low."

Shooting

"Square up!"

"BEEF!"

"**B**ase firm."

"**E**lbow under ball."

"**E**xtend arm."

"**F**ollow through or flip wrist."

Fitness Circle
(5 minutes)

Key Idea: Overload principle

Gather the team into a group. "Who can tell me what *overload* means?" Listen to their responses. "If your bodies do a little bit more work than they have done before, they will adapt and be able to do even more. We're talking about small amounts of work or activity—too much harms your body and causes injuries. Your fitness will improve and you'll be able to do more activity in practice before getting too tired. Let's use the acronym F-I-T—what do you think it stands for?" Listen to their responses. "F stands for *frequency*, or how often you practice the activity; I stands for *intensity*, or how hard you practice or play; and T stands for *time*, or how long you practice the activity. FIT is a good way to remember how to use the overload principle to improve our fitness."

Game 1 (10 minutes)

Goal

Players will pass and cut to the basket looking for return passes and good shots.

Description

Play 3 v 3 half-court games. Teams must make at least two passes before taking a shot. Shots must be within five feet of the basket. Offensive players pass and cut to the basket, presenting a target if they're open. If they receive the ball as they're cutting to the basket, they shoot. (See figure at the top of page 95.)

Coach: What was the goal of the game?
Players: To pass and cut; to present target if open.

Coach: What happened when you were able to get open?
Players: The ball was returned and the shot was attempted.

Coach: How did you get open?
Players: Used a ball fake, ran ahead of defender, kept body between defender and ball on way to basket.

Coach: What did the other offensive player do to create an open lane for you to attack the basket?
Players: Moved out of the lane.

Week 2, Practice 1

Skill Practice 1 (10 minutes)

1. Introduce, demonstrate, and explain how to execute a *give-and-go* (see page 240).
2. Practice the give-and-go.

Description

Play 2 v 1 half-court games with cooperative to active defenders. Another player serves as coach. The offense practices the give-and-go three times, using L-cuts or V-cuts toward the basket; then players rotate. (The defender goes to offense; one of the offensive players becomes the coach.)

Skill Practice 2 (10 minutes)

Description

Play 2 v 2 games with active to competitive defenders. Two other players serve as coaches. The offense practices the give-and-go three times; then players rotate. (The offense becomes the defense; the defense becomes the coaches; the coaches become the offense.) (See figure on page 163.)

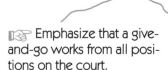

☞ Emphasize that a give-and-go works from all positions on the court.

☞ Make sure players cut *away* from the ball and *toward* the basket.

COACH's cues

"Pass and cut!"

"Target hand!"

"Keep the defender behind you!"

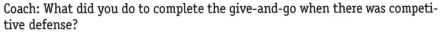

Coach: What did you do to complete the give-and-go when there was competitive defense?

Players: Used more fakes. Dribbled to create passing lanes. Got open to support player with the ball.

COACH's point

☞ Teach rules on technical fouls (see pages 277–278).

Game 2
(10 minutes)

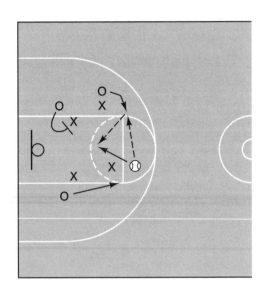

Goal

Players will execute the give-and-go play.

Description

Play 4 v 2, 4 v 3, or 4 v 4 games, depending on the skill proficiency of your players. Rotate players accordingly so that all players have a chance to play offense and defense. Teams must make at least two passes before taking a shot. Shots must be within five feet of the basket. Offensive players pass and cut to the basket, presenting a target if they're open. If they receive the ball as they're cutting to the basket, they shoot. Give the offense an extra point if they use the give-and-go to score.

Team Circle
(5 minutes)

Key Idea: Respect

Gather the team into a group. "Remember the scenario I talked about in the last practice? The opponent who wasn't playing fairly? If you play against a team that does those types of things, how should you handle the end of the game? Stand at this cone if you think you should still go to every player and the coach to shake hands. Stand at this cone if you think you should just walk away." Ask players why they voted as they did. Then separate the team into two groups. Practice an end-of-the-game line-up for both pleasant and fair opponents and for rude opponents. "You should always show your opponents respect by shaking hands at the end of the game, no matter what happens during the game."

Wrap-Up

Make summary comments about practice. Remind them of the next practice and give them a preview of the next practice's emphasis: off-the-ball defense.

Week 2, Practice 2

Warm-Up (10 minutes)

Players pair up and practice shooting off of various offensive moves. The shooter shoots 25 consecutive shots; the rebounder quickly returns the ball. After 25 shots they switch roles. The shooter follows this pattern:

- First 10 shots—no dribble
- Next 5 shots—dribble once
- Next 5 shots—dribble twice
- Last 5 shots—use a crossover dribble

The shooter keeps moving around the perimeter during all 25 shots.

COACH's cues

Crossover dribble

"Plant same-side foot as hand that's dribbling."

"V-cut in opposite direction."

"Change hands with the dribble."

"Cross the ball over in front."

"Keep the ball low."

PURPOSE

To win the ball through off-the-ball defense.

Equipment

- ☑ One basketball per two players, if possible
- ☑ Court space with three or four baskets
- ☑ Tape or markers
- ☑ Different colored vests or shirts to differentiate teams

Fitness Circle (5 minutes)

Key Idea: Overload principle

Gather the team into a group. "What does FIT stand for and when do we use it?" Listen to their responses. Discuss frequency, intensity, and time. "I want you to choose a letter of FIT and demonstrate it." As players give examples and demonstrate, encourage other players to try also. If frequency is chosen, increase repetitions. If intensity, they should try harder or faster. If time, lengthen the amount. Encourage basketball-related activities such as running and shooting. "You need to practice skills and running outside of practice and participate in other physical activities and exercise. This will give your body enough workload to overload and improve your fitness levels or abilities."

COACH's point

☞ Teach rules on holding, tripping, and hand-checking (see page 277).

Game 1 (10 minutes)

Goal

Defenders will prevent the offensive team from passing, receiving passes, and scoring.

Description

Play 4 v 4 half-court games. Players can't dribble except to drive to the basket or reposition to make a pass. They must make at least three consecutive passes before shooting. Defensive team receives one point for each turnover and two points for each steal without fouling. Treat fouls like violations—the other team gets the ball.

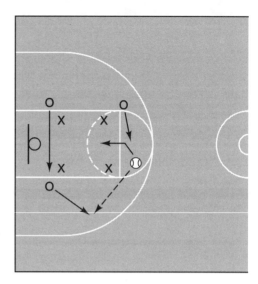

Coach: How did you position yourself to prevent the offensive team from passing?

Players: Overplayed toward potential passing lanes; closely guarded player with the ball.

Coach: How did you position yourself to deny a pass?

Players: Overplayed toward the ball; kept hand in passing lane.

Skill Practice 1 (10 minutes)

1. Introduce, demonstrate, and explain proper *off-the-ball positioning* (see pages 271–272).
2. Practice off-the-ball defensive positioning.

Description

Paired-up players practice off-the-ball defensive positioning (partners can also coach each other). As an option, you can have a player with the ball waiting to pass to his or her offensive teammate. (See figure on page 117.)

Week 2, Practice 2

Game 2 (10 minutes)

Goal

Defenders try to deny offense from making successful passes; offense tries to make six consecutive passes.

Description

Play 2 v 2 games using a competitive defense. For each 2 v 2 game, two other players serve as coaches. One offensive player begins at the point, the other at a wing position. The ball starts at the point. From a triple threat position, the ball handler uses a ball fake to give his or her teammate a chance to get open; or the ball handler dribbles to open a passing lane if necessary. Rotate after a turnover or after six consecutive passes. One player-coach gives feedback for the on-the-ball defense; the other player-coach gives feedback for the off-the-ball defense. (See figure on page 118.)

COACH's cues

"Medium body posture."
"Active hands and active feet!"
"See the ball!"
"Anticipate!"

Game 3 (10 minutes)

Repeat first game, except play 2 v 4, 3 v 4, or 4 v 4 games, depending on the skill proficiency of your players. Rotate players accordingly so that all players have a chance to play offense and defense.

COACH's point

☞ Remind players to stay focused on defense.

Team Circle (5 minutes)

Key Idea: Responsibility

Gather the team into a group. "What should be on your 'mental list' before you come to every practice?" Listen to responses and then lead a discussion about bringing proper equipment (a water bottle, workout clothes); being mentally prepared to work hard and learn new ideas; being well rested; and having eaten well and drunk water during the day. "Each player is responsible for preparing for each practice before practice starts. It's your responsibility to the team to come to practice prepared. Good players are prepared for all practices and games."

Wrap-Up

Make summary comments about practice, and remind them of the next practice: its emphasis is on rebounding.

Week 3

Warm-Up (10 minutes)

Groups of three players—a shooter, passer, and rebounder—play "Rapid Fire." The shooter has one basketball; the passer has another. The shooter keeps moving, shooting without dribbling (later you might add shooting off the crossover dribble). The shooter shoots, working on balance, position, and technique; the passer uses bounce and chest passes to pass to the shooter; and the rebounder outlets to the passer. After one minute, players rotate positions. The shooter becomes the rebounder; the rebounder, the passer; and the passer, the shooter.

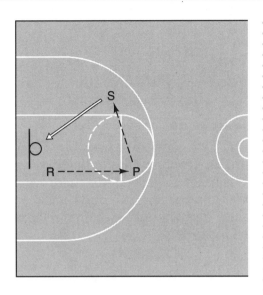

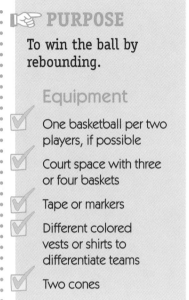 **PURPOSE**

To win the ball by rebounding.

Equipment

✓ One basketball per two players, if possible

✓ Court space with three or four baskets

✓ Tape or markers

✓ Different colored vests or shirts to differentiate teams

✓ Two cones

Fitness Circle (5 minutes)

Key Idea: Overload principle

Gather team into a group. "What does FIT stand for, and when do we use it?" Listen to their responses. Have a review discussion. "When we think about the second area of FIT, what is it? *Intensity*, or how hard you practice the activity. Raise your hand if you think that the only way to increase the intensity of an activity or make it harder is to go faster." Encourage all players to vote. "You can overload the work your body is doing by going faster and/or by going a longer distance, as in running, for example. Every time you run a greater distance or faster, your body will adapt and you'll be able to do more next time."

Game 1 (10 minutes)

Goal

Defenders try to prevent the offensive team from scoring—and from rebounding missed shots.

Description

Play 4 v 4 half-court games. Use a competitive defense. Players can't dribble, except to drive to the basket or to reposition to make a pass, and must make at least three consecutive passes before shooting. The defensive team receives one point for winning or rebounding the ball after only one shot. Treat fouls like violations—the other team gets the ball. (See figure on page 200.)

Coach: What was the goal of the game?
Players: To prevent scoring and prevent a second shot.

Coach: What did you do to prevent a second shot?
Players: Got the rebound after the first shot.

Coach: How did you position yourself to get the rebound?
Players: Moved between the offensive player and the basket.

(You could repeat this game with an offensive focus. In this case, the offensive team would earn a point for each shot attempt and rebound. You'd want to instruct your offensive rebounders to protect the ball, and to tip the ball to the basket or assume a shooting position as quickly as possible, like a pogo stick.)

Skill Practice 1 (15 minutes)

1. Introduce, demonstrate, and explain how to *box out* to rebound (see page 268).
2. Practice boxing out and rebounding.

Description

Play 3 v 3 games with 2 v 2 under the boards and a shooter and an outlet. The shooter shoots the ball. On the release, X_1 and X_2 turn and box out their offensive players. X_3 (the outlet) moves right or left, depending on which side of the basket the rebound occurs. The player rebounding the ball turns and passes to X_3. Repeat three times, then rotate offense to defense. The defenders try to outlet successfully three times in a row. (See figure on page 121.)

Week 3

COACH's cues

"Create a stable wall between opponent and ball."
"Elbows out—palms wide, feel for opponent."
"Put buttocks under opponents."

COACH's point

☞ Talk about the possible fouls that can occur (e.g., over the back; see page 277).

Game 2 (15 minutes)

Goal

Defenders try to prevent the offensive team from scoring—and from rebounding missed shots.

Description

Play 2 v 4, 3 v 4, or 4 v 4 games, depending on the skill proficiency of your players. Rotate players accordingly so that all players have a chance to play offense and defense. Players can't dribble and must make at least three consecutive passes before shooting. The defensive team receives one point for winning or rebounding the ball after only one shot. (See figure on page 200.)

Team Circle (5 minutes)

Key Idea: Honesty

Gather the team into a group near two cones about 10 feet apart. Identify three honesty situations that are important for your team to practice. These could be traveling, tripping, or another rule infraction. First, ask players how they would respond, and then discuss how you would prefer them to respond. "Being honest about a play during the game and in practice is an important part of the game. Good players are honest even when an official, coach, or opponent didn't see it happen."

Wrap-Up

Make summary comments about practice and give reminders for the first game.

☞ **PURPOSE**

To create space in the attack by setting screens.

Equipment

☑ One basketball per two players, if possible

☑ Court space with three or four baskets

☑ Tape or markers

☑ Different colored vests or shirts to differentiate teams

Warm-Up (10 minutes)

Groups of three players—a shooter, passer, and rebounder—play "Rapid Fire." The shooter has one basketball; the passer has another. The shooter keeps moving, shooting without dribbling (later you might add shooting off the crossover dribble). The shooter shoots, working on balance, position, and technique; the passer uses bounce and chest passes to pass to the shooter; and the rebounder outlets to the passer. After one minute, players rotate positions. The shooter becomes the rebounder; the rebounder, the passer; and the passer, the shooter. (See figure on page 203.)

Fitness Circle (5 minutes)

Key Idea: Flexibility

Gather the team into a group. "It's important to stretch our muscles. What area of fitness does that improve? Right—flexibility. It's also important to stretch muscles that have been used the most in a sport or activity. In basketball, what do we use the most? Our legs and arms. I am going to show you the proper way to stretch the different muscles in your legs and arms." Choose stretches that include quadriceps (front of thigh), hamstrings (back of thigh), calves and Achilles tendon (back of the lower leg and ankle), arms, and deltoids (shoulders). Remind players to get in position and hold their stretch, not to bounce, and they shouldn't feel pain.

Game 1
(10 minutes)

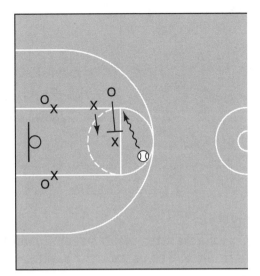

Goal

The ball handler tries to use teammates' positioning to lose his or her opponent and attack the basket.

Description

Play 4 v 4 half-court games. Have different players restart plays. Give one extra point for a basket scored off a screen. Players call their own fouls.

Coach: What were you trying to do in the game?
Players: Use teammates' positioning to lose opponent and attack the basket.

Coach: Why is the teammates' positioning so important?
Players: To create an open shot for the player with the ball.

Coach: What would be a good body position for the player trying to free his or her teammate.
Players: Wide base, bent knees, arms across body to protect self.

Skill Practice 1
(15 minutes)

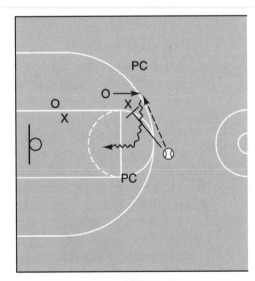

1. Introduce, demonstrate, and explain how to *set screens* (see page 238).

2. Practice setting screens.

Description

Play 3 v 2 games with two other players acting as coaches. Offensive players execute screens. The defensive player plays active defense. One coach will watch to see if the screen is set correctly; the other coach will watch to see if the ball handler uses the screen correctly. The goal is to successfully execute a screen three times in a row.

☞ Point out common errors: setting a screen with your side and setting a moving screen.

COACH's cues

"Stand firm, straddle feet."

"Hands across chest ready to take impact."

"Roll toward basket or roll to a passing lane."

Game 2 (15 minutes)

Goal

The offense attempts to screen the on-the-ball defender so the player with the ball can attack the basket.

Description

Play 4 v 2, 4 v 3, or 4 v 4 games, depending on the skill proficiency of your players. Rotate players accordingly so that all players have a chance to play offense and defense. Have a different player restart the play each possession. Give one extra point for a basket scored off a screen. Players call their own fouls. (See figure at the top of page 207.)

Team Circle (5 minutes)

Key Idea: Respect

Gather the team into two groups. "Think about professional teams. What ways do they show respect for their opponents?" Discuss with players. Lead discussion to talking about saying positive comments such as "good game" and "nice play today" along with a handshake. "Let's say this is the end of a game. Your two groups are professional teams that played against each other. Show me what you do at the end of the game." Use one of the discussion examples for players to try. "When you say positive comments to your opponents at the end of a game in addition to shaking or slapping hands, it shows you respect your opponents. Good professional players show they respect opponents."

Wrap-Up

Make summary comments about the practice and give reminders for the next game.

Week 5

Warm-Up
(10 minutes)

Players play "Rebound-Outlet." Player O_1 shoots the basketball, guarded by X_3. X_3 rebounds the shot and makes a strong outlet pass to O_2. As soon as 1 takes the shot, he or she moves quickly to play defense on 2. Player 1 then rebounds 2's shot and makes an outlet pass to X_3. After 2 takes the shot, he or she plays defense on X_3. The players continue the process for the duration of the warm-up.

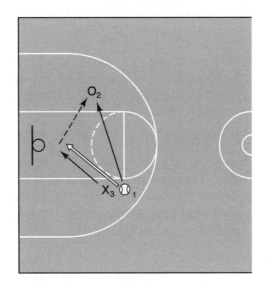

Fitness Circle
(5 minutes)

Key Idea: Flexibility

"Your muscles need to be stretched every day to prevent injuries. Lie down on your back with one leg up in the air. Stretch your knee toward your face and hold it there for 10 counts. Now let's try the stretch again. . . . See if you can use FIT. Repeat the stretch again, holding the stretch now to 15 counts and stretching your leg a bit farther. You should not stretch so far that you hurt yourself, lock your knee, or feel pain. Just stretch until you feel a gentle pull. Stretching helps to prevent injuries and improves your flexibility, an important part of fitness."

☞Teach rules on pushing.

Game 1 (10 minutes)

Goal

Offensive players will screen on-the-ball defenders so the player with the ball can attack the goal; defenders will effectively defend against the screen.

Description

Play 4 v 4 half-court games. The offense must make at least two passes before taking a shot. All shots must be within 5 feet of the basket. Have different players restart the play on each possession. Give an extra point for a basket scored off a screen. Give the defense a point for not allowing a shot. Players call their own fouls. (See figure at the top of page 207.)

Coach: What is the purpose of an on-the-ball screen?
Players: It allows the player with the ball to drive past the screener and lose the defender to set up a shot or a drive.

Coach: How can you get around the screen once it is set?
Players: Fight over the top (i.e., slide between the player setting the screen and the player you're guarding); duck behind the screener.

Skill Practice 1 (10 minutes)

1. Introduce, demonstrate, and explain how to *fight over the top of a screen* (see page 239).
2. Practice fighting over the top of screens.

Description

Play 2 v 2 games with a competitive defense. Offensive players execute screens; defenders being screened must fight over the top of screens, trying to keep the offense from shooting. Two player-coaches evaluate defenders' abilities to fight through screens. (See figure at the top of page 169.)

Skill Practice 2 (10 minutes)

1. Introduce, demonstrate, and explain how to *slide behind a screen* (see page 245).
2. Practice sliding behind screens.

Description

Play 2 v 2 games with a competitive defense. Offensive players execute screens; defenders being screened must duck behind the screens and stay with their opponents, trying to keep them from shooting. Two player-coaches evaluate defenders' abilities to slide behind screens. (See figure at the bottom of page 169.)

Week 5

COACH's cues

"Stay with your opponent!"

"Talk! Let teammates know the screen is there."

"Stand away from the person setting the screen to allow your teammate to move around the pick."

Game 2 (10 minutes)

Repeat Game 1. Rotate players accordingly so that all players have a chance to play offense and defense.

COACH's point

☞ Perform in slower motion, if necessary, to help players understand and perform the task.

☞ Take advantage of "teachable moments."

Team Circle (5 minutes)

Key Idea: Responsibility

Gather the team into two groups. Give one group a ball. Have them dribble and pass to each other. Have one player try to distract the rest of the group. Continue this for one minute. Bring the team together as a group. "How should you respond to someone who is trying to distract you?" Discuss their responses. "If you're at practice and talk to your teammates or distract other players, you're interrupting the practice. It's your responsibility to the team to pay attention at practices and games so you and your teammates can learn and play your best."

Wrap-Up

Make summary comments about practice and give reminders for the next game.

211

Week 6

☞ **PURPOSE**

To attack the basket by setting screens.

Equipment

☑ One basketball per two players, if possible

☑ Court space with three or four baskets

☑ Tape or markers

☑ Different colored vests or shirts to differentiate teams

Warm-Up (10 minutes)

Players play "Rebound-Outlet." Player O_1 shoots the basketball, guarded by X_3. X_3 rebounds the shot and makes a strong outlet pass to O_2. As soon as 1 takes the shot, he or she moves quickly to play defense on 2. Player 1 then rebounds 2's shot and makes an outlet pass to X_3. After 2 takes the shot, he or she plays defense on X_3. The players continue the process for the duration of the warm-up. (See figure on page 209.)

Fitness Circle (5 minutes)

Key Idea: Muscular strength and endurance

Gather the team into a group. Choose two players to demonstrate with one ball. Have the players pass to each other 10 times without telling them how hard or fast to pass. Then have them spread out farther. Direct them to pass as hard and as fast as they can 10 times. Have them come back to the group. "Did everyone see how during the second times they passed the ball harder and faster? When you do that, what area or component of fitness do you improve?" Listen to their responses. "Muscular strength and endurance. When you pass harder you are improving your strength; when you pass faster, you are improving your endurance."

Game 1 (10 minutes)

Goal

The offense attempts to screen (set a pick on) the on-the-ball defender so the player with the ball can attack the basket.

Description

Play 4 v 4 half-court games. Have different players restart plays. Give one extra point for a basket scored off a screen. Players call their own fouls. (See figure at the top of page 207.)

Coach: Why use a screen?
Players: To create an open shot for the player with the ball.

Coach: What is a screen?
Players: An offensive technique to take the defensive player guarding a team-mate out of the play, or to delay that player long enough to open a teammate for a pass or shot.

Coach: How do you execute a screen?
Players: Wide base, bent knees, arms across body to protect self.

Skill Practice 1 (15 minutes)

Description

Play 3 v 2 games with two other players acting as coaches. Offensive players execute screens. The defensive player plays active defense. One coach will watch to see if the screen is set correctly; the other coach will watch to see if the ball handler uses the screen correctly. The goal is to successfully execute a screen three times in a row. (See figure at the bottom of page 207.)

COACH's cues

"Stand firm, straddle feet."

"Hands across chest ready to take impact."

"Roll toward basket or roll to a passing lane."

☞ Point out common errors: setting a screen with your side and setting a moving screen.

Game 2 (15 minutes)

Goal

The offense attempts to screen the on-the-ball defender so the player with the ball can attack the basket.

Description

Play 4 v 2, 4 v 3, or 4 v 4 games, depending on the skill proficiency of your players. Rotate players accordingly so that all players have a chance to play offense and defense. Have a different player restart the play each possession. Give one extra point for a basket scored off a screen. Players call their own fouls. (See figure at the top of page 207.)

Team Circle
(5 minutes)

Key Idea: Caring

Gather the team and separate them into two groups, each with a ball. "Each group should pass the ball to each other. As you pass the ball I want everybody to be saying something good about the pass and the people passing and catching. I should be hearing constant talk." Encourage excitement about the activity by clapping and providing players with your positive comments. "We will keep the passing going until everyone has had two turns passing and catching. Let me know when you're done." Wait for players to signal that they are finished. "What are some of the positive comments that you heard? Saying positive comments shows you care."

Wrap-Up

Make summary comments about practice and give reminders for the next game.

Week 7

Warm-Up (10 minutes)

Players pair up and practice shooting off of various offensive moves. The shooter shoots 25 consecutive shots; the rebounder quickly returns the ball. After 25 shots they switch roles. The shooter follows this pattern:

- First 10 shots—no dribble
- Next 5 shots—dribble once
- Next 5 shots—dribble twice
- Last 5 shots—use a crossover dribble

The shooter keeps moving around the perimeter during all 25 shots.

Fitness Circle (5 minutes)

Key Idea: Cardiorespiratory fitness

Gather the team into a circle. "I want everyone to run to the opposite basket and back. Before you go, describe how your lungs feel and how fast your breathing rate is. How tired is your body?" Listen to their responses. "When you're done running, I'll ask you the same question and see if the answers are faster or slower or more tired than before. Ready? Go!" Repeat the question. Discuss their responses. "To strengthen your heart and lungs, you need to run and make your heart beat faster and breathe faster. You need to feel a little tired while running to improve your cardiorespiratory fitness. Checking how you feel tells you that you are running fast enough to improve the strength of your lungs and heart."

Game 1 (10 minutes)

Goal

The offense attempts to screen off-the-ball defenders so their offensive teammates can move to support the ball handler.

Description

Play 4 v 4 half-court games. Have different team members restart the play on each possession. Give an extra point for each basket scored off a screen. Players call their own fouls. (See figure at the top of page 175.)

215

Coach: How did you use the off-the-ball screen to free up your teammate?
Players: Setting a pick or screen on the defender, same as on the ball.

Coach: How did you know where to set the screen?
Players: Setting screen so teammate can get open to receive a pass, depending on where a passing lane can be opened; facing away from direction teammate needs to run.

Coach: How should you move to best use the screen?
Players: Cut toward the screen, brushing or nearly brushing shoulders as you pass the pick or screen.

Skill Practice 1 (15 minutes)

Description

Play 3 v 3 half-court games; two players act as coaches, one watching the offense, the other the defense. The offense screens off the ball. (See figure at the bottom of page 175.)

COACH's cues

"Anticipate ball movement!"

"Screen so the player can move *to* the ball or *to* the basket."

"Brush shoulders so the defender can't get through the screen."

Game 2 (15 minutes)

Goal

The offense attempts to screen off-the-ball defenders so their offensive teammates can move to support the ball handler.

Description

Play 4 v 2, 4 v 3, or 4 v 4 games, depending on the skill proficiency of your players. Rotate players accordingly so that all players have a chance to play offense and defense. Have different team members restart the play on each possession. Give an extra point for each basket scored off a screen. Players call their own fouls. (See figure at the top of page 175.)

Week 7

Team Circle
(5 minutes)

Key Idea: Respect

Gather the team into groups of three. Play a one-on-one game with the other player being the official. Play for one minute and rotate players so everyone gets a chance to referee. "How did it feel to be the official?" Discuss responses and importance of showing respect. "It can be difficult to be an official. It involves quite a few skills. Remember that it's a tough job, and always show respect for officials."

Wrap-Up

Make summary comments about practice and give reminders for the next game.

Week 8

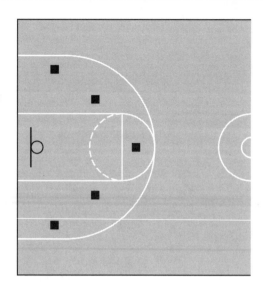

PURPOSE

To use space in the attack by rolling off a screen toward the basket.

Equipment

☑ One basketball per two players, if possible

☑ Court space with three or four baskets

☑ Tape or markers

☑ Different colored vests or shirts to differentiate teams

Warm-Up (10 minutes)

Players play "Spot Shooting," shooting five shots from each of the five areas. Player should run to get each rebound and then dribble back to the appropriate spot. Players should try to make at least 15 out of the 25 attempted shots.

Fitness Circle (5 minutes)

Key Idea: Cardiorespiratory fitness

Gather the team into a group. Have players run for two minutes with a partner without stopping. "During our run I want you to be able to run for the whole two minutes. Who remembers what a talk test is?" Listen to their responses. "You can use a talk test to pace yourself so you don't run too fast and get too tired before the two minutes are up. Say the words 'two points' to your partner. If you can say it without being out of breath, keep the same pace; if you're out of breath, slow down a little. Start running." Time for two minutes and gather team as a group. "Using a talk test helps you pace yourself. Pacing yourself when you run helps to improve your cardiorespiratory fitness."

Week 8

Game 1 (10 minutes)

Goal

The offensive player who sets a screen, either on or off the ball, cuts toward the basket.

Description

Play 4 v 4 half-court games. Have a different team member restart the play on each possession. Give an extra point for each basket scored off a screen. Players call their own fouls. The defense attempts to get around the screen and stay with the player cutting to the basket. (See figure below.)

Coach: After you set the screen, what do you do?
Players: Move toward the basket.

Coach: How did this movement create space in your attack?
Players: Created a passing lane, set up a potential high percentage shot (e.g., lay-up).

Coach: Which picks—high or low—provided more opportunities to shoot?
Players: High, because they allowed player to roll away from defense and kept defensive player from getting between offense and the basket.

Skill Practice 1 (15 minutes)

1. Introduce, demonstrate, and explain how to execute a *pick-and-roll* (see page 242).
2. Practice pick-and-rolls.

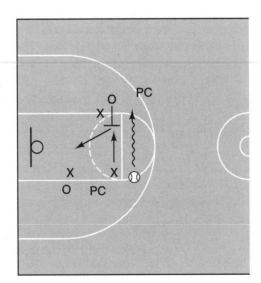

Description

Play 3 v 3 half-court games with two player-coaches evaluating the effectiveness of the offensive players. The offense tries to score twice off a pick-and-roll and then switches to defense.

☞ Focus on the offensive performance.

COACH's cues

"Open up to the ball when rolling to the basket!"

"Watch for the ball!"

"Show target hands!"

"Attack the basket quickly!"

Game 2 (15 minutes)

Same as Game 1, except play 4 v 2, 4 v 3, or 4 v 4 games, depending on the skill proficiency of your players. Rotate players accordingly so that all players have a chance to play offense and defense.

Team Circle (5 minutes)

Key Idea: Caring

Choose two players to demonstrate. Tell them they will role play a situation in which one player is dribbling the ball and passes to the other. The pass goes out of bounds and the player receiving the pass gets upset and yells at his teammate. Have them act out the situation with your assistance. "How would you feel if someone yelled at you for a bad pass?" Listen to their responses. "How about if you made a bad pass, but heard some encouraging words like 'It's okay. Maybe next time'?" Listen to responses, discuss comparisons. "You show you respect your teammates by not yelling at them for a mistake and encouraging them to make a better play the next time they have a chance."

Wrap-Up

Make summary comments about practice and give reminders for the next game.

Week 9

Warm-Up (10 minutes)

Players play "Spot Shooting," shooting five shots from each of the five areas labeled in the figure on page 218. Player should run to get each rebound and then dribble back to the appropriate spot. Players should try to make at least 15 out of the 25 attempted shots.

Fitness Circle (5 minutes)

Key Idea: Healthy habits

Gather players into two equal groups. "I want the first group to take a ball, then dribble and pass to each other, making sure everyone gets one chance with the ball, then attempt a basket." After players finish, ask them to come over to the sidelines. Have the second group go out and repeat the activity. "Following a play like that, and every time you come out of the game or during practice, what is one of the most important things you should do?" Listen to their responses. "Drink water during every break and especially when you need it. Drinking regularly prevents dehydration or when your body loses water. It's important to drink water *before* you feel thirsty. Drinking plenty of water is a healthy habit to do every day."

☞ **PURPOSE**

To defend space by communicating and to play good defense.

Equipment

☑ One basketball per two players, if possible

☑ Court space with three or four baskets

☑ Tape or markers

☑ Different colored vests or shirts to differentiate teams

☑ Three cones

Game 1 (10 minutes)

Goal

The defense will play effective player-to-player, competitive defense to keep the offense from scoring.

Description

Play 4 v 4 half-court games. Players call their own fouls. Players can dribble only to drive to the basket. The offense uses screens to score and create passing lanes in the attack. Use a jump ball to restart play after every basket. (See figure on page 200.)

Coach: How did you defend the offensive team?
Players: With player-to-player defense.

Coach: What are the advantages of player-to-player defense?
Players: All players are closely guarded, which increases the chance to win the ball; all defensive members know their responsibility.

Coach: What are the disadvantages of player-to-player defense?
Players: Defense can get spread out too far away from the basket; difficult to match players of equal ability.

Coach: How can you help your teammates while in player-to-player defense?
Players: Let them know when a screen is being set; pick up the player when there's a scoring threat.

Skill Practice 1
(10 minutes)

Description

Play 3 v 3 games, using two player-coaches. Begin by playing in slower motion, using a cooperative to active defense. Offensive players execute on-the-ball screens. Defensive players must fight through the screen and stay with their opponents; they transition into playing competitive defense. They attempt to keep the offense from getting a good shot. The player-coaches evaluate defenders' abilities in getting around screens.

Skill Practice 2 (10 minutes)

Description

The same as Skill Practice 1, except the emphasis here is on off-the-ball screens. (See figure on page 178.)

COACH's cues

"Call 'screen left' or 'screen right.'"
"Quick movements, jab steps and fakes."
"Stay between your player and the basket."

Week 9

Game 2 (10 minutes)

Goal

The defense, playing a player-to-player competitive defense, will keep the offense from scoring.

Description

Play 2 v 4, 3 v 4, or 4 v 4 games, depending on the skill proficiency of your players. Rotate players accordingly so that all players have a chance to play offense and defense. Players call their own fouls. Player can dribble only to drive to the basket. The offense uses screens to create passing lanes in the attack and score. (See figure on page 200.)

☞ Solid player-to-player defense is the foundation for all other facets of defense.

Team Circle (5 minutes)

Key Idea: Respect

Gather the team into a group near three cones about 10 feet apart. "What are three things you can do or not do that show you respect your body?" Listen to their responses. Main ideas might be not taking drugs, keeping emotional outbursts under control (swearing, pushing an opponent), and not doing dangerous plays in practices and games. As players give responses, have them and others with the same idea stand next to a cone. "Those are all great ideas. When you practice those ideas, you show yourself and others that you respect your body."

Wrap-Up

Make summary comments about practice and give reminders for the next game.

Week 10

To win the ball and use space in the attack by making a quick transition from defense to offense.

Equipment

☑ One basketball per two players, if possible

☑ Court space with three or four baskets

☑ Tape or markers

☑ Different colored vests or shirts to differentiate teams

Warm-Up (10 minutes)

Players play "Rebound-Outlet." Player O_1 shoots the basketball, guarded by X_3. X_3 rebounds the shot and makes a strong outlet pass to O_2. As soon as 1 takes the shot, he or she moves quickly to play defense on 2. Player 1 then rebounds 2's shot and makes an outlet pass to X_3. After 2 takes the shot, he or she plays defense on X_3. The players continue the process for the duration of the warm-up. (See figure on page 209.)

Fitness Circle (5 minutes)

Key Idea: Healthy habits

Gather the team into a group. "It's important to eat foods that give the most energy for basketball. What are the four main nutrients or parts of food that help you grow and stay healthy?" Listen to responses. Discuss how carbohydrates (breads, cereals, and fruits) give energy. Discuss how proteins (meats, nuts, and tofu) build muscle and bone. Mention that fats (fat and oils in meat, milk, and nuts) provide stored energy. Remind them that water (from the tap or in juice or milk) makes up 60% of their bodies. "One healthy habit you should be practicing every day is eating foods that keep your body healthy—that includes snacks. What are examples of each nutrient? Carbohydrates? Proteins? Fats? Water?" Discuss food choices.

Game 1 (10 minutes)

Goal

The defense will rebound and make an outlet pass.

Description

Play 4 v 4 half-court games. Defenders box out to rebound and use an outlet pass. Players call their own fouls. The defensive team gets one point for successfully rebounding and making an outlet pass. The offense scores as many points as possible. (See figure on page 200.)

Coach: **Why should you make an outlet pass after rebounding the ball?**

Players: To get ball out of lane and away from opponents; to get ball down the floor faster.

Coach: **Which player should get the outlet pass?**

Players: Player not involved in rebounding.

Coach: **Where should the outlet player go to receive the outlet pass?**

Players: To the sideline nearest the player rebounding the ball; move quickly to create a passing lane.

Skill Practice 1 (10 minutes)

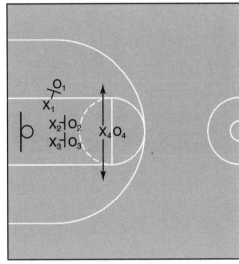

Description

Play 4 v 4 games half court, with one shooter and one outlet; O_4 shoots ball. On the release, X_1, X_2, and X_3 turn and box out the players they're guarding. X_4 (the outlet) moves right or left, depending on which side of the basket the ball is rebounded. The rebounder turns and passes to X_4. The defense tries to complete three successful outlet passes in a row; then the offense goes on defense, and vice-versa.

COACH's cues

"Rebound!"

"Protect the ball!"

"Pivot away from the basket!"

225

Skill Practice 2 (10 minutes)

Description

Extend Skill Practice 1. Go to full court. After the outlet pass is made, the point guard or off guard moves up toward center court to create a passing lane. The next available player fills the outside lane opposite the rebound. Trailing players move quickly down court and assume offensive positions. After rebounding the ball, the team outletting the ball tries to use no more than five passes to score.

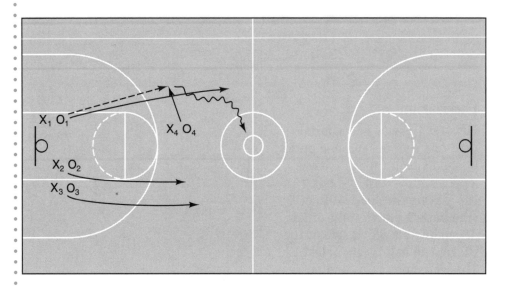

"Get and go!"

"Quick movement down court!"

"Stay wide and spread out to maintain passing lanes."

Game 2 (10 minutes)

Goal

The defense uses outlet passes after rebounding ball.

Description

Same as Game 1, except play 2 v 4, 3 v 4, or 4 v 4 games, depending on the skill proficiency of your players. Rotate players accordingly so that all players have a chance to play offense and defense.

Team Circle (5 minutes)

Key Idea: Responsibility

Gather the team into a circle. "I want everyone to count how many players we have in the circle." Wait while they count. "How many do you get, total?" Listen to their responses. "Well, that's good counting, but you know, the real total is *one*. That's right. We're one team with many contributions from each player. Remember there is no 'I' in team. If we don't play together as one, we will not play our best. To play together we all have individual responsibilities to the team like working hard on defense and offense, following rules, and getting good at ballhandling skills. Making sure each one of you takes that responsibility seriously is an important attitude to practice."

Wrap-Up

Make summary comments about practice and give reminders for the next game.

To win the ball by rebounding free throws.

Equipment

☑ One basketball per three players, if possible

☑ Court space with three or four baskets

☑ Tape or markers

☑ Different colored vests or shirts to differentiate teams

Warm-Up (10 minutes)

Groups of three players—a shooter, passer, and rebounder—play "Rapid Fire." The shooter has one basketball; the passer has another. The shooter keeps moving, shooting without dribbling (later you might add shooting off the crossover dribble). The shooter shoots, working on balance, position, and technique; the passer uses bounce and chest passes to pass to the shooter; and the rebounder outlets to the passer. After one minute, players rotate positions: the shooter becomes the rebounder; the rebounder, the passer; and the passer, the shooter. (See figure on page 203.)

Fitness Circle (5 minutes)

Key Idea: Healthy habits

Gather the team into a group. "Tell me some healthy habits you practice every day?" Responses may be brushing teeth, eating foods that help you grow, and getting enough sleep. If taking drugs or using alcohol is not a response, discuss this. If it was a response, lead discussion from the response. "You have been hearing 'say no to drugs' probably since you were very young. Let's talk about what it really means and if/where you might have to use that phrase. Tell me some situations where you think you might have to 'say no to drugs.'" Discuss responses—in school, from other kids you don't know very well, parties, etc. "It is an important healthy habit to stay away from drugs, alcohol, and tobacco."

Game 1 (10 minutes)

Goal

Players will learn correct positioning for free throws.

Description

Play 4 v 4. Begin each play with a free throw. A made free throw is worth one point; a rebound (for either team) is worth one point. Rotate so each player on both teams shoots a free throw. Team A shoots five free throws in a row; then team B shoots.

Coach: How should the offensive team line up for a free throw?
Players: Between defensive players on sidelines of the lane, one player at half court to defend against a potential fast break attempt.

Coach: How should the defensive team line up for a free throw?
Players: On the block next to the basket, with one player on other side of offensive player and one player close to shooter ready to box out.

Skill Practice 1 (15 minutes)

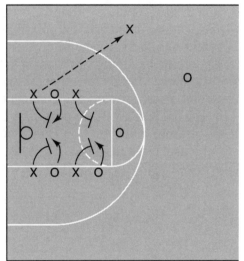

Description

Offensive and defensive teams alternate free throws. Practice defensive positioning after release of ball and practice making outlet passes, as in a fast break. If the offensive team gets the rebound, continue play until they score or the defense wins the ball.

COACH's point

COACH's cues

"Step in at the release!"
"Step in quickly and firmly hold position."
"Keep your body against your opponent."

☞ Teach free-throw rules (e.g., when players can enter the lane; see page 280).

☞ Emphasize the need to box out the shooter.

☞ Encourage free-throw shooting routines. For example: "see" the ball go in; bounce the ball; bend the knees; focus on the "BEEF" technique—**B**ase firm, **E**lbow under ball, **E**xtend arm, **F**ollow through.

Game 2 (15 minutes)

Same as Game 1.

Team Circle (5 minutes)

Key Idea: Caring

Gather the team into a group and choose three players to demonstrate. Have the three stand in a line. The two outside players should carefully lift the middle player. Have them problem-solve to find a way to hold the player up. Continue for about 30 seconds and then have them set the player down. "Did you see how Jared was supported by his teammates? Ben and Tyrone showed you how to give physical support, but it's also important to support your teammates emotionally. What are some examples?" Listen to responses (positive comments, identifying good plays, encouraging comments during losses) and discuss them. "When you support your teammates throughout the season, you show you care about them. You'll play better as a team when you show you care about each other."

Wrap-Up

Make summary comments about practice and give reminders for the next game.

Week 12

Warm-Up (10 minutes)

Play 1 v 1 games, starting at the foul line. Defense checks the ball and offense begins in a triple threat position. (See figure on page 108.)

Fitness Circle (5 minutes)

Key Idea: Reversibility principle

Gather the team into a group. "What happens to your body if you do not stay active and keep training and conditioning your body?" Listen to their responses. Discuss losing conditioning when you stop being active. "What is that called? Right—the 'reversibility principle.' What should you do to prevent losing your conditioning? Participating in physical activity or another sport after the season will prevent you from reversing your conditioning. How will you stay active after the basketball season is over?" Listen to their responses. "Remember the 'reversibility principle'—you use it or lose it! You worked hard all season to improve your Fitness, so keep it up for next year!"

Game 1 (10 minutes)

Goal

The offense will score within 10 seconds of inbounding the ball from the end line.

Description

Play 5 v 5, half court. Players can't dribble except to drive to the basket. Use a 2-1-2 defense to defend space around the basket. Restart play from the end lines.

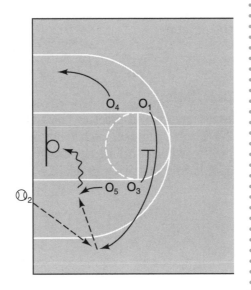

Coach: What did your team do to score within 10 seconds of the inbound pass?
Players: Passed quickly, moved quickly, set up screens and picks to create open passing lanes.

☞Teach the difference between a zone and player-to-player defense (players guard an area, not a person).

☞A zone defense protects the lane better than player-to-player.

☞Players need to communicate in the zone—they need to call cutters, shots, and so on.

☞The player inbounding the ball has five seconds to release the ball.

Skill Practice 1 (10 minutes)

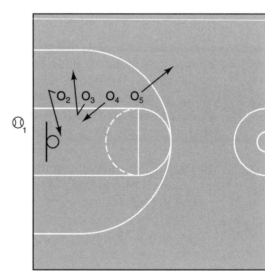

1. Introduce, demonstrate, and explain an end-line inbounds play (see page 243) against a 2-1-2 zone defense.

2. Practice the inbounds play.

Description

In a 5 v 5 half-court situation with an active 2-1-2 defense, the offense tries to score three times in a row on this inbounds play.

O_2 fakes outside, then cuts in the lane and sets a screen for O_4, who cuts toward the basket, hands held high, expecting the pass. O_4 is the first option. O_3 is the second option. O_3 fakes inside, then cuts toward the baseline.

Skill Practice 2 (10 minutes)

Description

Teams create and practice their own end-line inbounds plays against a 2-1-2 zone defense. Each team of five creates an inbounds play, then practices it against its opponent, which plays an active defense. The goal is to score three times in a row.

Week 12

"Know your role!"

"Execute your role!"

"Timing is everything!"

Game 2 (10 minutes)

Same as Game 1, except play 5 v 4 or 5 v 3. The offense earns an extra point when they score on the inbounds play. Rotate players accordingly so that all players have a chance to play offense and defense.

Team Circle (5 minutes)

Key Idea: Respect

Gather the team into a group near two cones about 10 feet apart. Choose two players to demonstrate. "Let's say you just scored a basket. Jack, show everyone a way to celebrate or congratulate your teammates that won't make the other team upset. Now, Kyle, show the team how you would celebrate if you wanted everyone to know how happy you were and that you thought you played much better than your opponents. If you think the best way to celebrate is like Jack, stand at this cone. If you think Kyle's is the better way, stand at this cone. . . . It's important to respect your opponents during games. You can do that by saying 'good play' or slapping hands calmly with your team. Now think about respected athletes—what do they do before, during, and after games?" Discuss.

Wrap-Up

Make summary comments about practice and give reminders about the final game.

Part IV

The Subject Matter

In part III we provided you with an instructional plan for the season and 14 practice plans for 8- to 13-year-olds, all using the games approach to teaching. In part IV we'll help you teach the subject matter that is contained in those practice plans. In chapter 13, we'll provide information on teaching the skills and strategies your players need to be able to execute them. In chapter 14, you'll review the rules of the game, along with a few unwritten traditions that are useful to know. In chapter 15 you'll learn more about the basic fitness concepts we want you to integrate into your teaching, and in chapter 16 you'll learn more about teaching character development.

We believe that the better you understand what you're teaching, the better you're likely to teach it. See the information here as a good starting point, but feel free to learn more by exploring some of the resources listed in appendix A at the end of this book.

Teaching Basketball Tactics and Skills

As your athletes play games in practice, their experience in these games—and your subsequent discussions with them about their experience—will lead them to the tactics and skills they need to develop in order to succeed. In the games approach to teaching basketball, tactics and skills go hand in hand.

In this chapter we'll provide information for you to teach your players team tactics and individual offensive and defensive skills. We'll also include suggestions for identifying and correcting common errors. Remember to use the IDEA approach to teaching skills—Introduce, Demonstrate, and Explain the skill, and Attend to players as they practice the skill. For a refresher on IDEA, see chapter 4. If you aren't familiar with basketball skills, rent or purchase a video to see the skills performed. You may also find advanced books on skills helpful; see appendix A for more information on additional resources.

We've only provided information about the basics of basketball in this book. As your players advance in their basketball skills, you'll need to advance in your knowledge as a coach. You can do so by learning from your experiences, by watching and talking with more experienced coaches, and by studying the advanced resources in appendix A.

Offensive Tactics

In basketball, the offensive team's primary objective is to move the ball effectively so they can score. A secondary goal is to maintain ball possession so the opposing team cannot score. The following tactics will help your team accomplish these goals.

Creating Passing Lanes

To move the ball effectively, your team needs to move well without the ball and create passing lanes. Players create passing lanes by using cuts and screens, by maintaining space and court balance, by keeping the middle open, and by quickly moving to a vacated spot. We'll address cuts and screens later in this chapter. Here we'll take a closer look at maintaining court balance, keeping the middle open, and moving to a vacated spot.

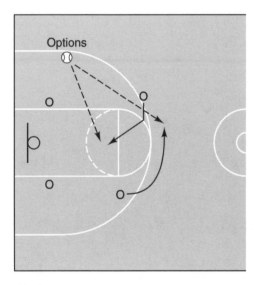

Figure 13.1 The player who is the next player away from a cutting player should quickly move to the vacated spot.

◎ **Maintaining court balance.** Players should start in an open formation, about 12 to 15 feet apart. They should be spaced high at the top, wide on the wing, and at the midpoint between the basket and corner on the baseline.

◎ **Keeping the middle open.** When a player cuts to the basket and doesn't receive a pass, he or she should continue through and fill an open spot on the side of the court with fewer players. This will keep the middle open and the floor balanced. Players shouldn't stay in the post area for more than one count.

◎ **Moving to a vacated spot.** The player who is the next player away from a cutting player should quickly move to the vacated spot (see figure 13.1). This is especially important when the player has cut from the point or top position. When replacing the player at the point, the new player should swing wide above the three-point line, creating a better passing angle from the wing.

Setting Screens

Screens may be set for a player with or without the ball; they help players get open for passes and shots. An offensive player who sets a screen, or pick, positions himself or herself as a stationary barrier on one side of a teammate's defender, blocking the defender's path as the teammate cuts around the screen to get open (see figure 13.2). The screening player stands erect with feet planted shoulder-width apart, keeping the arms down to the sides or crossed at the chest. The screen should be set perpendicular to the path of the defender. Against good defensive teams the cutter may often be covered, but the screener will often be open to receive a pass after setting the screen.

Direct players to "screen away" from the ball, meaning they should set screens for teammates who are on the opposite (weak) side of the court from the ball. That way the player for whom the screen is set will be moving toward the passer after coming off the screen. Players should cut right by (actually brushing by) the screeners.

Figure 13.2   Proper technique for setting a screen.

Transition Game

The fast break usually develops after a rebound, steal, or possibly after a made basket, and is the fastest way to make the transition from defense to offense. As soon as the defense gains control of the ball, they use the outlet pass or dribble to start the break—passing being the first option, because it moves the ball faster. On a rebound, the rebounder should pivot toward the wing area on that side of the court and hit the outlet (#1, #2, or #3 player). The player receiving the pass gets the ball to the middle of the court by either passing or dribbling; teammates should fill the lanes on either side as they proceed down court. The player with the ball in the middle wants to get to the free-throw line under control before passing to either lane for a shot or short drive.

It's important to stay spread out and run at top speed under control during the fast break. The last two players down the floor are called trailers (usually #4 and #5). They cut directly to the blocks on either side, looking for a pass from one of the outside lanes. Trailers often get passes on the blocks from the right or left lane cutters when the defense moves out to cover them on the wings. An example of the fast break is shown in figure 13.3.

239

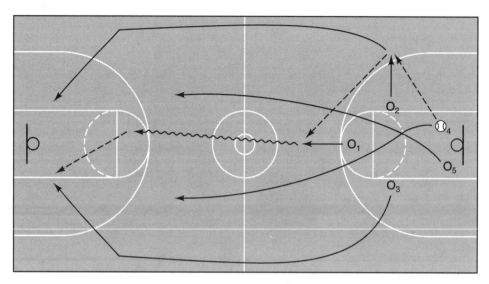

Figure 13.3 Fast break.

ERROR DETECTION AND CORRECTION FOR THE FAST BREAK

Error

Players anticipate a teammate will gain possession, and they run away from the ball to start the fast break before obtaining possession.

Correction

Players must first gain possession of the ball—*before* starting their fast break.

Error

After rebounding, a player is trapped or is in a congested area and unable to make the outlet pass.

Correction

Players should use one or two power dribbles up the middle and then look to pass. A point guard who sees that the rebounder is unable to make the outlet pass should come back to the rebounder to receive a short pass or handoff. They should call out "Ball!" to demand the ball.

Give-and-Go

The give-and-go is the most basic play in basketball. The name comes from the action: One player gives (passes) the ball to a teammate and goes (cuts) to the basket, looking to receive a return pass for a lay-up (see figure 13.4). The give-and-go exemplifies team play. By passing the ball and then moving without it, the player creates an opportunity to score on a return pass. If the player does not get open on the cut, the movement at least gives the teammate a better opportunity to initiate a one-on-one move, because the cutter's defender will be in a less advantageous position to give defensive help.

After a player initiates the give-and-go with a pass (see figure 13.4a), he or she reads the defender's position before cutting to the basket. If the defender moves with the passer, continuing to guard closely, the passer should simply make a hard cut to the basket. If the defender drops off, however, moving toward the ball on your pass, the passer should set the defender up with a fake before cutting (see figure 13.4b). The passer should fake by taking a step or two *away* from the ball, and then, as the defender moves with the passer, the passer should make a sharp cut in front of the defender toward the basket (see figure 13.4c). The passer can also fake by taking a step or two *toward* the ball, then make a sharp cut behind the defender. This is called a *backdoor cut*. The key is for players to read their defenders to know which type of cut—a front cut or a backdoor cut—will be most effective.

Figure 13.4 The give-and-go.

Pick-and-Roll

The pick-and-roll is another basic play that has always been a part of basketball. Its name, like that of the give-and-go, comes from the action of the play. A player sets a pick (screen) for a teammate (see figure 13.5a) who dribbles by it for an outside shot or a drive. The screener then rolls toward the basket (see figure 13.5b), looking for a pass from the dribbler for a lay-up. It's important that the dribbler take at least two dribbles beyond the screen to create space for the pass to the screener who rolls to the basket.

a

Figure 13.5   The pick-and-roll.   b

242

Error

A player doesn't wait for the pick to be set. The player dribbles off the pick while his or her teammate is still moving, causing a foul on the teammate for setting an illegal moving block.

Correction

Players must wait until a legal pick is set and until they have read their defender's position before they use the pick.

Error

As players roll or cut, they do not give a target with their lead hand.

Correction

After making a roll or cut, players should get their lead hand up for a target (see figure 13.6).

Figure 13.6 Players should get their lead hand up for a target after making a cut.

Inbounds Plays

Design most of your inbounds plays to create easy scoring opportunities when your team puts the ball in play from underneath your basket. Keep the plays simple and few. Consider aligning in the same manner for each play, so your players aren't confused about where to position themselves and the defense isn't tipped off by a change in formation.

Two options for offensive inbounds plays are shown in figure 13.7a and b. But you can design your own plays or use some from other coaches. The key is to have a good passer inbound the ball and for the rest of the team to cut hard to their designated spots.

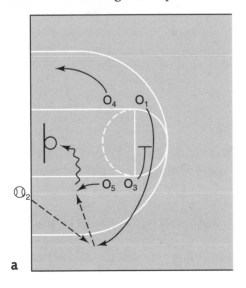

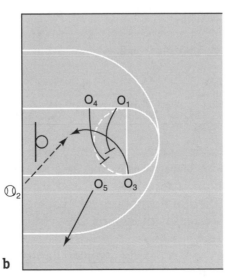

a

b

Figure 13.7 Offensive inbounds plays.

243

Jump Balls

How players are positioned for a jump ball depends on whether your team has the better chance of controlling the tip—that is, winning the jump ball. If the player jumping for you has the advantage, your team should align in an offensive formation and attempt to score off the play (see figure 13.8). If, however, it appears that the opposing team will gain possession, a defensive setup is appropriate (see figure 13.9). The jumper should tip the ball to an open spot where two teammates are next to each other without an opponent in between.

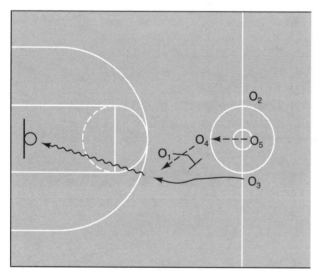

Figure 13.8   Offensive formation for a jump ball.

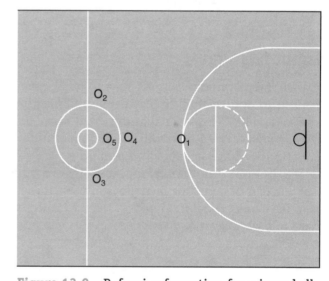

Figure 13.9   Defensive formation for a jump ball.

Defensive Tactics

Playing good defense involves using correct technique and working together with teammates. Good defense inhibits opponents by limiting the number of uncontested shots. Good team defense not only reduces scoring opportunities for the opponents; it opens them to your team.

Teams with less-than-average offensive talent can be successful by playing hard, intelligent team defense. Defense is more consistent than offense because it is based mostly on desire and effort. Players might have an off-game in shooting, but they should never have on off-game on defense, because they control their desire and effort.

In this section we'll focus on three aspects of defensive tactics: defending against screens, cutting off passing lanes, and helping out. Later in the chapter we'll address the individual skills of playing defense on the ball and off the ball.

Defending Against Screens

To defend against screens, players need to communicate and help each other. The defender on the opponent who is setting the screen must alert the defender being screened by calling out the direction of the screen: "Screen right!" or "Screen left!" Three ways to defend against a screen are to fight over the top of the screen, to slide behind it, and to switch.

Fight Over the Top

Players should fight over the top of a screen when there is room for the defender to get between the screener and the screener's teammate. The defender whom the screen was set on should let the teammate know to stay with his or her opponent by shouting "Through!" or "Over!" The defender being screened should work to get through the screen by first getting a foot over the screen and then the remainder of the body (see figure 13.10).

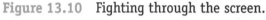

Figure 13.10 Fighting through the screen.

Slide Behind

When an opponent sets a screen on a player guarding a quick driver or when the action is outside the opponent's shooting range (see figure 13.11a), the player being screened should slide behind the screen (see figure 13.11b). In this case the player being screened slides between the screener and the teammate guarding the screener (this teammate should step back to allow the player to slide through).

a   b

Figure 13.11 Sliding behind a screen.

Switch

When teammates are of equal size and defensive ability, they can switch opponents (see figure 13.12a). If size and defensive ability differ, switching should be the last option, as it allows the offense to take advantage of a mismatch. Players who switch should call out the screen by yelling "Switch!" (see figure 13.12b). As players switch, one player must aggressively get in position to deny a pass to the cutter (the screener who rolls to the basket) while the other player gets in position on the ball side of the screener (see figure 13.12c).

a

b

c

Figure 13.12 Defensive switch.

Cutting Off Passing Lanes

The best defensive teams make it difficult for the offense to dribble and pass, much less shoot the ball. However, preventing passes is sometimes difficult.

The key to your players' denial of the opposition's passes is to have the off-ball defenders (those not guarding the ball handler) maintain ball-player-self position (see figure 13.13). Help your players learn to use their peripheral vision so they can see their player and the ball (without turning their heads)

ERROR DETECTION AND CORRECTION FOR DEFENDING AGAINST SCREENS

Error

A player attempts to fight over the top, but gets beat on a quick cut.

Correction

Players should step out into the path of the cutter to delay the cut or force the cutter to veer wide, allowing their teammate time to fight over the top of the screen. Players being screened should work to get a foot over the screen and then the remainder of the body.

Error

A player attempts to slide behind a screen but bumps into a teammate.

Correction

Players should call out the screen and drop back to allow room for their teammate to move between them and the screener, or squeeze so that their teammate can slide behind both the player and the defender.

at all times. When the offense cuts toward the ball, good defenders try to beat them to the spot and cut them off from receiving the pass. Playing good team defense means trying to prevent your opponent from ever receiving the ball!

It's not easy; even pros have difficulty cutting off the passing lanes. Help your players adjust their positioning when their player is one or two passes away from the ball. They'll be a stronger defensive unit if they can understand this concept.

Figure 13.13 Ball-player-self position.

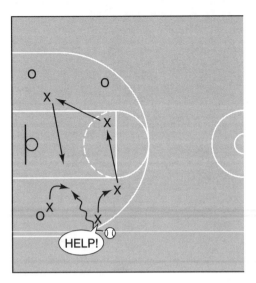

Figure 13.14 "Help" defense.

Helping Out

No matter how well your players position themselves and communicate on defense, an offensive player will at times spring free. Therefore, you must instruct your players on how to respond in these "help" situations.

Your instructions will vary depending on the type of help needed. For example, if one of your players spots an opponent wide open under the basket, waving for a teammate to pass the ball, that defender should leave an assigned opponent who is farther from the basket and sprint to try to prevent the pass. On the other hand, if a dribbler gets by a defender and is headed for a lay-up, the defensive player closest to the dribbler between the dribbler and the basket should immediately move in to cut off the lane to the hoop (see figure 13.14). Whatever the case, the defender who has been beaten, or who loses an offensive player and sees that recovery is impossible, should shout "Help!" All four teammates should be ready to respond if you have effectively taught them this very important defensive tactic.

Individual Skills

This section describes the basketball skills you'll want your players to learn during the season. The skills are categorized as follows:

◎ Footwork

◎ Dribbling

◎ Passing and catching

◎ Shooting

◎ Rebounding

◎ Playing defense

Footwork

Good footwork is important to both offense and defense. Offensive players have the advantage over defenders in knowing what moves they will make and when. Offensive players use footwork to fake a defender off balance, move off screens, cut to the basket, prevent charging into a defender, and to elude a block-out when going for a rebound. Next we'll look at six types of footwork: slides, cuts, pivots, jump stops, jab steps, and drop steps.

Slides

Defenders must be able to slide their feet and maintain an arm's distance from their opponent who is attempting to drive or cut to the basket. Younger players tend to cross their feet when attempting to move sideways. Instruct players to stand in the ready position and then move the leg nearest their intended direction about two feet to that side. Next they should slide the other foot until the feet once again are shoulder-width apart (see figure 13.15a-b). They should use short, quick steps, with their weight evenly distributed on the balls of their feet. Remind players to keep their toes pointed forward and to never cross their feet. They'll be able to slide more quickly if they keep their knees bent, rears down, and backs erect.

a   b

Figure 13.15   Lateral slide.

ERROR DETECTION AND CORRECTION FOR SLIDES

Error

Players cross their feet, preventing themselves from changing direction or moving quickly (see figure 13.16).

Correction

Instruct players to never cross their feet or bring them closer together than shoulder-width apart.

Cuts

The ability to change direction quickly and in balance—to "cut"—is important on both the offensive and the defensive end of the court. Offensive players will have trouble getting open for passes or shots if they cannot "lose" their opponents with quick cuts. Defenders will find it difficult to keep up with effective offensive players if they are unable to respond to various cuts.

Players execute cuts by planting one foot on the court at the end of a slightly shortened stride, then pushing off that foot to shift their momentum in another direction. For example, players push off with the left foot to cut to the right. Then they turn the unplanted foot in the direction they want to go and lead with that leg as they burst toward the new direction. When cutting, players should bend their knees to lower their center of gravity and provide explosiveness to their legs. After cutting, they should get their lead hand up as a target for a pass.

Figure 13.16   Crossing the feet during a lateral slide prevents a player from being able to move quickly.

249

Effective cuts are hard, sharp, and explosive. Three very effective cuts used by offensive players to get open are the L-cut, V-cut, and backdoor cut (see figure 13.17a-c). Players should use an L- or V-cut when a defender has a foot and hand in the passing lane to deny them from catching the ball. In this case, players should take the opponent to the basket, then sharply cut back to the outside. This is the most common way of getting open. Players should look to use a backdoor cut when a defender has a foot and hand in the passing lane to deny a pass from the outside. In this case, players should move to the outside, then quickly cut behind their defender and toward the basket.

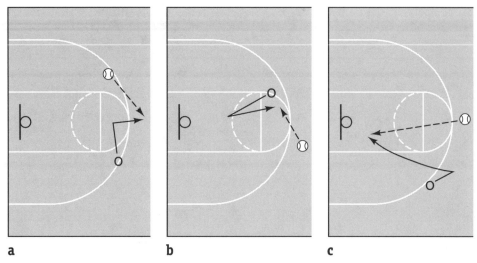

a   b   c

Figure 13.17 Cuts *(a)* L-cut, *(b)* V-cut, *(c)* backdoor cut.

ERROR DETECTION AND CORRECTION FOR CUTS

Error

Players slow up with short steps before cutting and thus are not deceptive.

Correction

Players should focus on a two-count move, stepping first with the inside foot, using a slightly shortened step, and then with the outside foot, without crossing the feet.

Error

Players circle on their cuts, rather than making sharp cuts.

Correction

On the first step, players should take a slightly shortened step, flex their knee to pivot sharply, and push off in the new direction. They should then shift their weight and make a long second step.

Pivots

Along with mastering the jump stop, learning to pivot correctly will give players a lot of confidence in their footwork. A pivot simply involves stopping, then turning on one foot to move forward (front pivot) or dropping one foot backward (back pivot), all while keeping the ball of one foot on the court (see figure 13.18a-b).

Remind players that after using a jump stop they may choose either foot as their pivot foot, but they may not change that pivot foot while in possession of the ball. When attempting a pass or shot, they may lift their pivot foot—providing they release the ball before their pivot foot again hits the floor. Each time they receive the ball, they should assume the ready position, and then they may use their pivot foot to

◎ pivot to protect the ball from the defense,

◎ pivot to pass to a teammate, or

◎ pivot to make a move to the basket.

a   b

Figure 13.18 Proper technique for the pivot.

ERROR DETECTION AND CORRECTION FOR PIVOTING

Error

Players move and switch the pivot foot while in possession of the ball.

Correction

Remind players that once they choose a pivot foot, they cannot lift that foot from or slide it across the floor.

Error

Players lose balance and lift or drag the pivot foot.

Correction

Players should keep their weight on the ball of their pivot foot as they move their nonpivot foot and maintain a balanced stance.

Jump Stops

One of the most common violations that younger players experience is traveling, usually due to poor stopping skills. You'll want to help your players learn how to start and stop with their bodies under control. They need to learn the jump stop so they can stop after moving quickly either with or without the ball.

Figure 13.19 Ready position.

To practice the jump stop, have players begin in the ready position, with arms relaxed and legs bent, feet shoulder-width apart, and weight shifted slightly forward to the balls of the feet (see figure 13.19).

Blow your whistle and have them sprint forward five or six steps. When they hear your whistle the second time, have them hop and stop quickly with both feet simultaneously hitting the floor, landing in a balanced and ready position.

By using the jump stop, players are able to gather and control their forward momentum and may use either foot as a pivot foot for offensive moves. The jump stop is particularly advantageous when players are moving under control without the ball, especially when they receive a pass with their back to the basket in the low-post area (within eight feet of the basket).

Jab Steps

A jab step (also called a *drive step*) is a short (8 to 10 inches), quick step with the nonpivot foot straight toward the defender. The weight should be on the pivot foot, with the knees flexed and the upper body erect. Players use a jab step to fake a drive and force their defender to react with a retreat step.

Drop Steps

The drop step, or reverse turn, is a basic pivoting move for pivoting backward. To perform a drop step, players' backs lead the way as they make a reverse turn. Players should maintain a balanced stance, keep the weight on the ball of their pivot foot, and drop their nonpivot foot back (see figure 13.20a-b).

Dribbling

Dribbling is an integral part of basketball and vital to individual and team play. To maintain possession of the ball while moving, players must dribble (tap or bounce the ball on the floor). At the start of the dribble the ball must leave the hand before the player lifts his or her pivot foot from the floor. Players may not touch the ball simultaneously with both hands while dribbling or allow it to come to a rest in their hand.

Dribbling is the most misused fundamental skill in the game. A pass travels much faster than a dribble, so before they dribble, players should look to pass to an open teammate. If players dribble too much, their teammates will

a   b

Figure 13.20   Proper technique for a drop step.

tend not to move, making the defense's job easier. Excessive dribbling can destroy teamwork and morale. Dribbling should have a purpose: The dribble should take the player somewhere.

The three most common errors in dribbling are slapping at the ball from the chest area and waiting for it to bounce back up; keeping the head down, with eyes riveted to each bounce; and using one hand exclusively to bounce the ball. The ability to dribble with the weak hand as well as the strong hand is a key to advancing a player's level of play. If players only dribble with their strong hand, they can be overplayed to that side and made to be virtually ineffective.

As you correct these dribbling errors and attempt to improve your players' dribbling skills, advise them to

◎ establish a feel for the ball with the pads of the fingers;

◎ maintain the ready position, keeping knees bent and rear down;

◎ keep the dribble under control and always bounce the ball below waist height, and even closer to the floor when being guarded closely;

◎ bounce the ball close to the body and protect the dribble from the defender with the nondribbling hand and arm;

◎ keep the head up and see the rest of the court (and teammates!);

◎ learn how to dribble with the right and left hands; and

◎ keep practicing!

Correct dribbling technique is shown in figure 13.21.

Figure 13.21   Proper dribbling technique.

253

Dribbling Dos and Don'ts

Dos

◉ Keep the dribble "alive" until you have a shot or an open teammate to pass to.

◉ Vary the speed and direction of the dribble so defenders are kept off guard.

◉ Protect the dribble from the defensive player with the nondribbling arm when being closely guarded.

◉ Cross over or switch dribbling hands to protect the ball after dribbling past the defender.

◉ Stay in the middle of the court and away from the sidelines and corners to avoid being trapped.

Don'ts

◉ Don't automatically start dribbling after receiving a pass. Look to see what shooting or passing options are available after squaring up to the basket.

◉ Don't pick up or stop dribbling with no other option (shot or pass) available.

◉ Don't dribble into a crowd—the ball is more likely to be stolen.

◉ Don't try to get fancy when good fundamental dribbling will do the job.

◉ Don't hesitate. Be assertive and confident when dribbling the ball.

There are many types and uses of dribbling. We'll look at three: the power dribble, the crossover dribble, and driving to the basket.

Power Dribble

A power dribble is a hard dribble that brings the ball up high and allows the player to get the ball high and make a move in a close space. It calls on many of the same fundamentals as described earlier for dribbling, combined with an explosive first step toward the basket or in whatever direction the player is dribbling.

The power dribble is most often used on a drive to the basket, but it can also be used to get out of a congested area (such as when rebounding and being surrounded by defenders with no open teammate to pass to). It's important that players using a power dribble keep their head up and see the rim so they can see open teammates and defenders. They should dribble off their finger pads with fingertip control, flexing the wrist and fingers to impart force to the ball without pumping the arm. Figure 13.22 shows a power dribble.

Crossover Dribble

The crossover dribble is important in the open court on a fast break, to get open on a drive to the basket, and to create an opening for a shot. Players should use a crossover dribble when their defender overplays them on the ball side. The effectiveness of the crossover dribble depends on how sharply the dribbler changes direction of the dribble.

Error Detection and Correction for Dribbling

Error

Players look at the ball when they're dribbling.

Correction

Tell players to keep their head up and see the rim.

Error

Players have trouble controlling the dribble.

Correction

Instruct them to use their fingertips for control.

Error

Players don't protect the ball while dribbling; they dribble too high and far away from their body.

Correction

Instruct them to protect the ball by keeping their nondribbling hand up and their body between the ball and the defender. They should dribble at knee level, close to their body.

Figure 13.22 Power dribble.

To execute the crossover dribble, players should cross the ball in front of them at a backward angle, switching the dribble from one hand to the other. They should keep the dribble close to their body and around knee level. As they make the change of direction, players should get their nondribbling hand up and change their lead foot and body position for protection (see figure 13.23a-c).

a   b   c

Figure 13.23   Crossover dribble.

ERROR DETECTION AND CORRECTION FOR THE CROSSOVER DRIBBLE

Error

Players dribble too high or wide as they change direction.

Correction

They should dribble at knee level and close to their body.

Error

Players do not protect the ball as they dribble.

Correction

They should protect the ball with their body and by keeping their nondribbling hand up.

Driving to the Basket

Ball handlers with an opening to the basket should take a longer step past their defender's lead foot, take a long dribble with their outside hand (the hand farthest away from the defender), and drive while keeping their head up and their eyes on the basket (see figure 13.24a). They should drive in a straight line to the basket, close to their defender, cutting off their defender's retreat by closing the gap between themselves and the defender's retreat step (see figure 13.24b). After driving by a defender, players should be alert for defensive help and see the basket. They should finish by going in strong for a lay-up or passing to an open teammate who can score (see figure 13.24c).

a   b   c

Figure 13.24   Proper technique for driving to the basket.

ERROR DETECTION AND CORRECTION FOR DRIVING TO THE BASKET

Error

Players make their drive step too long, or they lean and put weight on their drive-step foot (the right foot for right-handers).

Correction

They should keep their weight on their pivot foot as they execute the drive step. This enables them to move their lead foot quickly to shoot, pass, or drive.

Passing and Catching

Passing and catching are the keys to moving the ball effectively into position to take high-percentage shots. We'll address passing skills first.

Players pass the ball to maintain possession and create scoring opportunities. Passes should usually be short and crisp, because long or slow passes are likely to be stolen. However, players should avoid throwing too hard or using passes that are difficult to control. Players should pass the ball above the waist and within easy reach of the receiver. If possible, passes should be thrown to the receiver's side that is farthest from her or his defender. More skilled players can work on faking a pass one way, then passing another.

Here we'll focus on three types of passes:

◎ Chest pass

◎ Bounce pass

◎ Overhead pass

Chest Pass

Chest passes can be used quickly and accurately from most positions on the floor. The chest pass is so named because the ball is thrown with two hands from the passer's chest to the receiver's chest area. Players should begin in the ready position and step toward their target to initiate the pass (see figure 13.25a). While all players need to see their target, more advanced players should practice seeing their target without looking at it, by looking or faking away before passing. They should step in the direction of the target, extending their legs, backs, and arms. Emphasize forcing the weak hand through the ball; the strong hand tends to dominate (see figure 13.25b). Releasing it off the first and second fingers of both hands gives the ball backspin and direction. Players should follow through with their fingers pointed at the target, palms facing down (see figure 13.25c).

a   b   c

Figure 13.25   Proper technique for a chest pass.

Bounce Pass

Sometimes it is easier for a passer to get the ball to a teammate by bouncing the ball once on the court before it reaches the receiver. For example, a defender may be guarding a player with both hands overhead, preventing a pass through the air to a teammate. In that case a bounce pass may be the only route to get the ball to a teammate. Players should use bounce passes when they are closely guarded and may not have the space to extend their arms in a chest pass.

ERROR DETECTION AND CORRECTION FOR THE CHEST PASS

Error

Your players' chest passes lack force.

Correction

Have them start their pass with their elbows in and force their wrists and fingers through the ball.

Error

Your players' chest passes are not accurate.

Correction

They should point their fingers at the target. The pass will go where their fingers direct it.

Teach players to bounce the ball on the court two-thirds of the way between themselves and the receiver, as illustrated in figure 13.26. Remind them to use their legs and to step toward the target. Snapping their thumbs down and together as they release the pass will give the ball some backspin. Backspin will slow the pass down a little as it hits the floor and gives the receiver a chance to catch the ball at waist level in ready position.

Figure 13.26   Proper technique for a bounce pass.

Overhead Pass

Players use an overhead pass when they are closely guarded and have to pass over their defender—for instance, an outlet pass to start a fast break, or a lob pass to a player cutting backdoor to the basket. The overhead pass is also an option for feeding the low post. Players should start in a balanced stance, holding the ball above their forehead with elbows in and flexed at about 90 degrees (see figure 13.27a). Teach players not to bring the ball behind their heads, because it takes longer to make the pass and the ball is easier to steal in that position. Direct players to step in the direction of the target and extend their legs and back. They should quickly pass the ball, extending their arms and flexing their wrists and fingers, releasing the ball off the first and second fingers of both hands (see figure 13.27b). Follow through ends with fingers pointing at the target, palms facing down.

a   b

Figure 13.27   Proper technique for overhead pass.

ERROR DETECTION AND CORRECTION FOR THE OVERHEAD PASS

Error

Overhead passes lack force.

Correction

Make sure players don't bring the ball behind their head, because this tends to force their elbows out, leading to an incomplete follow-through. They should not break the plane of their body. Force comes from keeping the elbows in, flexing wrists and fingers, and extending legs, back, and arms.

Catching

Even the best passes are of little value if they aren't caught. Sloppy receiving technique is often the cause of turnovers and missed scoring opportunities. Emphasize the following receiving techniques:

◎ Show a target to the passer by putting an arm up or out to the side and call for the ball (see figure 13.28).

◎ Move to meet the pass—step toward the ball, not away.

◎ Watch the ball come into the hands (see figure 13.29).

◎ Use two hands, palms facing the passer, thumbs together.

In most situations after receiving a pass, players should come to a jump stop with their feet positioned shoulder-width apart in ready position. From this position, players should pivot to face the basket, looking for an open teammate, a shot, or a lane to dribble the ball to the basket.

Figure 13.28 The receiver of a pass should put a hand up to give the passer a target.

Figure 13.29 Proper technique for catching a pass.

Figure 13.30 The triple threat position.

Triple Threat Position

The triple threat position is a version of the ready position in which the player holds the ball to the side on the hip, with elbows out (see figure 13.30). This position gives the player the options of either shooting, passing, or dribbling. Such a position makes the defender uncertain of what the ball handler will do, and it gives the ball handler a number of choices.

To keep a defender off guard, players in the triple threat position should move the ball between shooting, passing, and driving positions, keeping it close to their chest and never lower than their waist. Their hands should remain in shooting position: A player must be a threat to shoot before the options of passing or driving become viable.

Shooting

Every player loves to put the basketball through the hoop. So your players will be highly motivated to learn proper shooting technique if you convince them that it will help them make more of their shots.

To get the fundamentals of shooting across and encourage your players to learn them, tell them they'll SCORE if they do these things:

S   Select only high-percentage shots (shots that are likely to go in).

C   Concentrate on their target.

O   Order movements: square up, bend knees and elbows, cock wrist.

R   Release and wave "good-bye" to the ball (have the shooting hand follow through).

E   Extend the shooting arm up and out toward the basket.

Players can shoot the ball in a variety of ways, including set and jump shots, free throws, lay-ups, and shooting off the dribble.

Set and Jump Shots

Although the most common shot at higher levels of play is the jump shot, young players who lack the leg strength and coordination to spring from the floor while shooting will more often shoot set shots. Teach younger players the mechanics of the set shot first, and they will be able to advance to the jump shot as they increase their strength and improve their coordination.

ERROR DETECTION AND CORRECTION FOR THE TRIPLE THREAT POSITION

Error

Players face to the left or right, limiting their moves with the ball in that direction.

Correction

Instruct them to square up to the basket with their body facing the basket and the defender, in a good position to shoot, pass, or drive to the right or the left.

Error

Players lower the ball, limiting their moves to a drive, or they raise the ball above their head, limiting their moves to an overhead pass.

Correction

Players should keep the ball moving close to their chest so they are a triple threat to shoot, pass, or drive.

Teach your players these shooting mechanics in this sequence:

1. *Lay the ball on the finger pads of each hand*, with the shooting hand behind and slightly underneath the ball and the nonshooting hand balancing the ball from the side.

2. *Focus on a specific target*, usually the rim or backboard. The middle of the rim should be the target for most shots, but when at a 30- to 60-degree angle from the hoop, sight the corner of the square on the backboard for a bank shot (see figure 13.31a).

3. *Align shoulders, hips, and feet square with (facing) the basket.* The foot on the shooting-hand side can be up to 6 inches in front of the other foot so that the base of support is comfortable and balanced.

4. *Bend the knees to get momentum for the shot.* Let the legs, not the arms, be the primary power source for the shot.

5. *Bend the shooting-arm elbow to approximately a 90-degree angle*, keeping the forearm perpendicular to the floor and in front of the cocked wrist as the ball is brought up to the shooting position above the forehead (see figure 13.31b).

6. *As you extend the legs, release the ball* by extending the elbow, bringing the wrist forward, and moving the fingers of the shooting hand up and through the ball (see figure 13.31c). The nonshooting arm and hand should maintain their supportive position on the side of the ball until after the release.

7. *Follow through after the release* by landing on both feet, extending the shooting arm and dropping the wrist, pointing the index finger of the shooting hand directly at the basket.

a   b   c

Figure 13.31   Proper technique for a set shot.

Check that your players aren't shooting "line drives" at the hoop. Help them to see how important proper arc is in allowing the shot a reasonable chance to go in. Remind them to shoot the ball up, then out, toward the basket.

A jump shot is similar to shooting a set shot except for two adjustments:

◎ You align the ball higher and shoot after jumping, rather than shooting with the simultaneous extension of your legs; and

◎ Because you jump first and then shoot, your upper body, arm, wrist, and fingers must generate more force.

Players should jump straight up off both feet, fully extending their ankles, knees, back, and shoulders (see figure 13.32). The height of the jump depends on the range of the shot. On shots close to the basket when they are closely guarded, players will have to jump higher than their defenders. On longer-range jump shots, players usually have more time and defenders are not quite as close. Therefore players don't have to jump as high for long-range shots. More force from the legs can be used for shooting the ball rather than for jumping high. Balance and control are more important than gaining maximum height on a jump. Smooth rhythm and complete follow-through are also important.

Figure 13.32   Proper technique for a jump shot.

Error Detection and Correction for Shooting Set and Jump Shots

Error

Shots are short.

Correction

Players should generate more force from their legs. They may also need to speed up their rhythm or make it more even-paced.

Error

Shots are long.

Correction

Players need to put more arc into the ball. Their shoulders should be relaxed and in a forward position; they should move their hands closer together if they are too far apart; and they should raise their shooting arm higher to provide more arc.

Error

Shots hit the sides of the rim.

Correction

Players should square up to the basket, setting the ball on the shooting side of their head between their ear and shoulder with their elbow in. Their shooting arm, wrist, and fingers should go straight toward the basket.

Free Throws

Success in free-throw shooting requires sound mechanics, a routine, relaxation, rhythm, concentration, and confidence. Routine, relaxation, and rhythm contribute to concentration and confidence.

A routine helps players relax, focus, and shoot with confidence and rhythm. A routine can include a set number of dribbles, checking mechanics, using visualization to practice mentally shooting the free throw just before shooting it, and taking a deep breath to relax (see figure 13.33). The same form as described for the set shot should be used for free throws.

Figure 13.33 Having a routine before a free throw helps a player relax, focus, and shoot with confidence.

Figure 13.34 Proper technique for a lay-up.

Lay-Ups

The highest percentage shot, and therefore the most desirable shot, is a lay-up. A lay-up is a one-handed shot taken within 3 feet of the basket (see figure 13.34). Teach players to use their left hands when shooting lay-ups from the left side of the basket and their right hands when shooting from the right side of the basket. The lay-up motion begins with the player striding from a 45- to 60-degree angle to the hoop and planting and exploding—much like a high jumper—off the foot opposite the shooting hand. The player explodes off the planted foot straight up into the air. At the top of the jump, the player releases the ball by bringing the shooting hand, which is underneath the ball and near the shoulder, up toward the basket. As in the set shot, the index finger of the shooting hand should be pointed directly at the basket or the appropriate spot on the backboard.

Your right-handed players are likely to find left-handed lay-ups troublesome, just as your left-handed players are going to find right-handed lay-ups difficult. Point out to them the reason for using the hand farthest from the basket to shoot the ball: The ball is more easily protected.

ERROR DETECTION AND CORRECTION FOR SHOOTING LAY-UPS

Error

Players swivel the ball to the side before shooting, allowing it to be blocked or stolen.

Correction

Instruct them to lift the ball straight up as they shoot.

Error

The ball hits low on the backboard and, with slight contact on the arm, falls short.

Correction

Players should shoot high off the backboard so the ball drops in the basket. This way, even if they are fouled on the shot, the ball will have a chance to go in.

Shooting Off a Dribble

When shooting off a dribble, players should pick up the ball facing the basket in position to shoot. They shouldn't reach for the ball, but should pick it up in front of their shooting knee with the knees flexed to gain balance for the shot.

When players are dribbling to their strong-hand side, they should jump behind their last dribble and pick the ball up in front of their shooting knee. When players are dribbling to their weak-hand side, they should use a crossover dribble on their last dribble to pick the ball up in front of their shooting knee.

ERROR DETECTION AND CORRECTION FOR SHOOTING OFF A DRIBBLE

Error

Players float forward, backward, or to a side when shooting.

Correction

Have them pick the ball up in front of their shooting knee with their knees flexed to gain balance for the shot.

Rebounding

Possession of the ball comes more often from missed shots than any other way. The team that controls the backboards usually controls the game. Offensive rebounding adds to your team's chances to score, and defensive rebounding limits your opponent's scoring opportunities.

More than any other basketball skill, rebounding relies on a player's desire and courage. Good rebounders are also able to anticipate missed shots, determining how hard or how soft, or to what side of the rim, the ball will rebound. They also know where their opponents are at all times, and are able to "box out" their opposing player by getting between the opposing player and the basket and putting their rear in contact with the opponent's body (see Figure 13.35).

Players may use a front or rear pivot to turn and box out their opponent. A front pivot allows the defense to turn while watching the offense move toward the rebound. A rear pivot is used to move into the path of the offense without the same visual contact. Encourage defenders to use whichever method gets them in position in front of the offense, sealing the offensive player away from the basket.

Figure 13.35 Boxing out.

Players should avoid reaching over an opponent when they get boxed out; they'll get called for a foul if they do. Emphasize the importance of jumping straight up for the rebound. Not only will a vertical jump achieve greater height, but players will avoid needless fouls if they go straight up.

Here are some additional rebounding tips to share with your players:

◎ A shot taken from the side is likely to rebound to the opposite side of the basket. Therefore, players should try to get positioned on the opposite side of the basket when such a shot is taken.

◎ Once contact is established with an opposing player, the defensive rebounder wants to maintain that contact until releasing to jump for the rebound.

◎ After controlling a rebound, players should keep the ball at chin level with their elbows out (see figure 13.36).

Use the following guidelines in coaching your players to rebound free throws:

◎ Have your best rebounders in the positions closest to the basket.

◎ Remind players to block out the players next to them when the opposing team is shooting.

◎ Designate a player to block out the shooter when the opposing team is shooting.

Figure 13.36 Proper position after controlling a rebound.

◎ Have one player near midcourt when your team is shooting, to prevent easy fast breaks by the opponents.

ERROR DETECTION AND CORRECTION FOR REBOUNDING

Error

Your players watch the ball, and their opponents gain position for the rebound.

Correction

Instruct players to locate their opponent first, get inside position, block out, and then go for the ball.

Error

Players have trouble holding onto rebounds.

Correction

They need to catch it firmly with two hands.

Error

After gaining rebounds, your players have the ball stripped by an opponent.

Correction

They must protect the ball, keeping it above their forehead, with their elbows out and away from their opponent.

Playing Defense

Individual defensive skills are sometimes less appreciated than individual offensive techniques, but they are just as important. Your players need to learn the basics of player-to-player defense, both on the ball and off the ball, to compete successfully.

On the Ball

Defenders can best keep their opponents with the ball from scoring by staying between them and the basket. Defenders should try to maintain an arm's distance from the offensive player with the ball.

Tell your players to consider these things about their bodies and court positions when guarding a player with the ball:

◎ Body position

—Am I in ready position and alert?

—Am I arm's distance from my player with the ball and able to put pressure on his or her ability to shoot, pass, or drive?

◎ Court position

—Is my player close enough to attempt a good shot?

—Am I close enough to the player to prevent an easy shot?

—Am I too close, so the opponent can drive around me?

—Will a teammate be able to help me if the player beats me with the dribble?

269

a

Have your players focus on their opponent's midsection (see figure 13.37a). If defenders watch the ball or their opponent's head or feet, they are likely to react to a fake that will put them out of position. As the offensive player begins to dribble, the defender should react by sliding the feet and maintaining an arm's distance from the opponent, trying to beat the offensive player to the spot that the player wants to reach (see figure 13.37b). If the defender can get the offensive player to stop and pick up the ball, the defender can then move closer and crowd the offensive player by blocking the passing lanes, applying extensive pressure with the arms (see figure 13.37c).

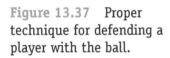

Figure 13.37 Proper technique for defending a player with the ball.

b

c

More advanced defenders can focus on four defensive strategies when playing defense on the ball:

◉ **Turning the dribbler.** Defenders who establish position a half body ahead of the dribbler can force the dribbler to turn or reverse direction.

◉ **Forcing the dribbler to the sideline.** By forcing the dribbler to dribble toward the sideline, the dribbler can pass in only one direction. Defenders can do this by working for position a half body to the inside of the court, with the inside foot (the one closer to the middle of the court) forward and the outside foot back.

◉ **Funneling the dribbler to the middle.** By taking position a half body to the outside of the court, a defender can force a dribbler to the middle. This strategy will move the dribbler toward one of the defender's teammates off the ball.

◎ **Forcing the dribbler to use the weak hand.** By overplaying the strong hand, defenders can force the dribbler to use the weak hand. Defenders can overplay the strong hand by being a half body to the dribbler's strong-hand side.

Off the Ball

Defending an opponent without the ball is just as important as guarding a player with the ball, but it is a bit more complicated. Whether an opponent is one pass or two passes away from the ball, defensive players need to apply the defensive concept of ball-player-self (see figure 13.38). Defenders should position themselves so they can see the ball (and know if they need to come and help a teammate on a pass or drive), and they must keep track of a moving opponent (their player) who may be trying to get open to receive a pass. The closer an opponent is to the ball, the closer the defender should be to that opponent. The farther the ball is from an opponent, the farther away a defender can play that opponent and be able to give help to the teammate guarding the ball.

Figure 13.38 Proper positioning for defending a player off the ball.

ERROR DETECTION AND CORRECTION FOR GUARDING OFF THE BALL

Error

Defenders off the ball lose track of their offensive player.

Correction

Position players to see the ball and their player without turning their head. They should establish and maintain the ball-player-self relationship. Have players point at the ball with one hand and their player with the other. Players must adjust positions as the offensive player or ball changes position. A player two or more passes away needs to be alert to help out on a drive or deflect a long pass attempt to their opponent in the corner (see figure 13.39).

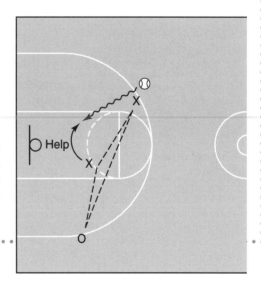

Figure 13.39 Proper ball-player-self positioning.

Denial Position.   Players should use the denial position when their opponent is one pass away from the ball. The space between two offensive players where a pass can be made is called the *passing lane*. A defender wants to have an arm and leg in the passing lane when guarding a player who is one pass away (see figure 13.40). This denial position allows the defender to establish the ball-player-self relationship and discourages the offensive player with the ball from attempting a pass.

Open Position.   When offensive players are two or more passes away from the ball, the defensive player wants to establish an *open position* that still maintains the ball-player-self relationship. In the open position the defender is farther away from the offensive player, pointing to the ball with one hand and the opponent with the other hand (see figure 13.41). Using peripheral vision, the defender moves to react as the ball penetrates toward the basket (to help out on the drive) or into denial position if the offensive player cuts hard to receive a pass. In both the denial and open positions, the key is remembering always to maintain the ball-player-self relationship.

Figure 13.40 Denial position.

Figure 13.41 Open position.

Teaching Basketball Rules and Traditions

This is where we'll introduce you to some of the basic rules and traditions of basketball. We won't try to cover all the rules of the game, but rather we'll give you what you need to work with players who are 8 to 13 years old. Some of the rules we'll be explained just so you understand the game better; those that should be taught to your players have been incorporated into the practice plans. We'll give you information on equipment, court size and markings, player positions, actions to start and restart the game, fouls, violations, and scoring. We'll recommend rules modifications to make the sport more appropriate for youngsters. In a short section we'll show you the officiating signals for basketball. We also will talk briefly about a few of the "unwritten rules," or traditions, of basketball, those that good players follow to be courteous and safe.

Equipment, Court, and Game Length

Basketball requires very little player equipment. Players should wear basketball shoes so they have proper traction on the court. They should wear clothing such as athletic shorts and tank tops or loose-fitting shirts so they have the freedom of movement needed to run, jump, and shoot. Players may choose to wear safety glasses or goggles to protect their eyes from injury. Also, if desired, players who have conditions affecting the knees or elbows may want to wear soft pads to protect them. Players may *not* wear jewelry during games.

In table 14.1 we present rules that cover many of the basics of the game.

TABLE 14.1

Rules Modifications for Basketball

	8- to 9-year-olds	10- to 11-year-olds	12- to 13-year-olds
Players on team	9	9	9
Ball size	Junior (#5)	Women's (#6)	Regulation (#7)
Court size	Short court	Short court	Full court
Free-throw distance	9 ft	9 ft	12 to 15 ft
Game length*	24 min	24 min	32 min
Time-outs	4	4	4
Players on court	5 v 5	5 v 5	5 v 5
Basket height	7 ft	8 ft	9 to 10 ft

*Many leagues run the clock continuously. In such cases, instead of playing, for example, a 12-minute half and stopping the clock, you might play a 16- to 20-minute half without stopping the clock.

Figure 14.1 shows standard basketball court markings.
Several areas of the court are referred to with special basketball terminology:

◎ *Frontcourt* refers to the half of the court where your team's offensive basket is located.

◎ *Backcourt* includes the midcourt line and the half of the court where your opponent's basket is located.

◎ The *three-second lane* is an area that extends from the baseline under the basket to the free-throw line; it's also called the *key*. The semicircle that extends beyond the free-throw line designates the *top of the key*.

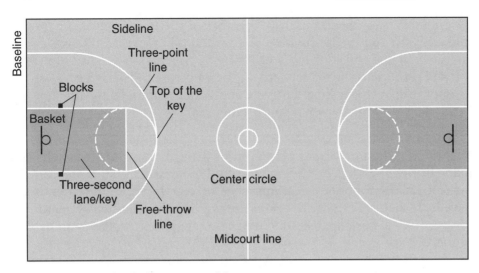

Figure 14.1 Basketball court markings.

◎ The area outside the three-second lane area is called the *perimeter*.

◎ The *three-point line* marks a semicircle that is 19 feet, 9 inches from the basket at all points. Shots that are made from behind this line count for three points instead of two.

◎ The square markings six feet from the baseline on each side of the lane are referred to as the *blocks*.

 ## Player Positions

Basketball is usually played with five players on a team. Some leagues for 8- and 9-year-olds might consider playing 3 v 3 or 4 v 4, and some leagues for 10- and 11-year-olds might consider playing 4 v 4. We do recommend that 12- and 13-year-olds play 5 v 5 in competitions. Each player is assigned a position, which is often referred to by number (1 through 5). The types of positions are guard, forward, and center.

◎ **Guards.** Guards usually are the best ball handlers and outside shooters on the team. They tend to be shorter and quicker than the other players and have good dribbling and passing skills. Guards play farthest from the basket, on the perimeter.

A basketball team usually has two guards in the game at all times. The point guard, who is in the #1 position, is played by the team's best dribbler and passer. The second guard is the off-guard, who is in the #2 position. He or she is often the team's best long-range shooter and second-best dribbler.

◎ **Forwards.** Forwards typically are taller than guards and play closer to the basket. They should be able to shoot the ball accurately from within 12 feet of the basket and rebound the ball when shots are missed.

A team usually plays with two forwards in its lineup. The small forward (also referred to as the wing) is in the #3 position. This position often is filled by the most versatile and athletic member of the team. The small forward must be able to play in the lane and on the perimeter on offense, and to guard small and quick or big and strong opponents on defense. The other forward position is the big forward, or the #4 position. This is a good spot to assign to one of your bigger players and better rebounders—who can also shoot the ball from anywhere in the lane area.

◎ **Center.** The center, or #5 position (also called the *post position*), is frequently the tallest or biggest player on the team. That extra size is helpful in maneuvering for shots or rebounds around the basket. A tall center can also make it difficult for opposing teams to shoot near the basket. A center should have "soft" hands to catch the passes thrown into the lane area by guards and forwards. Most basketball teams designate one player on the court as their center.

 ## Starting and Restarting the Game

In regulation play, a jump ball at center court is used to start games and overtime periods, which are played when teams are tied at the end of regulation time. During jump balls, the official tosses up the ball between two players, usually each team's center or best leaper. Each player attempts to tip the ball to a teammate (who must be outside of the center circle) to gain possession of the ball. Another jump ball situation is simultaneous possession of the ball by players from opposing teams. In this case, teams alternate possession; the team that did not win the first jump ball takes the ball out of bounds in the next jump ball situation.

Play stops during intermissions and time-outs, but also when the ball goes out of bounds and when an official calls a violation or a foul. The clock restarts when the ball is touched following an inbounds pass or a missed free throw.

 ## Fouls

Basketball is a contact sport, with players in close proximity and in constant motion. The rules of the game discourage rough play or tactics that allow a team to gain an advantage through brute force. Therefore, fouls are called when officials see illegal physical contact between two or more players based on these general principles:

◎ The first player to establish position (to become stationary or set) on the court has priority rights to that position.

◎ A body part cannot be extended into the path of an opponent.

◎ The player who moves into the path of an opponent—especially an airborne opponent—when contact occurs is responsible for the contact.

◎ All players have the right to the space extending straight up from their feet on the floor. This is called the *principle of verticality.*

Types of Fouls

Based on the general principles concerning player contact, these specific fouls are called in a regulation game:

- *Blocking*—physically impeding the progress of another player who is still moving.
- *Charging*—running into or pushing a defender who is stationary.
- *Hand-checking*—using the hands to check the progress of an offensive player when that player is in front of the defender who is using the hands.
- *Holding*—restricting the movement of an opponent.
- *Illegal screen*—a form of blocking in which the player setting the screen is still moving when the defender makes contact.
- *Over-the-back*—infringing on the vertical plane of, and making contact with, a player who is in position and attempting to rebound.
- *Pushing*—impeding the progress or otherwise moving a player by pushing or shoving.
- *Reaching in*—extending an arm and making contact with a ball handler in an attempt to steal the ball.
- *Tripping*—extending a leg or foot and causing an opponent to lose balance or fall.

The fouls just described are called *personal fouls*. This list covers most common ones, although there are others. Another type of foul is a *shooting foul*, in which a defender makes contact with a player who is shooting the basketball. Emphasize to your players the importance of keeping hands off the shooter, establishing position, using the feet to maintain position rather than reaching in with the hands, and not attempting to rebound over an opponent who has established position.

Other types of fouls exist, such as a *technical foul;* this is a foul that does not involve contact with the opponent while the ball is alive (use of profanity, delay of game, unsporting conduct).

Intentional and *flagrant fouls* relate to extreme behaviors by players and should hopefully not come up with YMCA Winners players. If they do, we recommend that players who are guilty of unsporting conduct during a game be ejected, assessed a technical foul, and counseled by the coach. In such a case the opposing team should be awarded two free throws and possession of the ball.

Consequences of Fouls

A team that fouls too much pays for it. Fouls carry with them increasingly severe penalties. A player who has five fouls is taken out of the game. In regulation play, a team that has more than a specified number of fouls in a quarter or half gives the opposing team a bonus situation: the member of the team who was fouled is allowed to shoot free throws. If the foul is a nonshooting foul, the player shoots one free throw and, if he or she makes it, shoots a second one (this is called *one-and-one*). If the foul is made during shooting, then the player shoots two free throws.

Table 14.2 lists the types of fouls and their consequences.

TABLE 14.2

Fouls and Consequences

Type of foul	Team fouled in bonus?	Penalty
Shooting	Yes/No	Two free throws
Personal	No	Ball out of bounds
Personal	Yes	One-and-one free throws

Violations

The turnovers—the loss of the ball to the defense—caused by violations will be one of your continuing frustrations as a basketball coach. Violations can be categorized as ballhandling violations and clock violations.

Here are common violations committed by ball handlers:

◎ *Double dribble*—resuming dribbling after having stopped (when no defender interrupts the player's possession of the ball) or dribbling with both hands at the same time.

◎ *Over-and-back*—the return of the ball to the backcourt when last touched by an offensive player in the frontcourt.

◎ *Traveling*—taking more than one step without dribbling; also called *carrying the ball* or *palming the ball,* as a player turns the ball a complete rotation in the hand between dribbles.

Here are common clock violations:

◎ *Inbounds*—on any inbounds play the thrower-in has 5 seconds to release the ball.

◎ *Lane*—an offensive player cannot be in the lane (in the key) for more than 3 seconds at a time.

◎ *Backcourt*—a team must advance the ball into its frontcourt within 10 seconds after gaining possession in the backcourt.

◎ *Shot clock*—the ball must leave an offensive player's hands before the shot clock expires. The ball must subsequently hit the rim on that shot or it will be a violation.

Table 14.3 shows our recommendations for modifying the rules for these violations.

TABLE 14.3

Modified Rules for Violations

Violation	8- to 9-year-olds	10- to 11-year-olds	12- to 13-year-olds
Double dribble	Allow one violation per player possession; gradually tighten up this allowance.	Allow one violation per player possession; gradually tighten up this allowance.	Call.
Over-and-back	Don't call.	Don't call.	Call.
Traveling	Give an extra step for starting and stopping; gradually tighten up this allowance.	Given an extra step for starting and stopping; gradually tighten up this allowance.	Call.
Inbounds (5-sec)	Don't call.	Give warnings early in season; call after mid-season.	Call.
Lane (3-sec)	Don't call.	Give warnings early in season; call after mid-season.	Call.
Backcourt (10-sec)	Don't call.	Give warnings early in season; call after mid-season.	Call.
Shot clock	Don't use.	Don't use.	Don't use.

Table 14.4 shows modified rules for defensive play.

TABLE 14.4

Modified Rules for Defensive Play

Defense may . . .	8- to 9-year-olds	10- to 11-year-olds	12- to 13-year-olds
Use player-to-player defense	Yes	Yes	Yes
Use zone defense	No	No	No
Use full-court press	No	No	No
Strip ball handler of ball	No	Yes	Yes
Draw charges	No	No	Yes

 ## Scoring

In regulation play, teams are awarded 2 points for every field goal inside the three-point line, and 3 points for shots made beyond the three-point stripe. A successful free throw is worth 1 point. (Players may not enter the lane until the free throw has hit the rim. If the free throw doesn't hit the rim, the ball is awarded to the opposing team out of bounds.) The team that scores the most points over the course of the game is the winner.

 ## Officiating

Games are officiated by one or two officials who should know the rules and enforce them to ensure a safe, fair, and fun contest. Officials should also require good sporting behavior from all players and coaches. You can be a big help to officials by respecting their efforts and emphasizing to your players the need to play with respect for the rules.

Figure 14.2a-t shows some common officiating signals. Familiarize yourself with these signals and explain them to your players.

Figure 14.2 Officiating signals for *(a)* starting clock, *(b)* stopping clock for jump ball, *(c)* beckoning a sub in on dead ball, *(d)* stopping clock for foul, *(e)* scoring one point, *(f)* scoring two points, *(g)* scoring three points, *(h)* blocking.

(continued)

Figure 14.2 *(continued)*   Officiating signals for *(i)* bonus situation, *(j)* over-and-back or carrying the ball, *(k)* pushing, *(l)* illegal use of hands, *(m)* technical foul, *(n)* three-second violation, *(o)* designating out-of-bounds spot.

(continued)

Figure 14.2 *(continued)* Officiating signals for *(p)* traveling, *(q)* holding, *(r)* no score, *(s)* illegal dribble, *(t)* hand check.

 ## Basketball Traditions

YMCA Winners basketball players need to know a couple of "unwritten laws" for basketball, both of which are based on the core values of caring, honesty, respect, and responsibility. First, players should raise their hands if they know they've fouled someone. Admitting when you've committed a foul is an example of being honest. Second, players should play cooperatively with those on their team and should show respect to their opponents. This is showing respect for others. They should shake hands with their opponents after the game to thank them for playing hard and providing a good game. Players usually line up on the sideline next to the benches to shake hands with each other.

Teaching Fitness

One of our long-term goals in having young people play any sport in YMCA Youth Super Sports is for them to learn to enjoy not just that sport, but to enjoy physical activity and to appreciate the value of being physically fit. As a basketball coach, your short-term goal is to get your players fit to play the game. Your long-term goal is to help your players appreciate basketball as a physical activity that they can do for a very long time to stay fit.

One of your responsibilities as a coach is to get your players in shape to play the game. When your players are not fit, their fatigue leads to more errors and they are more likely to get injured. Playing basketball will help your players get fit, but your players can further improve their fitness through specific training apart from the practice setting. In this chapter we'll show you how to guide that training.

An old coaching tradition was to use fitness activities like running and push-ups as punishment when players made errors or misbehaved. Thank goodness that tradition is almost dead, because it certainly doesn't develop an appreciation for physical activity for a lifetime. Make practice and playing games fun, and you'll achieve both our short-term and long-term fitness goals.

Because we want to help young people develop an appreciation for physical activity and fitness, we not only want you to make practice fun, but we want you to teach your players the principles of fitness. In addition, we want you to educate them about other healthy habits. We'll explore these principles and habits in this chapter.

Cardiorespiratory Fitness

As you might guess from its name, *cardiorespiratory fitness* is fitness of the heart (cardio) and circulatory system as well as the lungs (respiratory). It's also known as *aerobic fitness, endurance,* or *stamina.* Cardiorespiratory fitness involves storing and using fuels to power muscle contractions.

Training for aerobic fitness helps toughen ligaments, tendons, and connective tissue and reduces the risk of injury while developing the toughness and endurance needed for more intense training. Good aerobic training includes these components:

- Low-intensity, long-duration activity (running, bicycling, swimming)
- Natural intervals (medium distance with occasional periods of increased intensity)
- Resistance effort (such as hills in running) once a week

As endurance grows, you can increase the aerobic overload with greater distance or intensity.

In working to improve your athletes' aerobic foundation, remember that prepubescent athletes differ from young adults in several respects. Whether or not their aerobic fitness is low, they are less efficient and less able to withstand high temperatures. Therefore, intense aerobic training can be more difficult and risky, especially in hot weather. And while training of aerobic energy pathways is less effective before puberty, aerobic training provides neuromuscular benefits, helping athletes relax and become more efficient, using less energy to cover the distance. So prepubescent athletes can do aerobic training, but it shouldn't be hard training until they've reached puberty.

 Muscular Strength and Endurance

Muscular fitness includes strength, endurance, power, speed, and flexibility. We'll focus here on two components of muscular fitness: muscular strength and muscular endurance.

Muscular strength is the ability of a muscle to exert force against resistance, such as a weight. Strength improves when a muscle is overloaded. Prior to puberty, the difference between boys and girls is small, but at puberty boys increase in strength more rapidly because they add more muscle tissue than girls do.

Muscular endurance is the ability of a muscle to exercise for an extended period of time without too much fatigue. Muscular endurance is developed through repeated use of the movement for which it is needed—that is, to develop muscular endurance, players should practice a skill repeatedly. Performing a skill in practice more often than it's called on in a game will help build muscular endurance.

Prepubescent athletes can increase their strength, enhance their motor skills, and improve their athletic performance through resistance training without significant injury risk. In fact, a properly designed resistance training program can help *prevent* injuries, and it can improve the psychological and social well-being of youngsters, as well as enhance their overall health. The YMCA of the USA Medical Advisory Committee recommends the following:

◎ Strength-training facilities should be made available to youth under the age of 16 only with adult supervision and proper training for youth.

◎ Youth strength-training programs and facilities should be integrated to include education and activities that reflect the YMCA's commitment to the health and fitness of spirit, mind, and body.

◎ Youth strength-training programs should include all components of fitness.

◎ The strength-training component of a youth fitness program should concentrate on muscular endurance with the use of low weights and high repetitions.

 Flexibility

Flexibility involves the joints and muscles. It is the ability of the muscles around a joint to allow the joint its full range of motion. Being flexible makes movement easier. The way to gain flexibility is to stretch—which your players will be doing at the beginning and end of each practice. Figures 15.1 through 15.10 illustrate stretches to incorporate into your practices and your warm-ups for contests. For all stretches, use these guidelines:

◎ Warm up with 5 to 10 minutes of low-intensity aerobic activity (this is built into your practice plans).

◎ Perform two repetitions of each stretch.

◎ Stretch to the point of a gentle pull, then hold 10 counts without bouncing.

◎ For cooldowns, walk around to allow the heart and breathing rates to return to normal.

◎ Then perform three to five repetitions of each stretch before the muscles cool.

Figure 15.1 Shoulder stretch.

Figure 15.2 Triceps stretch.

Figure 15.3 Elbow and forearm stretch.

Figure 15.4 Quadriceps stretch.

Figure 15.5 Iliotibial band stretch.

Figure 15.6 Hamstring stretch.

Figure 15.7 Hip flexor stretch.

Figure 15.8 Calf stretch.

Figure 15.9 Trunk stretch.

Figure 15.10 Lower back stretch.

Training Principles

Knowing the following principles of training will help you work with players at the YMCA Winners age levels:

◎ The warm-up and cooldown principle

◎ The overload principle

◎ The reversibility principle

◎ The specificity principle

The Warm-Up and Cooldown Principle

Before beginning strenuous activity, players should perform some moderate warm-up activity that will increase body temperature, respiration, and heart rate and help prevent muscle and tendon strains and ligament sprains. We have built warm-up games and activities into the practice plans for you, followed by stretching.

Once strenuous activity is over, players should then slow down gradually with a cooldown activity. Stopping heavy activity abruptly can cause blood to pool in the legs and feet and can slow the removal of waste products created by muscle use. Light activity such as jogging or walking and then stretching helps to keep blood circulating.

The Overload Principle

Luckily for us, our bodies are very adaptable. We can present them with a workload a bit higher than what we've done before, and they will, over time, adapt to it. Each time our bodies adapt, we can then add more to what we've done before. This is how we can improve our fitness.

Overloading the body can be done in three different ways:

◎ *Frequency*—doing an activity more often;

◎ *Intensity*—doing an activity harder; and

◎ *Time*—doing an activity longer.

To remember these methods of overloading, think of the acronym FIT. Increasing one or more of these aspects of activity or exercise will put a heavier load on the body.

The FIT principle can be used in all kinds of training. One player might increase her number of sit-ups and push-ups as she grows stronger, adding intensity. Another might add more minutes of jogging or running. Either one might choose to exercise more often during the week, increasing the frequency.

Overloading stimulates the body to make changes. Such changes involve the nervous system, which becomes able to recruit more muscle fibers; the circulation, which becomes better at distributing the blood to the working muscles; and the muscles, which produce new protein to meet working demands.

One caution about overloads—don't increase them too quickly, or you could cause injuries. A gradual approach is always safer.

290

The Reversibility Principle

To state this principle briefly: Use it or lose it! Just as the body can make adaptations when given an overload, it can also lose its capabilities when it is not used. It takes three times as long to gain endurance as it does to lose it. If you stayed in bed for a week, you would lose nearly 10 percent of your fitness. Your strength would also decline, although not as fast. This is why you want to encourage your players to be active, both during and after the basketball season.

The Specificity Principle

This principle simply means that the type of training a person chooses to do should relate to his or her goal. For example, heavy weight training will not make a runner run faster. Bicycling will not improve swimming performance as much as additional swimming would. Performance improves most when the training done is specific to the desired activity.

 # Healthy Habits

In addition to getting your players physically fit, we want you to help your players appreciate other healthy habits. These habits include eating well, managing stress, staying active year-round, and staying away from tobacco, alcohol, and other drugs.

Eating Well

Disordered eating and unhealthy dietary habits are problems for youngsters as well as adults. Let players and parents know the importance of healthy eating and the dangers that can arise from efforts to lose weight too quickly. Players need to supply their bodies with the extra energy they need to keep up with the demands of practices and games. Ask your YMCA Youth Super Sports director about information that you can pass on to your players and their parents, and include a discussion of basic, common-sense nutrition in your parent-orientation meeting.

Good nutrition is not the first thing most of your players think about when they choose foods. At this age, they may not even know which foods are good for them and which are not. You can start to make them aware of which foods will make them healthier and why good nutrition is important.

A simple guide for a good diet is the U.S. Department of Agriculture's food pyramid (see figure 15.11). This is a guide that encourages us to eat lots of breads, cereals, rice, pasta, vegetables and fruits; a smaller amount of meat, cheese, eggs, dried beans, or nuts; and only a very little bit of fats, oils, and sweets. Eating this way cuts down on the amount of fats in the diet and helps ensure an adequate amount of vitamins and minerals.

A serving of the foods in each of these groups is equal to the following:

◎ 1/2 cup of fruit or vegetables

◎ 3/4 cup of juice

◎ 1 slice of bread

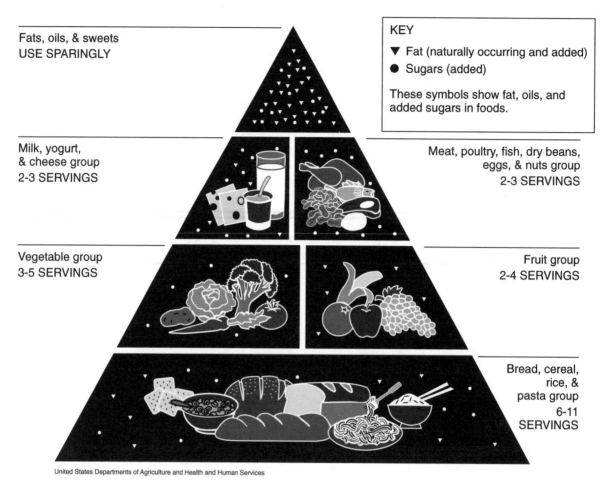

Figure 15.11   The food guide pyramid.

◎ 1 cup of milk

◎ 1 average piece of fruit

◎ 1 cup of salad greens

◎ 1/2 cup of cooked pasta

◎ Lean meat about the size of a deck of cards

The number of servings your players should eat depends on their age, height, weight, and level of physical activity. One exception is milk; kids need to have three milk group servings a day.

Managing Stress

Stress is not something that is reserved only for adults; kids feel stress too. However, what's stressful for one player may not be stressful for another. Why? Stress is not caused directly by a demanding situation, but by how the person interprets the situation. For instance, your next game is against a tough team that will be hard to beat. Derek, one of your players, is excited and looking forward to the challenge. Derek's teammate Sam is nervously anticipating it, worried about both individual and team performance. He hasn't been playing well lately. His Aunt Kristi is going to be at the game. The other team has bigger kids. He has a cold. And on and on.

Derek can't wait to play, and Sam wishes the game would go away. The point is, the situation alone doesn't dictate the stress. Nevertheless, most people who experience stress tend to blame their situations as the cause, not their interpretations of them. So what can you do as a coach to help your players manage stress?

You can guide your players through two options: They can either change the situation, or they can change their perception of the situation.

Sam can change the situation in two ways to relieve his stress: he can ask his Aunt Kristi not to attend the game, and he can (we hope) get over his cold. However, doing these two things will likely not fully relieve the stress he feels.

The better option is to help Sam interpret his situation differently. Once you find out what he's stressed about, help him focus on the good things he's done in practices and games, on the skills that he has. Remind him of how the team has prepared for this contest. Help him focus on his own performance and not worry about who's watching on the sidelines. And remind him that the bigger team doesn't always win and isn't always the better team.

The best way to manage stress is to change habitual negative thinking to more realistic and constructive thinking. Help kids who often feel stressed by negative thinking to think more realistically and constructively. This isn't easy, and it's often a complex issue, but you can help youngsters manage stress by helping them to interpret their situation in a more realistic and constructive vein.

Staying Active Year-Round

Basketball is a great way to get in shape and have fun. As the season progresses, your players will be getting in better shape. However, the fitness that is gained through participating will rapidly vanish if players aren't active in the off-season. One of the goals of YMCA Youth Super Sports is to introduce kids to the value of fitness. We want kids to enjoy training, to want to become fit on their own, and to stay fit for a lifetime. As the season nears an end, encourage your players to stay active and fit in the off-season. Tell them about the benefits of being active year-round:

◎ It improves strength and endurance.

◎ It helps build healthy bones and muscles.

◎ It helps control weight.

◎ It reduces anxiety and stress and increases self-esteem.

◎ It may improve blood pressure and cholesterol levels.

◎ It helps people feel and look better.

Kids need to be active year-round just as much as adults do. The percent of kids ages 6 to 11 who are overweight has more than doubled in the past 30 years. In fact, kids today are more sedentary, weigh more, and have more body fat than their counterparts 20 years ago. Kids under 10 spend twice the time watching television as they do actively playing. It's no wonder that half of all youngsters don't get enough exercise to strengthen their heart and lungs.

That's why youngsters need coaches to encourage them to be active in the off-season. Offer a variety of examples for remaining active throughout the year, and encourage a moderate amount of physical activity on most, if not all, days of the week. Examples of moderate activity include

◎ Walking 2 miles in 40 minutes

◎ Running 1-1/2 miles in 15 minutes

◎ Bicycling 5 miles in 30 minutes

◎ Playing basketball (shooting baskets) for 30 minutes

◎ Playing volleyball for 45 minutes

◎ Jumping rope for 15 minutes

Not Using Tobacco, Alcohol, and Other Drugs

Neither sports participation nor, to a lesser extent, age insulates kids from tobacco, alcohol, and other drug use. Alcohol is the most widely used drug at the upper ages (14 to 16) of YMCA Winners. In the past 30 days (30-day use is commonly used as an indicator of current drug use), 26 percent of eighth-graders will have used alcohol, 17 percent will have smoked cigarettes, 7 percent will have used smokeless tobacco, and 5 percent will have smoked marijuana. The good news is that athletes are less likely to smoke cigarettes than nonathletes. But even among athletes, cigarette and alcohol use tends to double in the off-season. This is one more good reason to encourage remaining active in the off-season: Those who remain active are less likely to use tobacco, alcohol, or other drugs.

While these facts pertain to kids at the upper levels of YMCA Winners, the risks of using tobacco, alcohol, and other drugs permeates all ages of kids in YMCA Winners. It's to your advantage to understand why kids use tobacco, alcohol, and other drugs, and to be able to tell your players the benefits of not using these substances.

Why Kids Use Tobacco, Alcohol, and Other Drugs

There are many reasons why kids use tobacco, alcohol, and other drugs, but here are five important motives:

◎ **To experience pleasure.** Certain drugs give pleasurable feelings. Young athletes may like these feelings associated with drug use and may find that drugs quickly produce these desired sensations.

◎ **To take risks.** Some athletes are more likely to have a thrill-seeking personality, looking for excitement and stimulation through physical activity. This same quest for adventure may encourage some athletes to choose other risky behaviors, including the use of tobacco, alcohol, and other drugs.

◎ **To belong.** People often emulate the standards and actions of their peers. Young athletes may use tobacco, alcohol, and other drugs to fit in with others.

◎ **To be like their heroes.** Beer is advertised extensively during televised sporting events. Champagne corks pop in locker-room celebrations on TV. Major league baseball players come to bat with the unmistakable imprint of a smokeless tobacco canister showing in their back pocket. Major league baseball players and managers are often seen in public—sometimes even in the dugout!—smoking cigarettes. Tobacco, alcohol, and other drugs are very closely linked to professional sports in a number of ways, leading perhaps to the idea that usage must not be so bad.

◎ **To cope with stress.** Many people use tobacco, alcohol, and other drugs to cope with stress or to escape from stressful situations. As we've mentioned earlier in this chapter, youngsters feel stress just as adults do.

Benefits of Not Using

If you want to make an impact on kids, don't just tell them that tobacco, alcohol, and other drugs are bad for them. Tell them about the benefits of *not* using tobacco, alcohol, and other drugs. Following are some of the benefits of not using:

◎ Their performance—not just in sports, but in academics and all other activities—won't be hampered.

◎ They won't encounter legal problems because of underage use of tobacco, alcohol, or illicit drugs.

◎ They are less likely to encounter the numerous health problems associated with usage.

◎ They won't become dependent or addicted.

◎ They will be less likely to be involved in accidents.

◎ They can better develop their skills in managing stress and solving problems.

◎ They will achieve normal physiological and hormonal growth and development.

◎ They can develop honest relationships.

Of course, it's of utmost importance that you be a good role model here. You have two choices: Either abstain from tobacco, alcohol, and other drug use, or use those substances moderately, appropriately, and legally. However, understand that as a YMCA Winners coach, you must abstain from the use of tobacco, alcohol, and other drugs (other than prescription or over-the-counter drugs) while coaching your team.

Teaching Character Development

This final chapter will deal with character development, the teaching of values to players. Teaching values is as important a part of YMCA Winners basketball as teaching game skills. As a YMCA Winners coach, we ask you to take on the responsibility of helping your players learn about and use four core values: caring, honesty, respect, and responsibility. Here are just some of the ways you can do this:

- ◎ Communicate to your players that character development is an important part of the program.

- ◎ Teach the four values to players so they know what those values mean. Give them examples.

- ◎ Include the values in each practice session (character development discussions appear in each practice plan).

- ◎ Consistently model those values in your own behavior so players can see what those values look like.

- ◎ Celebrate those values and hold them up to players as what is right to help them learn to believe in these values.

- ◎ Ask players to practice the values over and over again.

◎ Consistently reinforce and reward behaviors that support the values, using the specific value word that is relevant: "Cindy, thanks for helping Amy find the ball. That shows caring."

◎ Consistently confront a player whose behavior is inconsistent with the values, but do so in a way that does not devalue him or her. Focus on the player's behavior, not on judging him or her.

◎ Be prepared to talk to parents about the character development portion of the basketball program.

Teaching players values takes a different approach than teaching skills. Here are four keys to teaching values:

◎ Be a good role model. Set an example with your words and actions.

◎ Understand at what level your players are capable of understanding and applying values. Kids do not think about moral decisions in the same way as adults. They gradually develop the ability to understand values as they grow.

◎ Identify situations during practice that relate to the four values. Many everyday occurrences provide a chance for you to demonstrate to players that values are relevant to their daily lives.

◎ Use the Team Circle discussions suggested in the practice plans or use similar discussions and activities that emphasize values.

 ## Being a Good Role Model

Most of us believe in the YMCA's core values of caring, honesty, respect, and responsibility, but we don't always follow our own beliefs. Our character is measured by our behavior. We judge ourselves by our good intentions. Other people judge us only by our behavior. Consider the following lists of coaching behaviors for each value. These aren't meant to be comprehensive lists; they're meant to get you thinking about what it means, in practical terms, to be a good role model as it applies to these four important values.

Caring

◎ You spend time after practice helping a player learn a skill.

◎ You comfort a player who is dejected after a loss.

◎ You help a player who is stressed manage that stress.

◎ You inform your players of the benefits of not using tobacco, alcohol, or other drugs.

Honesty

◎ You tell a player that he's not executing a skill correctly, and that you'll help him.

◎ You tell a player when you don't know a rule (but you'll find out).

◎ You tell a player when you make a mistake, such as misinterpreting who instigated minor misbehavior during practice.

◎ You tell your team that you haven't been as physically active in the off-season as you'd like to be, but you're trying to improve here.

Respect

◎ You don't blow your cool when a referee blows a call.

◎ You shake hands with the opposing coach and players after a game.

◎ You bring the same energy and enthusiasm for teaching skills to all your players, no matter how skilled they are.

◎ You don't criticize players in front of their teammates.

Responsibility

◎ You show up on time—and prepared for—all practices and contests.

◎ You provide appropriate first aid for injured players.

◎ You supervise all practice activities closely.

◎ You intervene when players are misbehaving.

Understanding Kids' Moral Reasoning

As you discuss character development issues with your players, keep in mind that they approach moral questions much differently than an adult would, and that their perspective changes as they grow. Kohlberg (Bee, 1995; Crain, 1992) has developed a set of stages for thinking about moral questions that he believes youngsters move through as they mature.

Children through the age of 9 generally think about moral questions in terms of obedience and punishment. They assume that fixed rules are set by powerful adults who can enforce those rules by punishment. They are doing right when they obey rules unquestioningly. Actions are judged by their outcomes, not by the person's intentions. Moral reasoning for children 9 and younger is very "black and white." In basketball, you might expect to see 8- and 9-year-olds interpret an opponent's personal foul *personally*—as an intentional attack—when it is most likely unintentional and a result of poor skill or lack of experience.

Around the age of 10, most youngsters think about moral questions in terms of what works best for them. The right thing is the thing that brings pleasant results. They also think about making deals with others—If I do something for you, then you may in turn do something for me. Making fair deals is important. A 10-year-old and an 11-year-old may agree to congratulate their opponents on good plays or at the end of a game because they know that that behavior pleases most adults and most other kids. However, if their opponents either don't congratulate *their* good play in return, the young athletes may stop that behavior because it doesn't generate a pleasant or "fair" result.

Near the age of 16, most athletes have started thinking about moral questions in terms of how those questions relate to the expectations of their family and community. The key focus is behaving in good ways, having good motives and good feelings toward others. At this point, athletes also start to take into account people's intentions when judging actions. They can better understand their roles as representatives of their team or their YMCA and as role models for younger players. This is particularly true when their coach, parents, and teammates encourage them. Such encouragement would likely cause them to modify their game behaviors to fulfill others' expectations.

Moving from one type of thinking about morality to another happens gradually and may occur at different ages for different kids. However, this overview gives you some broad guidelines for how the majority of the players on your team may look at character development questions when you bring them up in Team Circles or during practices or games.

 ## Using "Teachable Moments"

During practices, you may find that a situation arises that gives you a chance to point out how values apply. This is known as a *teachable moment*. Examples of teachable moments include one team's behavior toward an opponent, one player's behavior toward another or toward a referee, or a violation of team rules. Use teachable moments when they occur. Stop a drill or game to comment on an incident. Don't do this too frequently, but it can be effective when a good opportunity arises to illustrate a value discussed earlier.

Teachable moments can be triggered by either good or bad actions; you can praise an individual's or group's supportive, fair behavior, or stop an activity briefly to talk about negative behavior. Try to balance positive and negative instances; don't use just negative situations. Here are some examples:

- If one player yells at another for a mistake in play, talk to that player about respect.

- If a player does something dangerous during a practice or game, discuss responsibility and caring for others with that player.

- If a player helps a teammate or opponent who is hurt, praise that player for being caring.

- If a player raises her hand to admit committing a foul that wasn't called, congratulate her for being honest.

Teachable moments are occasions when you can hold up the right value and explain why it is the acceptable thing to do. Doing this illustrates to players what values look like beyond the words and how values are a part of our everyday lives.

 ## Using Values Activities

We've already included a Team Circle in each practice plan. This gives you a topic for brief discussion of one or more of the core values. Just as practice games focus on physical skills, Team Circles focus on character development.

They help players realize that participating in basketball also teaches them about themselves and others.

Here are some tips on leading Team Circle discussions:

◎ Begin discussions by reviewing the YMCA House Rules: Speak for yourself; listen to others; avoid put-downs; take charge of yourself; and show respect. Repeat these rules in your first three or four Team Circles; after that you'll probably only need to reinforce the House Rules occasionally.

◎ Be yourself. Kids respect an adult who listens to them and who talks honestly.

◎ As a role model for your players, be willing to admit mistakes; it will make players more likely to be open about themselves.

◎ Give players a chance to respond, but allow them to pass if they want to. Reinforce their responses with a nod, smile, or short comment like "Thanks," "Okay," "That's interesting," or "I understand." Give the player speaking your undivided attention.

◎ After all players have had a chance to respond to your Team Circle question, briefly summarize the responses and add your own comments. Try not to lecture.

You might also include activities of your own that reinforce values. The YMCA of the USA has created a number of character development resources; ask your YMCA Youth Super Sports director if they can make those available to you. Here are a few ideas taken from the YMCA Character Development Activity Box:

◎ *Ask your players what they should do if they think a referee made a bad call.* Allow time for responses. Say, "If you say something bad to the referee, make a face, kick the ball, or in any way complain, how do you think that makes the referee feel?" Emphasize that because the referee doesn't care who wins, he or she did not make the bad call on purpose. And it's only the player's opinion that the call was bad—it may have been the right call. End by saying it's important to respect referees because they're helping the players learn the game.

◎ *Place four cones in a line about 10 feet apart.* As your players sit in a circle, tell them this story:

> You want to play on a team with your friends, but they're all one year younger than you. You'll have to join a team at the next age level, where the players are much better than you. However, the league doesn't require proof of age.

Give the players four options; each cone symbolizes an option. Tell them to stand by the option they choose. Cone A: Since the league doesn't require proof of age, you'll just sign up with your friends. No one will know the difference. Cone B: You'll sign up to play in your correct age group. Cone C: You won't play at all. Cone D: You'll check with league officials to see if you have other options available before making a final decision. Once players make their decisions, ask them why they chose the option they did. What are the consequences of choosing that option? Conclude by pointing out the importance of being honest even though at times we may not be able to do what we want as a result of our honesty.

◎ *Point out to your players that one way to demonstrate caring is to volunteer to do things for other people.* Ask your team to brainstorm different things they can do for others. Examples might include raking leaves, mowing lawns, washing cars, carrying groceries, and so on. Encourage players to volunteer for one hour during the season and bring a note verifying they did it. At the final practice or game, ask each player to tell about their volunteer experience.

Any activities you use should meet these criteria:

◎ Be age-appropriate.

◎ Account for varied personal backgrounds and differing views on values.

◎ Focus on players' attitudes as well as actions.

◎ Focus on long-term results.

◎ Be planned and intentional.

◎ Fit logically with what you are doing.

◎ Be positive and constructive.

◎ Be inclusive.

◎ Be meaningful, not trivial or corny.

◎ Be fun!

Where to Find More Information

Books (Basic to Intermediate Level)

American Sport Education Program. 1996. *Coaching youth basketball (second edition)*. Champaign, IL: Human Kinetics.

> For coaches and parents working with 6- to 14-year-olds. Describes in detail how to teach kids important basketball skills and strategies at a level that's just right for them.

Krause, Jerry V. 1991. *Basketball skills and drills (second edition)*. Champaign, IL: Human Kinetics.

> Explains fundamentals so coaches can start beginners off right and reinforce basic skills in more advanced players.

YMCA of the USA. 1999. *Coaching YMCA Rookies Basketball*. Champaign, IL: Human Kinetics.

> The first level of YMCA Super Sports, for 4- to 7-year-olds.

Books (Advanced Level)

Wissel, Hal. 1994. *Basketball steps to success*. Champaign, IL: Human Kinetics.

> A program for expanding and refining basketball tactics and skills. Through skill instruction and 113 drills, helps players of all levels of ability add dimensions to their game in a step-by-step approach.

Wootten, Morgan. 1992. *Coaching basketball successfully*. Champaign, IL: Human Kinetics.

Covers every facet of building a successful basketball team. Breaks sophisticated techniques down into practical skills, strategies, and drills that coaches can apply in their own program.

 Videos

American Sport Education Program. 1995. *Teaching Youth Basketball Basics*. Produced by the American Sport Education Program. 23 minutes.

Shows how to teach skills using the IDEA method to Introduce, Demonstrate and Explain, and Attend to players as they practice the skills.

Teaching Basketball Fundamentals. With Morgan Wootten. n.d. 55 minutes.

Features passing, shooting, dribbling, and footwork fundamentals and workouts.

Becoming a Basketball Player: Ball Handling. 1990. 21 minutes.

Becoming a Basketball Player: Defense and Rebounding. 1990. 20 minutes.

Becoming a Basketball Player: Offensive Moves. 1990. 21 minutes.

Becoming a Basketball Player: Offensive Moves Off Dribble. 1990. 21 minutes.

Becoming a Basketball Player: Shooting. 1990. 21 minutes.

These five *Becoming a Basketball Player* videos teach the basic individual skills.

 Organizations

USA Basketball
5465 Mark Dabling Blvd.
Colorado Springs, CO 80918-3842
Phone: 719-590-4800

Youth Basketball of America
P.O. Box 3067
Orlando, FL 32802-8201
Phone: 407-363-YBOA

Preparticipation Screening for YMCA Youth Super Sports Programs

 **A Statement of the YMCA of the USA Medical Advisory Committee**

The YMCA believes in providing a safe experience for all youth participating in YMCA sports programs. Although staff and other program leaders are primarily responsible for the health and safety of the children during training and competition, it is equally important for parents to determine that their children participating in YMCA sports have no medical conditions that would preclude their participation or result in further injury or harm.

The YMCA of the USA Medical Advisory Committee recommends that YMCAs encourage parents of youth participating in YMCA sports programs to have their children screened for the purpose of (1) determining the general health of the child, (2) detecting medical or musculoskeletal conditions that may predispose a child to injury or illness during competition, and (3) detecting potentially life-threatening or disabling conditions that may limit a child's participation. The following 10 questions are particularly important for a physician to ask during a sports preparticipation exam:[1]

1. Have you ever passed out during or after exercise?

2. Have you ever been dizzy during or after exercise?

3. Have you ever had chest pain during or after exercise?

4. Do you get tired more quickly than your friends do during exercise?

5. Have you ever had racing of your heart or skipped heartbeats?

6. Have you ever had high blood pressure or high cholesterol?

7. Have you ever been told you have a heart murmur?

8. Has any family member or relative died of heart problems or a sudden death before age 50?

9. Have you had a severe viral infection (for example, myocarditis or mononucleosis) within the last month?

10. Has a physician ever denied or restricted your participation in sports for any heart problems?

Although not a complete list, these questions address the most likely areas of concern and are helpful in identifying individuals at high risk. A yes answer to any question should result in further evaluation and a discussion between physician and parent about appropriate sports participation for the child.

On the registration form for each youth sports program, there should be a statement requiring a parent's or guardian's signature, indicating that the child has been properly screened and there are no medical conditions or injuries precluding his or her participation in that sport.

---

[1] *Preparticipation Physical Evaluation*, Second Edition, American Academy of Family Physicians, American Academy of Pediatrics, American Medical Society for Sports Medicine, American Orthopaedic Society for Sports Medicine, American Osteopathic Academy of Sports Medicine, 1997.

Emergency Information Card

Athlete's name _____ Age _____

Address _____

Phone _____ S.S.# _____

Sport _____

List two persons to contact in case of emergency:

Parent or guardian's name _____ Home phone _____

Address _____ Work phone _____

Second person's name _____ Home phone _____

Address _____ Work phone _____

Relationship to athlete _____

Insurance co. _____ Policy # _____

Physician's name _____ Phone _____

IMPORTANT

Is your child allergic to any drugs? _____ If so, what? _____

Does your child have any other allergies? (e.g., bee stings, dust) _____

Does your child have _____ asthma, _____ diabetes, or _____ epilepsy? (Check any that apply.)

Is your child on any medication? _____ If so, what? _____

Does your child wear contacts? _____

Is there anything else we should know about your child's health or physical condition? If yes, please explain. _____

_____

_____

_____

_____

_____

Signature _____ Date _____

Emergency Response Card

Information for Emergency Call (be prepared to give this information to the EMS dispatcher)

1. Location _____

   Street address _____

   City or town _____

   Directions (cross-streets, landmarks, etc.)_____

   _____

2. Telephone number where the call is being made _____

3. Caller's name _____

4. What happened _____

   _____

   _____

   _____

   _____

   _____

5. How many persons injured _____

6. Condition of victim(s)_____

7. Help (first aid) being given_____

Note: Do not hang up first. Let the EMS dispatcher hang up first.

Injury Report

Name of athlete _____

Date _____

Time _____

First aider (name) _____

Cause of injury _____

Type of injury _____

Anatomical area involved _____

Extent of injury _____

First aid administered _____

Other treatment administered _____

_____

Referral action _____

_____

_____
First aider (signature)

Resources and Suggested Readings

American Sport Education Program. 1996. *Coaching youth basketball.* 2nd ed. Champaign, IL: Human Kinetics.

American Sport Education Program. 1997. *Sport first aid course instructor guide.* Updated ed. Champaign, IL: Human Kinetics.

Bee, Helen. 1995. *The developing child* (7th ed.). New York: HarperCollins College.

Bergeron, J.D., and Greene, H.W. 1989. *Coaches guide to sport injuries.* Champaign, IL: Human Kinetics.

Berk, Laura E. 1998. *Development through the lifespan.* Needham Heights, MA: Allyn & Bacon.

Christina, R.W., and Corcos, D.M. 1988. *Coaches guide to teaching sport skills.* Champaign, IL: Human Kinetics.

Clifford, C., and R.M. Feezell. 1997. *Coaching for character.* Champaign, IL: Human Kinetics.

Crain, William. 1992. *Theories of development: Concepts and applications* (3rd ed.). Englewood Cliffs, NJ: Prentice Hall.

Flegel, M.J. 1997. *Sport first aid.* Updated ed. Champaign, IL: Human Kinetics.

Griffin, L., Mitchell, S. and Oslin, J. 1997. *Teaching sport concepts and skills.* Champaign, IL: Human Kinetics.

Kalish, Susan. 1996. *Your child's fitness: Practical advice for parents.* Champaign, IL: Human Kinetics.

Krause, J. 1991. *Basketball skills and drills (second edition).* Champaign, IL: Human Kinetics.

Martens, R. 1997. *Successful coaching.* 2nd ed. Champaign, IL: Human Kinetics.

Ringhofer, K.R. and Harding, M.E. 1996. *Coaches guide to drugs and sport.* Champaign, IL: Human Kinetics.

Winning respect. 1998. Produced by the American Sport Education Program. 15 min. Human Kinetics. Videocassette.

Wissel, H. 1994. *Basketball steps to success.* Champaign, IL: Human Kinetics.

YMCA of the USA. 1997. *Character development activity box.* Chicago, IL: YMCA of the USA.

YMCA of the USA. 1999. *YMCA youth super sports director's manual.* 3d ed. Champaign, IL: Human Kinetics.

YMCA of the USA. 1997. *Recommendations YMCA of the USA medical advisory committee.* Chicago: YMCA of the USA.

YMCA of the USA. 1990. *YMCA youth fitness program.* Champaign, IL: Human Kinetics.